FINDING, ENTERING, AND SUCCEEDING IN A FOREIGN MARKET

Seamus G. Connolly, Ph.D.

PRENTICE-HALL, ENGLEWOOD CLIFFS, NEW JERSEY 07632

Prentice-Hall International, Inc., *London*
Prentice-Hall of Australia, Pty. Ltd., *Sydney*
Prentice-Hall Canada, Inc., *Toronto*
Prentice-Hall of India Private Ltd., *New Delhi*
Prentice-Hall of Japan, Inc., *Tokyo*
Prentice-Hall of Southeast Asia Pte. Ltd., *Singapore*
Editora Prentice-Hall do Brasil Ltda., *Rio de Janeiro*
Prentice-Hall Hispanoamericana, S.A., *Mexico*

© 1987 *by*

PRENTICE-HALL, INC.

Englewood Cliffs, N.J.

All rights reserved. No part of this
book may be reproduced in any form or
by any means, without permission in
writing from the publisher.

Library of Congress Cataloging-in-Publication Data

Connolly, Seamus G.
   Finding, entering, and succeeding in a foreign market.

   Includes index.
   1. Export marketing—Management. 2. International business enterprises—Management. I. Title.
HF1009.5.C59 1986   658.8'48   86-25395

ISBN 0-13-316951-0

Printed in the United States of America

ABOUT THE AUTHOR

Dr. Seamus Connolly works in International Marketing Communications in the MSD AGVET Division of Merck & Co. He has worked for extended periods in Europe, Asia, and the Middle East. As vice-president of a New York-based international management, technical assistance, and research firm, he has conducted business and negotiations with private investors, governmental agencies, and international banks in Brazil, Venezuela, Mexico, Paraguay, Peru, Colombia, Honduras, Guyana, Indonesia, The Republic of the Philippines, Saudi Arabia, Egypt, The Yemen Arab Republic, Ghana, Somalia, Kenya, Belgium, and Ireland. Between 1982 and 1985 he was coordinator of International Business Studies at the Rutherford campus of Fairleigh Dickinson University, New Jersey.

Dr. Connolly earned his Ph.D. from Fordham University, New York City; his M.Sc. Econ. from the University of Wales, Great Britain; and his B.A. from University College Dublin, Ireland.

ACKNOWLEDGMENTS

I wish to acknowledge the dozen or more business people of many nationalities, on four continents, who shared their ideas, successes, and failures with me. Their experiences have enabled me to make this book a hands-on guide to overseas business.

I am grateful to Bette Schwartzberg at Prentice-Hall for her encouragement and helpful suggestions throughout the writing of this book.

Above all, I am grateful to my wife, Evelyn, who typed the original manuscript and whose critical comments added depth and clarity to the overall document.

DEDICATION

To my wife, Evelyn

INTRODUCTION

THE WORLD IS YOUR MARKETPLACE

The world is fast becoming one large marketplace, and the exporter, the investor, and the service contractor are traders in that global market. Many U.S. companies, big and small, are making large profits from international operations. Yet, it is estimated that there are more than 25,000 firms in the United States with exportable products that shun foreign sales. Why? The reasons most often given are the increased risks, lack of expertise, and the difficulty of operating in new and unfamiliar environments.

THE PROBLEMS YOU FACE

The problems are legion and very distinctive. Your agent in Jakarta starts selling a competing Japanese product. You are exposed for 90 days on a receivable for a large shipment to France. Brazil insists that you export spare parts to Cuba. You have millions of pesoes in Mexico as their dollar value plunges from 25 cents to less than 1 cent. You spend thousands of dollars on a feasibility study in Malaysia that the government would have financed. You need insurance for a rewarding but risky investment in Jamaica. What do you do?

The problems sound formidable but, in practice, are quite manageable. Managers with the expertise to handle them are scarce because the domestic market is so large and American companies are so focused on that market that it is difficult for their international or export division to get the personnel and support they need. But this is changing. Almost every corner of the domestic market faces foreign competition. Competitors are relocating to areas where labor is cheap. Foreign producers are investing here. In the last decade alone the dollar value of U.S. exports has increased eightfold, and it is now estimated that more than 80 percent of new manufacturing jobs being created are linked to exports. In short, markets, profits, production, and employment are becoming internationalized.

WHAT THIS BOOK WILL DO FOR YOU

Some years ago it was a bit easier for the international manager. Most U.S. foreign investments and exports went to Canada and Europe. This is still true, but the areas of opportunity are changing and so is the degree of risk and the strangeness of the environment. China and the Indian subcontinent now have half the potential customers in the world. There has been a massive transfer of purchasing power to several Middle Eastern, Asian, and African nations through increased oil revenues. The Pacific Rim countries of Asia are the fastest growing in the world. They have abundant cheap labor and large populations. How to find your place in this marketplace, how to enter it, and above all, how to succeed in it is what this book is all about.

FINDING THE RIGHT MARKET FOR YOUR PRODUCT

Finding the right market for your product or service is the foundation on which the success of the whole venture depends. Many companies spend thousands of dollars on visits to different countries while most of the information they need for such an initial screening is available right on their own doorstep. You can probably learn more about the Brazilian market in one week in New York than in one month in Brazil. By using the information available from government and other sources and by analyzing it correctly, it is possible to eliminate, select, and concentrate

Introduction

on a few markets where an on-site investigation will be justified. The first section of this book will show how to project demand, evaluate the competition, determine the economic and financial risks involved, and assess the likely impact of the political situation on the success of the venture. The result will be savings in time and money as the focus is narrowed to the best opportunities.

The analysis done at this stage is an essential part of the preparation for an on-site visit and will familiarize the manager with the business practices, the negotiating techniques, and the cultural factors of the foreign market that will make the visit worthwhile. I saw a cloud of formality and distance descend on a friendly negotiating session with a Saudi businessman when a member of the visiting team rushed to get agreements on paper. The signing of the formal agreements was set back for months.

HOW TO ENTER THE MARKET

The method of supplying a foreign market can range from simple exporting to full-scale direct investment. Each method has its advantages and disadvantages and different degrees of risk and proportionate rewards. Most companies begin by exporting and proceed from there to the more rewarding method of foreign manufacturing.

In the second section of this book a step-by-step approach will take the reader through export procedures and the different means even the small exporter must use to protect receivables in foreign currencies. In exporting, a good agent or distributor is invaluable. Guidelines will be given on selecting an agent and on the important areas that should be included in a formal contract to avoid future conflict. For companies who do not want the risk or hassle of foreign investment but have a distinct trademark or technology, licensing or management or technical assistance contracts are alternative routes to the international market. As in the case of an agent, the details of the contract agreement are extremely important, especially if there are differences in language, legal practices, and business customs.

Guidelines will be given to assess the attractiveness of joint ventures, and we will see how successful the Japanese have been in using this route, especially in Asian countries. They have limited their risk, visibility, and exposure and yet have maintained substantial control. This is a possibility that could be very attractive to U.S. firms in, for example, food or raw-material processing in Thailand with the added advantage of access to the Asian market.

The greatest payout comes, of course, from owning and controlling a foreign plant, and there are many situations where this may be the best form of entry as long as the investment is correctly planned, structured, and secured. The chapter on direct investment will take you step by step through all the factors that you need to take into account in making that decision.

The success of the foreign enterprise depends on three things: management, management, and management. Overseas, the experience of American companies is full of examples of misfits, repatriations, and failures. These managers are often highly successful in the domestic environment, but a different set of skills are an added requirement in a foreign post, and many of the sacred principles of an American business education may not only be irrelevant but harmful. The culture is different; the work ethic is different; the business environment is different. The role of the manager is often enlarged so that he or she represents not only the foreign company but a foreign nation in the position of manager of a foreign work force and a possible agent of change. The concluding section of this book will tell you how to find the right manager and how to train him or her and what you and the manager need to know to manage foreign currencies, different cultures, and different work forces successfully.

CONTENTS

INTRODUCTION *vii*

1   THE WORLD IS YOUR MARKETPLACE 1
    Where Are Your Customers? 3
    What Can They Afford To Pay? 7
    Do They Want What You Have or Do You Have
      What They Want? 13
    Who Are Your Competitors? 17
    Conclusion 20

2   HOW TO NARROW YOUR CHOICES 21
    Five Steps To Predict Demand 22
    How UNCLE SAM Can Help You 28
    Narrowing Your Choices 33
    Other Sources of Information 43
    Can You Supply the Market? 49

3   **A STEP-BY-STEP APPROACH TO EVALUATING FINANCIAL RISK**   *53*

   What You Can Learn from the Balance of Payments   *54*
   The World's Money: As It Was, As It Is, and As It Will Be   *61*
   Managing Foreign Exchange   *65*
   Conclusion   *70*

4   **POLITICAL RISK: WHETHER THE CAT IS BLACK OR WHITE MAKES NO DIFFERENCE AS LONG AS HE CATCHES MICE**   *71*

   Four Myths About Political Risk   *72*
   Important Steps in Packaging Your Program   *75*
   How To Assess Levels of Risk   *79*
   Ways To Minimize Risk   *86*
   Summary   *88*

5   **VISITING THE COUNTRY**   *90*

   Homework Completed   *92*
   Business Advice   *92*
   Finding Out Who's Who   *94*
   On-site Research or Feasibility Study   *103*
   The Basics of Negotiation   *109*
   Conclusion   *114*

6   **HOW TO ENTER THE MARKET: THE COSTS AND THE BENEFITS**   *115*

   What Are Your Choices?   *116*
   Direct Exporting   *119*
   Licensing and Contracting   *119*
   Joint Ventures   *120*
   Wholly-owned Subsidiary   *121*
   How Do You Decide?   *122*
   Conclusion   *129*

7 THE OLDEST PROFESSION IN THE WORLD: TRADING 130

Finding the Right Agent or Distributor 131
Profile of the Agent or Distributor 133
Avoiding Future Problems—The Details of
  the Agreement 134
Outline of the Agreement 135
Getting Paid 142
Steps in Setting Up a Letter of Credit 144
How To Beat the Paper Chase 147
Conclusion 152

8 REWARDING OPPORTUNITIES WITH LOW RISK 153

Licensing: Is It the Best for You? 154
What's In It for the Licensee? 156
Putting Some Icing on the Cake 159
The Licensing Agreement—The Most Important
  Components 163
Outline of the Licensing Agreement 164
Payment 166
Contracting without a License 167
Conclusion 171

9 HOW THE JAPANESE DO IT: JOINT VENTURES 172

Joint Ventures: Different Countries, Different Partners 173
Joint Ventures: Your Choices 173
The Pros and Cons of Joint Ventures 175
Making the Joint Venture Decision: Ten Questions To
  Answer 178
Exercising Control as a Minority Partner 182
Conclusion 186

10 DIRECT FOREIGN INVESTMENT: BIGGER RISKS, BIGGER REWARDS 188

Extra Risks, Greater Returns 189

The Pull and the Push in Direct Foreign Investment 193
How To Decide on the Bottom Line: The Return on
   Investment 196
Capital Budgeting 198
Methods of Ranking Investments 201
Conclusion 206

11 THE SECRETS OF SUCCESS IN AN OVERSEAS MARKET: THE MANAGER AND THE WORKFORCE 208

Where Do You Find Overseas Managers? 209
The Advantages and Disadvantages of Hiring
   Local Managers 212
How Do You Select Them? 213
How You Can Prepare Them: Outline of
   a Training Course 215
Compensation: How Much Will the Manager Cost You? 219
Managing a Foreign Workforce: What You Need To
   Know 220
Know the Labor Laws 221
Motivation, Compensation, and Performance 222
Working with Foreign Labor Unions 225
Conclusion 226

12 BREAKING THE CULTURAL BARRIER 228

From Here to China: A Long Cultural Distance 229
Breaking the Communication Barrier 231
Ten Steps for Easier Communication 233
The Constitutents of Culture and How They Affect Your
   Business 234
Technology 236
Values and Attitudes 236
Religion 240
Social Organizations 240
Some Basic Do's and Don'ts 242

Contents

Doing Business in the Arab World 244
Doing Business in the Philippines 245
Conclusion 246

13 PROTECTING YOUR PROFITS: PRICES, TAXES, AND EXCHANGE RATES 248

How To Set Your Price 249
The Role of Governments in Pricing 251
Transfer Pricing 253
You Got Your Price; Where's the Money? 254
Minimize Your Maximum Regret 256
Facing the Inevitable: Taxes 259
How the Government Can Help in Financing and Protecting the Investment 262
Conclusion 263

EPILOGUE 265

SELECTED BIBLIOGRAPHY 266

INDEX 267

1

THE WORLD IS YOUR MARKETPLACE

Ninety-five percent of your potential customers live outside the United States, and they have 75 percent of the purchasing power of the world. Half the people of the world live in Asia, and if you add Latin America and Africa they comprise three quarters of the world's population. These people need everything from basic foodstuffs to nuclear technology. But when you look at actual markets and where U.S. firms now export or invest, you see that nearly 70 percent is concentrated in Europe, Canada, Japan, and a few other countries that have only a quarter of the world's population.

In deciding to investigate and enter a foreign market, you could react to these facts in two ways: You could say: "I am going to follow the leaders to where most of the markets now are because these must be the best and safest places" or you could say, "The world is my marketplace, everyone in it is my potential customer, and there may be many undiscovered and rewarding opportunities out there." Yes, many of these countries are farther away, they are underdeveloped and have a very different culture and way of doing business. But although most American firms concentrate on Europe and Canada, many other firms sell in more than 100 countries. H. J. Heinz, the multinational food giant has seen the potential of these larger markets and has recently announced its plans to increase its Third World operations tenfold by 1990. They made this decision on the basis that they now serve only 15 percent of the world's population, mainly in Europe and the United States.

Moreover many companies don't or won't have much choice. For firms from smaller countries the world is their marketplace right from the word go. Their domestic markets are often small, and the cost of development of new products makes sense only in a world market. There is only so much Valium that Hoffman-La Roche could sell to the 6 million people in its home country, Switzerland. But U.S. firms start off with the largest domestic market in the world. They have not had to seek out foreign markets or to worry too much about foreign competition. But that is changing, and changing rapidly. The domestic U.S. market is now very much part of the world marketplace for firms that come not only from countries in Europe and from Japan, but from countries in Asia and South America producing everything from steel to shoes to computers to sugar.

U.S. firms can react negatively by buckling down and trying to keep their market share or by trying to get protection from imports from the U.S. government. Alternatively, they can look at this large and dynamic world marketplace and see it as an opportunity for bigger sales and bigger profits in a variety of goods and services.

In this and the following chapter we are going to examine this world marketplace to see where the best opportunities lie for you and your product. This chapter will take an overall look without prejudging any situation and without eliminating any market because it is unfamiliar or too distant, or because it appears uninteresting at first glance. This is global market scanning, and by the end of the chapter you should have narrowed your choices to a dozen or less attractive areas that demand closer attention. This closer examination will be the subject of the second chapter.

So far we have been talking as if this is a completely new international venture and that the firm has no prior experience in a foreign market. However, the procedures to be followed here are valid for first-time entry as well as for firms that already have significant foreign operations. Whether you are old or new in foreign markets, there is a need to regularly scan the world to find the best markets and to make sure you are not missing any new or changing opportunities where markets may be lost or competitors may gain advantage.

To do this scanning in a systematic way and without foreclosing any possibility you should first ask and answer the following questions:

1. Where are your customers?
2. What can they afford to pay?
3. Do they want what you have or do you have what they want?
4. Who are your competitors?

What you are doing at this stage is matching your product with the customers who need it and can afford to pay for it. You are systematically trying to narrow your focus to a few of the most interesting markets, and you are trying to do so as cheaply as possible using information that is available either free or at a very low cost.

WHERE ARE YOUR CUSTOMERS?

Without people there is no market, so the first thing to do is to take a quick look at where your potential customers are. Of course, even in a country with a large population you still may not have a market because of the nature of your product, or levels of income, or the country won't let you in. But you cannot prejudge that.

At first glance the larger the population the greater the attractiveness of the market, especially if your product is a mass-consumption necessity or a low-priced item that meets particular needs such as transport or education.

In the world market, there are more than 155 countries and a population in excess of 4.8 billion. The first thing you do is see how the population is distributed by country and region. The following list shows the ten most populated countries that together have more than half the population of the world. What is perhaps most significant is that of these top ten only the United States and Japan can be classified as developed market economies. All the rest are less developed countries and the Soviet Union.

There are three things you should take into account in looking at these figures. First is the realization that the top three countries are currently very small markets for U.S. firms. In 1981 China, with over a billion people, imported $3.6 billion worth of goods from the United States or about a billion less than South Korea with a population of only 41 million. Nevertheless, the ten largest developing country markets for U.S. goods took in more than 41 percent of total U.S. exports in 1981. Second, the importance of regional markets is not clear. Even excluding China and India, Asia is a very important region for U.S. firms, with

TABLE 1.1 THE TEN MOST POPULOUS NATIONS—1983

Country	Population	Increase from 1982
1. China	1,059,802,000	14,984,000
2. India	730,572,000	15,503,000
3. Soviet Union	272,308,000	2,286,000
4. United States	234,193,000	2,136,000
5. Indonesia	160,932,000	3,337,000
6. Brazil	131,305,000	3,022,000
7. Japan	119,205,000	756,000
8. Bangladesh	96,539,000	2,937,000
9. Pakistan	94,780,000	2,638,000
10. Nigeria	85,219,900	2,823,000

Source: U.S. Census Bureau

large markets in Korea, Taiwan, Indonesia, Thailand, Singapore, Malaysia, and Hong Kong, while the European Economic Community is the most densely populated and richest market in the world. Third is the significance of the population growth rates. Some of these countries are increasing their population at an annual rate faster than the total population of some of the medium-sized countries of Europe. In general, the low-income countries are growing the fastest. While this means more potential customers, it also may mean lower average levels of income. If per capita income is growing at a faster rate than the population, you may have an expanding market and, depending on your product and the country, greater demand for durable goods and consumer items usually associated with an expanding economy.

Market Segments

Although the sheer size of a national market is important, from your point of view what may be more important is one particular group or segment in a particular market. Populations can be broken down into several categories including occupation, sex, levels of income, levels of education, and place of work. Depending on your product, you may be interested in a particular segment, and while the overall population figures may not appear very interesting, they may conceal attractive subnational markets. Or several adjacent countries may have segments that, when combined, offer an attractive opportunity. For example, the oil-producing countries of the Middle East, although thinly populated, have provided excellent market opportunities in particular areas like con-

The World Is Your Marketplace

FIGURE 1.1

AGE STRUCTURE OF DEVELOPING AND INDUSTRIALIZED COUNTRIES:

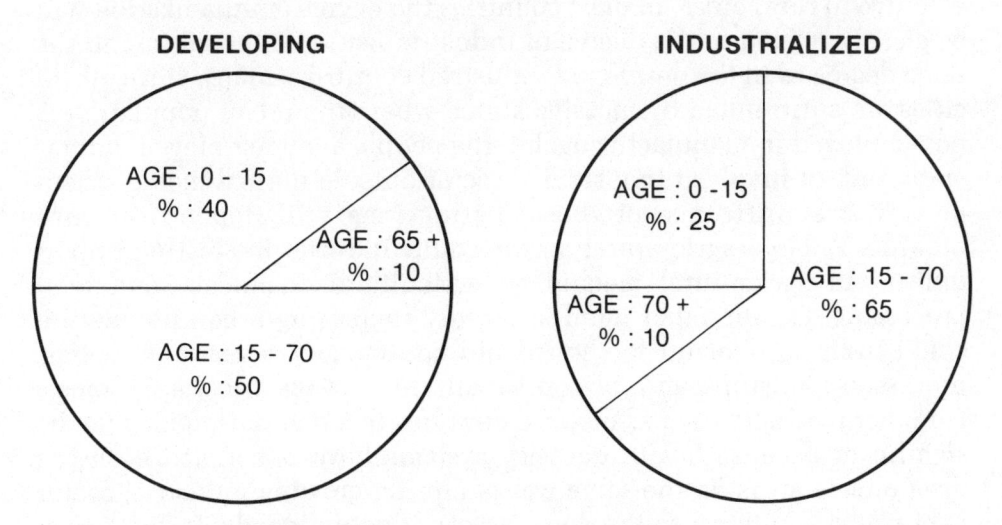

DEVELOPING

- AGE: 0 - 15 — %: 40
- AGE: 65 + — %: 10
- AGE: 15 - 70 — %: 50

INDUSTRIALIZED

- AGE: 0 -15 — %: 25
- AGE: 70 + — %: 10
- AGE: 15 - 70 — %: 65

struction supplies, irrigation equipment, and high-priced consumer items.

In other heavily populated countries like Mexico or Indonesia the age structure of the population may be of great interest to you. In general, the population of Asia, Africa and Latin America can be illustrated by a pie chart, showing that more than 40 percent of the population is under 15 years of age and less than 10 percent is over the age of 65. In contrast, the population of the more developed, industrialized economies is more evenly distributed by age.

Just as many firms have been positioning themselves in the United States to take advantage of the demand associated with the so-called "Graying of America," the opposite is significant in the developing countries where there will be an exploding demand for foodstuffs, clothing, health, and educational supplies. It is important to remember that the 40 percent of the under 15's at the base of the pyramid in the less developed countries is more than the total population of the United States, Canada, Japan, Australia, Europe, and the Soviet Union. And the number is getting bigger: 80 percent of the world's population of 6.3 billion will be living in the countries of Asia, Africa, and Latin America by the year 2000.

Rural or Urban

One of the most important divisions of a country's population for scanning purposes is the number of people who live in cities versus those who live in rural areas. In most countries the degree of urbanization will be closely related to the degree of industrialization although not to the same degree as in the developed industrial countries. Many Third World cities are surrounded by massive slums where the urban population is not employed in manufacturing, but the people are unemployed, underemployed, or involved in a service sector outside normal market channels. The significance of these distinctions will depend on your product. A large agricultural sector could indicate interesting opportunities in agricultural machinery, agricultural chemicals, and food processing. On the other hand, a rapidly increasing urban population could indicate demand for household appliances, recreational goods, processed foodstuffs and, of course, all kinds of electrical appliances. For other products such as medical supplies this distinction may not be significant because health delivery systems have penetrated even the most remote areas. In the same way, a rapidly growing industrial sector is of primary interest to the supplier of industrial goods. In looking at the large markets of the less developed countries, it is a useful starting point to look at how the urban/rural division has affected consumption in the home markets. In the United States, for example, sales of cameras are much lower for farmers than for the nonfarm population. In Europe consumption of margarine is usually much higher in urban areas. But it is important to re-examine these assumptions very carefully in a different market environment because they can be greatly affected by other factors such as levels of income or education.

Population Density

Closely related to the urban/rural division is the question of population density. In general, the more people are concentrated in one area, the easier it will be to promote, sell, and service your product.

The trend is toward rapid urbanization. As an example, it is estimated that Mexico City will have more than 30 million inhabitants by the year 2000. So population density is very important in determining demand for your product. If you were selling an agricultural machine or products related to rural electrification in Egypt, it is very significant that most of the population are concentrated in the Nile delta. On the other hand, Bangladesh has the highest population density in the world with more than 1,500 people per square mile. In contrast, the rural population of the Philippines or of many countries in Africa are spread over vast areas and often divided by sea, mountains, or impassable rivers.

POPULATION: WHAT'S IMPORTANT FOR YOU?		
Characteristic	Yes	No
Size		
Distribution (rural/urban)		
Density		
Age		
Occupation		
Educational Levels		
Income Levels		

These are some of the clues that readily available population statistics can give you to market potential. Already you probably will have enough information to screen out many countries, either because they are too small or the segment you are interested in is too small, or because there is very low demand, for example, for machine tools in a mainly agricultural economy. In the case of the rural sector the demand may be there, but the population is too scattered. Of the countries that remain the next big question is even if demand is there, can they afford to pay?

WHAT CAN THEY AFFORD TO PAY?

What makes a potential customer an actual customer is the money in his or her pocket. We have just seen where the potential customers are but, in general, there is little money where most of the people are. This is why, as we will see later, most of the trade and investment takes place between a small group of rich countries. But that does not mean that the poorer countries are not important. Indeed, of the 20 largest U.S. trading partners 11 are developing countries, and in 1983 they bought more than $50 billion from U.S. firms. The reason is that although *average* incomes are low because of the large populations, there are significant segments with high incomes, or there is even a mass market for cheap products, and often the government itself or the enterprises it controls are large purchasers of goods and services.

To get a handle on what people in a particular country can afford, the first step is to compare the size of the economies of the different countries because *in general* the larger the economy, the greater the potential market. But, although an economy is large, the people may be poor because of the large population. So a second step is to see what is the per capita income of the population as a whole. Finally, it is necessary to see how this income is distributed in the country and how the distribution will affect your sales because what one group can afford to pay may bear no resemblance to what another group can pay.

The size of the economy gives you an idea of what the gross purchasing power in the economy is likely to be. The most common measurement used across nations to compare their size is the Gross National Product (GNP), or the market value of all goods and services produced in the country over a set period. This is a crude measurement and needs to be carefully qualified, but it is one on which information is available for most countries. In sheer size economies range from the $3 trillion worth of goods and services produced annually in the United States to the $500 million produced in Chad or Lesotha. Of the 15 largest economies in the world, 10 are the industrialized market economies of the United States, Canada, Europe, and Japan with Russia, China, Brazil, India, and Mexico making up the rest.

Per Capita Income

In order to compare these nations' purchasing power, it is necessary to go beyond the gross national figures to per capita income, or in other words, divide the gross national figures by the size of the population. Now a different picture begins to emerge as some of the large countries in total output have very low per capita incomes, while some of the smaller economies have large per capita incomes (see Figure 1.2).

Kuwait has a GNP of only $30 billion and a population of 1.5 million, but it has the highest per capita income in the world at over $20,000. Brazil has an economy 8 times larger and a population 90 times larger, but a per capita income of only about $1,800. Which is the most attractive for your product? To answer this question, it may be helpful to classify the major countries of the world as in Table 1.2.

FIGURE 1.2 TOP TEN COUNTRIES RANKED BY GROSS NATIONAL PRODUCT AND PER CAPITA INCOME

Gross National Product	Per Capita Income
United States	Kuwait
U.S.S.R.	Switzerland
Japan	Sweden
Germany, Federal Republic	Denmark
France	United States
United Kingdom	Germany
Italy	Norway
China, Peoples Republic	Canada
Brazil	Belgium
Canada	Netherlands

As you scan countries, it will greatly simplify matters and narrow your focus if your customers can be slotted into one of these groups. For higher priced consumer products that, for example, presume an urban lifestyle or a high educational level, the primary focus will be on the developed economies of Europe and Japan. The NICs (New Industrializ-

TABLE 1.2 WHAT CAN THEY AFFORD TO PAY?

Category	Per Capita Income (Approx.)
1. Developed Market Economies of the Americas, Europe, and Japan	$6,000–$15,000
2. Centrally Planned Economies of U.S.S.R. and Eastern Europe	$2,000–$6,500
3. Oil-Rich, Developing Nations of the Middle East: Kuwait, Libya, Saudi Arabia, Quatar, and the United Arab Emirates	$8,000–$20,000
4. New Industrializing Countries, e.g., Brazil, Singapore, South Korea, Venezuela, Mexico	$1,500–$4,000
5. Developing Countries comprising the vast majority of the world's population	$100–$1,000

ing Countries) will be attractive for industrial goods and supplies as well as for an offshore location for production. But even the very low-level countries have mass needs for buses, health supplies, steel, and housing equipment.

How Is the Income Distributed?

There is no such thing as an average income. In most countries the vast majority of the people are significantly below the average and a small minority significantly above it. This is true in both the rich and poor countries, but income is generally much more unevenly distributed in the latter. It is difficult to accurately compare distribution of income across countries, first, because these are not statistics that governments are most interested in collecting or publicizing, and second, because there is a great difference in the way information is collected. It is an extremely important aspect of market scanning, however, because the average per capita income may give a very misleading impression. It is possible to get some information on most countries, and although the information may be dated, this is not too important because income distribution changes very slowly. Indeed, in most developing countries it appears to get worse as the economy and average per capita income expands.

The distribution of income is usually measured by the share each percentile, or each 20 percent, of the population has. In most countries the distribution is heavily skewed toward the top 40 percent as illustrated by the following chart.

Such a breakdown may tell you a lot about the potential demand for your product. In France, for example, the top two percentiles, or 40 percent of the population, have almost 70 percent of the national income, while the bottom 40 percent has only 14 percent. Even more can be told about a country when you combine these income-distribution figures with the earlier population and Gross National Product figures. For example, in the case of the Philippines the Gross National Product in 1980 was $34 billion, and with a population of 48 million, the average per capita income was $708. But the bottom 40 percent of the population got only 14 percent of the total income so their incomes were much, much lower than the $708 average. If your product is expensive, has low margins, and presumes high volume you know this segment of the market cannot afford it. On the contrary, the fact that the top 20 percent of the population receive 54 percent of the national income could indicate an attractive market for low-volume, expensive goods.

FIGURE 1.3

INCOME DISTRIBUTION BY PERCENTILE OF POPULATION

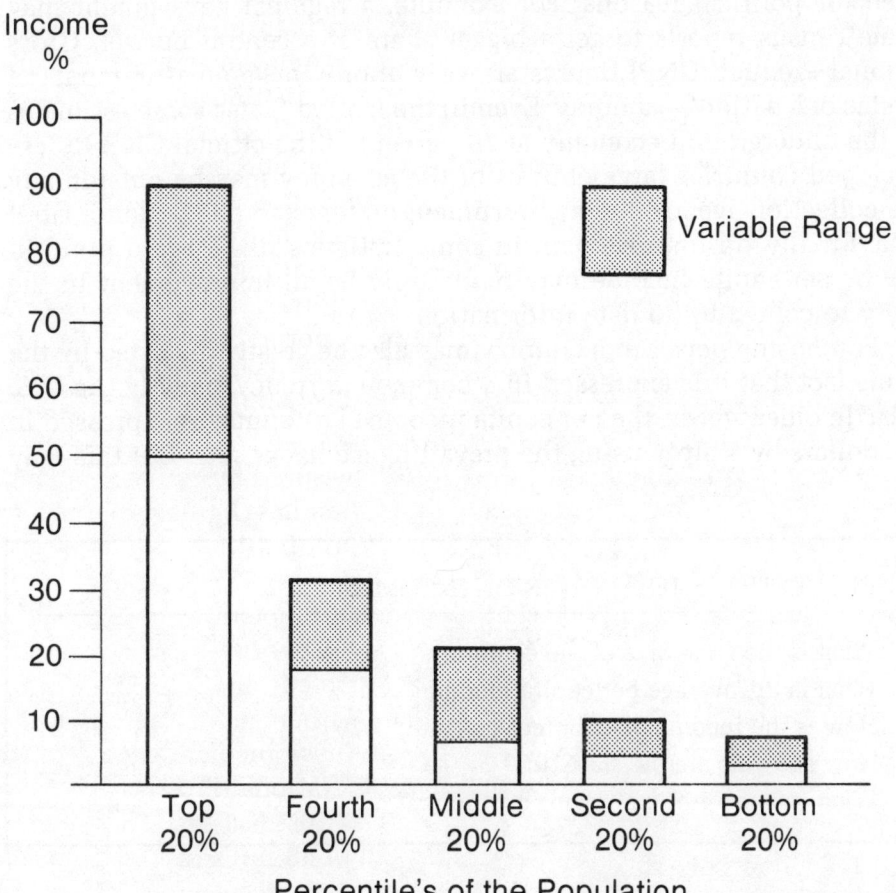

Income %

Percentile	Income % (solid)	Variable Range (top)
Top 20%	50	90
Fourth 20%	18	~31
Middle 20%	7	~21
Second 20%	4	10
Bottom 20%	3	~7

Percentile's of the Population

Telling Lies with Statistics

Having just outlined what you can learn about a foreign market from readily available statistics, it is time now to look at some of the pitfalls in using these statistics. Gross or national statistics are notoriously inaccurate in some developing countries. A developed country has a developed statistical service. A less developed country does not.

Statistics on income distribution and population are often distorted for political reasons. For example, a regional government may inflate census reports to get a bigger share of a central budget. Gross National Product (GNP) figures are very approximate measurements of the size of a nation's economy. Even in the United States some estimates put the underground economy at 20 percent of the official GNP. In less developed countries large chunks of the economy may be outside any data-collection agency of the government in, for example, barter or rural trade. Finally, an improvement in some statistics like a rapid jump in GNP or per capita income may really only be an improvement in the ability to collect up-to-date information.

Purchasing power in a country may also be greatly distorted by the simple fact that it is expressed in a common currency, usually the U.S. dollar. In other words, the per capita income of a country is expressed in U.S. dollars by simply using the prevailing exchange rate. But this may

---

FIVE QUESTIONS TO ANSWER ON INCOMES

1. What is the gross size of the economy?
2. What is the average per capita income?
3. How is the income distributed?
4. How accurate are the statistics?
5. What income group are your customers?

---

not at all express the real purchasing power of the local currency in that country. The exchange rate is often controlled, or if it is not, it only reflects the relative prices of those products that trade internationally. Everyone who has traveled overseas has observed the differences in purchasing power. If you buy a suit in Hong Kong or an eight-course

The World Is Your Marketplace

meal in Rome, your money goes a long way. In contrast, locally produced food may be very expensive in Saudi Arabia. When you see that a particular country has a per capita income of less than $1,000, it may mean little in terms of the real purchasing power of the local people in their currency. One study has indicated that in the case of India, for example, the real purchasing power would have to be multiplied by three times the official exchange amount. This difference in purchasing may be particularly significant if you are planning to produce all or part of your product inside the country in question.

DO THEY WANT WHAT YOU HAVE OR DO YOU HAVE WHAT THEY WANT?

In scanning world markets you are caught in the old dilemma of which comes first, the chicken or the egg? That is, does your product determine the market or does the market determine your product? In following the foregoing outlined steps, you need to be guided by the product or products you expect to sell in these countries, but as you go along you may find that other products you have or even products you don't currently produce may be the best candidates for a foreign market. Or you may find opportunities for different products in different markets. What this means in practice is that you have initial product screening and initial market screening continually interacting with continuous feedback loops as you look at where the customers are, what they can afford to pay and what they want.

FIGURE 1.4

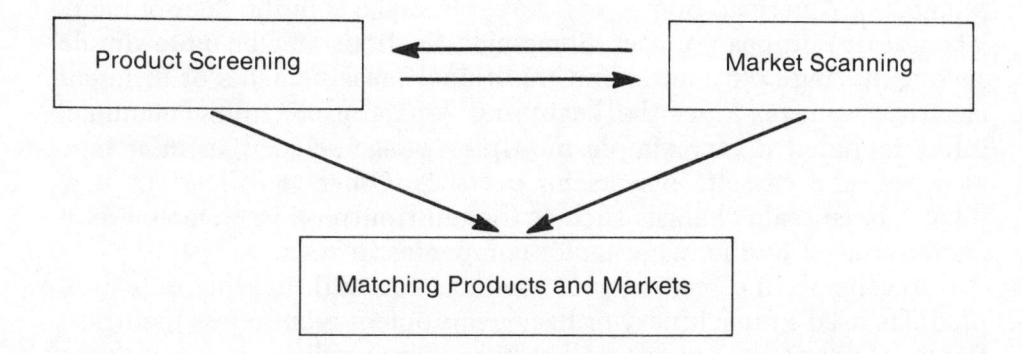

```
┌──────────────────┐                    ┌──────────────────┐
│ Product Screening│  ⇄                │  Market Scanning │
└──────────────────┘                    └──────────────────┘
           ↘                              ↙
            ┌──────────────────────────────┐
            │ Matching Products and Markets│
            └──────────────────────────────┘
```

Many firms make their first sale of a product to a foreign market by accident rather than by design. The product is recommended by someone or another U.S. company needs it for export or it is purchased under a tied loan or grant. When the firm begins to examine foreign markets in a more systematic way, it is natural to start with existing products that have sold well domestically and have a good profit margin. It is a useful exercise to select your product systematically by answering the following questions:

What product or products in my domestic product line can I sell overseas? The focus here is on exporting and on using existing production facilities to increase volume, sales, and profits at little extra marginal cost. The assumption is that the product will fill the same needs in a foreign market as it does in the domestic market and that it can be used in more or less the same way without modification. Examples include products like frozen foods, specialty tools, or office furniture.

Do I have products that satisfy one set of needs in the domestic market and may satisfy a very different set of needs in a foreign market? For example, kerosene stoves or lamps are recreational goods in the United States while they are necessities, required for cooking or light, in many less developed countries. Bicycles are a recreational vehicle in the United States but a basic means of transport in other countries.

What products could I modify for sales in a foreign market? Because of the size and overall uniformity of the U.S. market, most U.S. firms have standardized products, and there has been little need to modify products for different regions. The large kitchen appliances of American homes will not even make it in the door of many Japanese or European houses. Some modifications may be quite simple such as having both metric and traditional measurements or different electrical voltage. From the beginning, Japanese electronic manufacturers included a very simple multiple voltage selector in their tape recorders and cassette players for overseas. Other modifications may involve large-scale changes such as the multipurpose basic motor vehicle introduced by the major motor companies in Asia.

In general, in screening your products you will find that industrial products used in machinery or heavy equipment require less modification while consumer goods will require more modification, but at the same time this is likely to be less costly.

Where does my product fit into its life cycle in different countries? Certain manufactured products follow a fairly standard series of steps within the domestic market. The first involves the introduction of an innovative product, for instance, the instant camera, which is a major improvement on previous products. It goes through a period of rapid growth with high prices as development costs are recovered. After a certain length of time it matures and sales begin to even out. Competitors have entered the markets and price, rather than a brand name or the newness of the technology, determines sales. The product has become standardized, the market becomes saturated, and sales begin to decline. The cycle begins all over again with a new replacement product such as a small hand-held video camera. Many firms only begin to seek foreign markets for their product when it reaches the saturation stage in the domestic market and when they begin to face severe competition. In looking at your product line you may find that although the product has peaked or even is in decline in the U.S. market, it may be at a much earlier stage in its life cycle in other countries. Most new products are developed in the United States, Europe, and Japan, but the speed at which they spread from one country to another may vary depending on price, levels of income, and how the product is perceived. So while your sales may have begun to decline for a product in the U.S., it may still be at the mature stage in several markets in Europe. In some of the newly industrializing countries it may be at an earlier stage and have a lot of growth potential. In less developed countries it might not even be introduced yet, and it could reach an important segment of those markets.

Another twist to the product life cycle is that because of severe price competition in the U.S. market you may decide not only to pick up the life cycle at an earlier stage by exporting to other countries, but in certain products you may decide to locate production overseas to reduce costs and remain competitive in the domestic U.S. market by importing the product back into the United States. Under intense competition from competitors in video games and home computers Atari decided the only way they could retain their market share in the United States was by moving production to the Far East. As you scan world markets and view the world as one large market place that includes the United States, this is an option you may want to consider now or for a later stage.

Do you have services you could sell? Most manufacturers never consider selling services, yet in their own firms they may have valuable technical, management, and production skills that are a scarce and valuable asset in other countries. These skills may be marketable as part of a joint venture or to foreign entrepreneurs who are going into production themselves. They could also be sold in conjunction with production equipment or a "turnkey" project where the equipment is sophisticated or quality control is important. There is also a large market for certain types of services, for instance, construction design and engineering associated with the large multilateral lending agencies.

Do you have a patent or production secret or trade name that is marketable? This may be an opportunity where a market is attractive for your product, but import controls or the risk of foreign investment exclude you from the market. Very often the sale of a patent or trademark can be tied to the sale of services in order to use the technology involved in the production or to maintain the level of quality you require for use of your trade name.

This area of services, high-level skills, and patents needs careful attention because it is an area where the United States has distinct advantages, and as the competitive forces shift in different countries, it may be a way of entering a market or staying in a market where exporting is too costly.

Are there products you could sell that you don't currently produce or products that could be sold in conjunction with your own product? For example, General Tire saw the possibility of selling fan belts to their tire customers. It was a related product they did not produce in their home market but that offered attractive opportunities overseas. In the last decade there has been a big market in the Middle East for equipment to reconstitute concentrated fruit juices. Associated with it is a market for plastic and paper containers as well as supplies of the concentrate itself. These are the types of situations where the sale of one component of a process could easily lead to the sale of other components even if you do not manufacture the product yourself.

In screening your product or product line, what you are doing, in effect, is taking a fresh look at the inventory of products, services, skills, patents, and other goods that you have at your disposal for foreign markets. You may even find a market for your used machinery. But what is important is that as you can scan the various countries you have a clear idea of the full range of what you can sell. In this way you are less likely to miss any major opportunity in any major market. It is possible that all you are looking for is one good market for one product or several attractive markets for one product. But you also may find you have different products suitable for different markets or different products for one market. Once you are collecting the information and scanning

WHAT CAN YOU SELL?		
	Yes	No
1. Can my domestic product line be sold overseas?		
2. Do any of my products satisfy a different need overseas?		
3. Can I modify my product for foreign use?		
4. Are any of my old products still new elsewhere?		
5. Do I have a skill or service I can sell?		
6. Can I sell a secret or technology or trade name?		
7. Can I produce a new product for a foreign market?		
8. Are there other products I can sell with my own line?		

markets at all, it is well worthwhile to have a clear inventory of what you could sell.

WHO ARE YOUR COMPETITORS?

The Ivory Coast gets a large loan from the World Bank. The government is bound to advertise and purchase the goods and services, financed by the loan, under international competitive bidding. Do you respond and incur considerable expense putting together a bid? Probably not, because the contract is likely to go to a French company that already has experience in French West Africa or has contacts into the "French Connection" that runs from Paris, to the French civil servants in the Ivory Coast government to the French loan officers in the World Bank. If your plant is located several hundred miles from the nearest East Coast port, can you sell PVC pipe to satisfy the large construction and agricultural demand in the Middle East? The answer is that the inland and overseas shipping costs make your fairly standardized product too costly. Part of the process in scanning world markets and screening your product is not to fight the wrong battle, trying to enter markets where the competition is in a very strong position. Rather, at this stage you are interested in selecting the countries that show the greatest potential for you and your products. At a later stage you will need to take a much closer look at the competition in markets which you are considering entering. Now you are trying to eliminate markets by looking at the situations where the competition is so strong it is not worth looking any further.

Will the competitors please stand up? The first step is to identify the competitors or likely competitors in the various markets. Are they from the United States or already inside the prospective market or from a third country? As the world becomes one large marketplace, the competition is more intense for shares in that market. If your competition is from the United States, this means you can probably compete in price and quality and get your share of the market unless your competitor has some special arrangements or has already locked up a large share of the market. If the main competition comes from within the foreign country itself, then your product will have to succeed by being different or distinctive or having an established trademark or quality. If the competition comes from third countries, especially Third World countries, your product may not be able to withstand the price pressure especially if these products are already successful in U.S. markets. Even the Japanese domestic market is now being penetrated by textiles, electronics, and chemicals made elsewhere in Asia, while large chunks of the construction business in the Middle East have been taken by Korean firms. But these facts in themselves do not eliminate markets. They make it impossible to enter by one means, namely exporting, but may make entry possible through a joint venture or direct foreign investment. A Cleveland-based construction company successfully won a large construction contract in Kuwait in a joint venture with the Chinese who will supply a cheap and hard-working labor force.

What advantages do the competitors have? Very often, but not always, price determines your chances of succeeding in a foreign market. The most obvious factor in determining price is your cost of production, and there are situations where you can only be competitive by producing inside the market itself or using a cheap third location. For example, the European countries have traditionally been large export markets for U.S. firms, but the rise and expansion of the European

The World Is Your Marketplace

Economic Community and the elimination of internal tariff barriers combined with some large mergers have given European firms a very large advantage. So competitors may have a tariff advantage by being part of a regional trading group or may have an advantage in transport costs by being close to the market. They may also have an advantage because of political favoritism, either formal or informal. Formal favoritism would include such things as tariffs to protect a local industry or subsidies or specific tax advantages. It would be informal if it involved preferences in purchasing by the government or state agencies or obstruction of the competition by stricter enforcement of regulations.

WHAT YOU NEED TO KNOW ABOUT YOUR COMPETITORS

1. Who are they?
2. Foreign or local?
3. What advantages do they have?
4. What advantages do I have?
5. Is there room for me and my competitors?

What advantage do I have over the competition? In screening your product and in scanning the markets you will certainly be conscious of the distinctive advantages you have. These may include one or other of price, quality, newer technology, brand name, or, if you are already in the market with other products you may have valuable support facilities you can use in the introduction of the new product. The most obvious place to start in evaluating your advantages is on the home market because if your product is doing well there in the face of what is now both domestic and world competition, it is likely to have similar advantages in foreign markets. Your distinctive advantage is what will enable you to gain your share of the new market.

Is there room for me and my competitors? Competitors may look formidable, but the market may be large and have room for you. In order to judge this you will have to have some idea of the market potential versus the share of the market that competitors now have. You may also feel that having penetrated the market, you will be able to take some of their market share away by, for example, providing better support services or a better quality product or a lower price. Your experience in the domestic market or in another market will give you a good idea of how well you are likely to succeed. One of the major ways you may overcome a competitor that is either inside or outside the market, is by adopting an entry strategy that gives you a distinct advantage such as, for instance, forming a joint venture with a local firm. It is important, therefore, to look at the competition, especially if it is local, not just from the point of view of exporting to the country but also if you are thinking of gaining access through other means. Admittedly, most companies make their first entry through exporting, but in looking at the competition, you may have to look early on at other entry options. This is a subject that will be looked at in detail later on.

CONCLUSION

At this stage the world that was your marketplace has probably shrunken to a dozen or more countries at which you are going to look closer and that warrant a greater investment of time and money. You have seen where the customers are, and you have identified important segments of the market for your product. You have determined what the purchasing power is in each market and, perhaps of more importance, how it is distributed among the population and how this is related to the segment of the population you are interested in and the products you want to sell. You have examined the range of products you have, and you have looked beyond them to services or valuable rights or other products you could provide to different markets. Finally, you have looked at competitive products and firms and you know what you are up against.

The number of markets you are now looking at are much fewer and the stage is set for a more detailed look to find the market or markets that offer you the best opportunities.

2

HOW TO NARROW YOUR CHOICES

Many companies sell their products in more than 100 different countries and many of them make more than 50 percent of these profits from international operations. But most companies don't have the products or resources, at least initially, for such a broad involvement. Moreover, there are often external obstacles that make entry into many markets impossible.

The task is to narrow your choices, step by step, so that you select the best markets to match your product. To do this you need to predict demand for your product in the countries you have now selected.

Moreover, you want to do this at the lowest possible cost. Once you start an on-site investigation or decide to visit the country or countries, you are already incurring large expense. The challenge is to make sure you are going to the right markets for your product and, at the same time, that you have not left out any important market by default. From your preliminary market scanning you probably have your eye on a dozen or so countries. But you want to narrow your choices to a few that will justify a larger investment of time and money. There is a series of steps that can help you to do this, and there is a lot of information available to enable you to do it. Your most urgent need at this stage is easily available, low-cost information that preferably is processed in a form that is useful to you. The best source of help is your own government and in particular the Department of Commerce. Many companies are unaware or even surprised that their government wants to help them sell overseas. But it is true, and the reasons are very real. It is estimated that every billion dollars of exports sustain 20,000 jobs here at home. Additionally, the government is worried about the growing imbalance between exports and imports.

In 1984 alone imports exceeded exports by $130 billion, and the gap is growing. That is a lot of jobs, a lot of taxes lost, a lot of payments to manufacturers overseas. So, the government is an eager partner in your effort to export, and one of the most valuable assets they can give you at this stage is information.

You need as much accurate information as you can get your hands on. Although the best source is the U.S. government, there is also a lot you can get from the targeted countries and from other sources. These sources of information will be useful not only for narrowing your choices, but also for the market scanning that should be an ongoing procedure and also for evaluating financial or political risk. At the end you should have a good idea of the country or countries where you are going to make a major effort.

FIVE STEPS TO PREDICT DEMAND

On-site market research is expensive and in certain cases may be impossible because of language differences or because of cultural or political restraints. When you have decided on a target market in one of the rich industrialized countries, many of the advanced research techniques of the domestic market can and should be used if you intend to make a large investment such as, for instance, setting up a foreign plant. But if you are primarily interested in exporting or if you cannot afford the cost or if there is a scarcity of reliable information, you can use other means to forecast demand. These are particularly useful if your preselection process has focused on several developing countries where accurate statistics are a problem. Taken singly, these steps can be misleading, but taken together they can give a good idea of expected demand. It is like looking at an object from five different angles. If it looks the same from all sides, you are fairly certain that what you are seeing is real, but if it looks different from two or three different angles, you know you need more accurate information before making any big decisions.

How To Narrow Your Choices

Step One: Predict the Future from the Past. In other words examine the trend in sales over a number of years and project this trend into the future. In many cases finding actual sales figures for different countries will be difficult, but you could get a fairly good idea of consumption by using the following equation:

Consumption = Domestic Production + Imports − Exports

For this you need trade and production statistics for your product in each country. Trade statistics are often the most accurate even in less developed countries because, historically, collecting taxes on imports was a major source of revenue. The problem, however, will be that the categories of imports may be too broad to identify your particular product. You may be able to offset this by statistics on exports from major exporting countries that might provide the detail you need.

But even if you know the actual sales figures, there are a few other factors to take into account. When you are thinking of going into a foreign market you will probably be thinking of a long-term investment, but the further you project present trends, the more risky the projection becomes. This is because you are assuming that present trends will continue more or less the same. But all kinds of things could change. A country may find a new and unexpected source of income, or all imports might be stopped, or your type of product could be targeted for special taxation. Obviously, projecting past trends in the Middle East, when oil was $2 a barrel, to 1980, when it was $30 a barrel, would have given a very false picture. Therefore, the projection has to be over a fairly short period especially if economic or political conditions in the country are uncertain.

Another problem is that present consumption may be greatly underestimated if most of it is supplied by imports. If you could supply that market from within with a cheaper product because of the absence of shipping costs and tariffs, you might have a much higher level of consumption than existing sales figures indicate. The danger is that based on present sales you pass up the market altogether, of if you do set up a manufacturing plant or supply facilities in the country you may find yourself without sufficient capacity to supply the demand. This danger will probably be lessened by the other steps you will take to estimate demand.

Step Two: Predict the Unfamiliar from the Familiar. Predict demand in other countries from what you know has happened to demand in the home market or in other countries at a similar stage of development. For example, if the sales of an electrical appliance have been tied to the rate of expansion of electrification in the home country, the same rate of increase can be projected to the target market to get an estimate of future demand. What you are doing is taking one factor that you know for most countries and presuming demand will change in a uniform way for all countries as change occurs in that factor. Usually, the factor taken is Gross National Product or per capita income or some other easily obtainable statistic. If you don't have actual demand for your product, you should be able to get historical sales data for its broad sector and be able to identify how demand has behaved as, for example, GNP or per capita income has increased. Research has shown that as per capita income has increased in certain countries, the percentage of total manufacturing in different sectors expands at very different rates. For example, there is a sharp increase in the demand for metal products and chemicals as gross domestic product per head increases, whereas the percentage of food or textiles in total manufacturing output decreases.[1]

This projection from one country to another has to be done with caution. There may be significant differences in culturally determined tastes from one country to another, or a very different income distribution pattern may seriously alter demand. Nevertheless, there is a lot you can learn about your product's potential by transferring the experience of one country to another. For example, the trend away from basics like food, beverages, and textiles toward more industrial-type production, as incomes increase, creates opportunities for suppliers of industrial inputs or machine tools.

Step Three: Determine the Factors that Are Associated with Levels of Sales in Your Home Market or Another Foreign Market and See to What Degree They Are Present or Are Beginning to Come into Play in the Market in Which You Are Interested. Let's say you are selling office furniture and office equipment. In the home market your level of sales is associated with a whole series of factors, for instance, the total size of the work force, the number of white-collar workers, the size of the service sector, the degree of urbanization, or the percentage of the work force involved in manufacturing. You could very simply rank these factors on a scale of low, medium, and high to get an idea of the attractiveness of different markets, such as in Figures 2.1 and 2.2. If, for example, Saudi Arabia is low on several counts then the market is unlikely to be large for office furniture.

How To Narrow Your Choices

FIGURE 2.1

	(1) LOW	(2) MEDIUM	(3) HIGH
Size of Work Force	6 million	6–12 million	12 million+
Number of White Collar Workers	1.5 million	1.5–6 million	6 million+
Service Sector % of GNP	5–10%	10–15%	15%+
Urbanized Population %	10–15%	15–25%	25%+
Work Force in Manufacturing %	8–15%	15–30%	30%+

One of the problems with this is that it gives you a static picture that is useful but not sufficient. You also need to see how changes in these factors have affected levels of sales so that you can project that onto your targeted country. If you have the necessary information, you can use regression analysis of historical information to determine, for example, how much unit sales of a product in your line increased for every increase in the white-collar work force or every jump in size of the service sector. In a more complicated use of this statistical technique, growth in sales is related to several factors together.

As usual, the problem here is the availability of information, not for the home market only. You also need similar information in the target market and some idea of the pace and direction of change in key factors. But if the information is at your disposal, this could be an extremely useful technique. One of the first major studies using regression analysis related some gross economic measurements to demand for certain products and was able to predict, for example, that for every $100 increase in per capita GNP, on average ten cars, ten refrigerators, 17 televisions, and 27 radios were purchased per 1,000 population.

Step Four: Predict Demand from Change in Income. This technique, called income elasticity of demand, tries to measure what changes will occur in consumption as changes occur in income. The increases in income and demand are measured in percentages, and you get the formula by dividing the percentage increase in demand for the product by the percentage increase in income. Let's take an example: Again, you want to predict the demand for office furniture as change occurs in income in a particular country. Follow these steps.

FIGURE 2.2

	Size of Work Force	Number of White-Collar Workers	Size of Service Sector	Urban Population	Work Force in Manufacturing
Brazil					
West Germany					
Indonesia					
Saudi Arabia	Low	Low	Medium	Low	Low
Australia					

How To Narrow Your Choices

Step I: Find out the level of income of either individuals or families in the country.

Step II: Find out what change in income is expected over your planning period.

Step III: Divide the expected change in income by existing income levels to get the percentage increase. For example, if average income per year is $10,000 and it is expected to increase by $500 per year over the next five years, you divide $500 × 5 = $2,500 by $10,000 to get a 25 percent increase.

Step IV: Next, find out the present demand for office furniture.

Step V: Find out how the demand for furniture has increased relative to the increase in incomes in the past. For example, if incomes increased by 25 percent in the past and office furniture increased by 45 percent, you divide 45 by 25 to get an income elasticity of 1.8.

Step VI: Next multiply the expected increase in income, i.e. 25% by the income elasticity for office furniture, i.e. 1.8 and you can expect that future demand for office furniture will increase by 45% or 25 × 1.8.

If the income elasticity for office furniture is only 0.75, then you can expect an increase of 25 × 0.75 = 18.75 or, in other words, a rate of increase slower than the increase in income. As incomes rise, it is to be expected that basic necessities like food and clothing will increase at a slower rate than other consumer, industrial, or recreational goods.

There are two important limitations to watch out for in using this technique:

1. You are using the income elasticity of the past and projecting it onto the future, but all kinds of things could change this such as a lower price, higher tariffs, or rapid unexpected increases in incomes.

2. Remember the rate of increase in sales does not necessarily mean a large market. The income elasticity for office furniture may be high, but total sales volume is low. The income elasticity for clothing may be low, but the sales volume very high.

Step Five: Find Out What Government or Semi-State Bodies are Purchasing Especially in Less Developed Countries Where There May Be a Large Public Sector. In many countries this is a large demand area, often financed by loans from multilateral lending agencies like the World Bank or the United States Agency for International Development. Government purchases of goods and services was and is a very large part of demand in the Middle East, but other countries like Indonesia, Thailand, and the Philippines have ambitious ongoing plans to develop their infrastructure with a large demand for goods and services in construction, engineering, and technical services. As we will see later on, many of these targets are made quite explicit in 5- or 10-year national plans, and very often the funding agencies have done some detailed market projections required for the approval of the loans. An added attraction is that most of the goods and services must be supplied under international competitive bidding. But apart from specific projects themselves, the governments' plans can give a key to expanding demand, for example, for household appliances in areas not previously having electricity.

FIVE QUESTIONS THAT INDICATE FUTURE DEMAND

1. What do past sales tell you about future demand?
2. What does the experience of other countries tell you about future demand?
3. What changes in the economy are important in changing demand?
4. Will demand for your product increase slower or faster than incomes?
5. Is the government going to be a large customer?

HOW UNCLE SAM CAN HELP YOU

In scanning markets and narrowing your choices down to a few interesting targets, what you need is information, information, and more information. Moreover, it needs to be cheap and easily available, and you need the same type of information for a large number of countries. For the developed industrialized economies this is not as big a problem as for the less developed countries. A developing country also has a developing ability to collect information. A straightforward census, for

How To Narrow Your Choices

example, in a large, mainly rural country is very expensive and may be postponed continuously because of scarce resources. In the United States market research has been greatly assisted by the willingness of people to reveal information about incomes, tastes, and expectations. In many of the developing countries that were colonized the usual purpose of any such information-collecting exercise used to be to raise rent or taxes, and responses were distorted accordingly. In several countries even the population figures are inflated, sometimes by a significant factor in order, for example, to intimidate a neighboring country. Sometimes the motive is more political. In the Middle East there are few countries with reliable population figures because some of them try to lower the number of foreigners working in their country or increase their own size to even the balance. But if there is a problem of quality and so much information is required, what do you do? The first thing you do is turn to Washington. This is true for firms interested in markets in the less developed countries and particularly true for the smaller- to medium-sized firms that are most suited for, and most acceptable in, these markets. The large multinational corporations will, of course, use this information also, but because of their existing international operations and their own in-house capacity many of them are independently and continuously looking at new markets anyway.

If scanning markets and measuring your choices as outlined here appears like a rather daunting task, it will come as a pleasant surprise to learn how much of it the government has already done for you and how easy it is to apply their information to your product. Generally speaking, the information is as accurate as you will get; it is easily available in libraries and regional offices of the various government departments, and for a very reasonable cost you can get a regular flow of the type of information you need in your firm by writing to the U.S. Government Printing Office in Washington, D.C. One of the problems with the government's information is that it is scattered among many different agencies and departments of the federal government. In running down the information you need, the best place to start is the Department of Commerce and the U.S. Government Printing Office. They have the bulk of the information.

Several other federal agencies can give you valuable assistance, and most of their information is also published by the Government Printing Office.

In order to put some order into the mass of information that is available, we will retrace some of the steps we have taken so far in global-market scanning and in narrowing our choices and see where we can find the information we need.

Where are your customers and what can they afford to pay? To get information on population worldwide, the first place to start is the U.S. Bureau of the Census. They cover social and economic data as well as information on population. The bureau is working on a computerized data base for all countries in the world, which covers many aspects that will be of interest in global scanning. Those include population growth rates, age structure, levels of education and literacy, urban/rural residence, and economic activity. In other words, it includes most of the information you need to break the market into broad segments and to determine economic size and levels of income. The Census Bureau also publishes detailed information on specific countries in the "Country Demographic Profiles." The next best source for the kind of broad information you need for global-market scanning is the State Department and in particular the "Background Notes" on each country that give summary information on population, geography, government, and the economy. They include information on per capita income, GNP, sizes of the different sectors, and an overall breakdown of imports and exports. The front page of "Background Notes" for Thailand, for example, shows how much information you can get from this concise and low-cost publication of the State Department.

Do they want what you have, and who is the competitor? The place to start here is the Department of Commerce. Each year their "Market Share Report" gives an overall view of what is being imported and by whom and how import demand is changing for different products. It gives information on the competitive position of the United States compared with foreign suppliers and identifies potential new markets for U.S. products. The reports are divided into the "Commodity Series" and the "Country Series." The former provides data on exports of particular products from the major exporting countries and shows the U.S. market share over a number of years. The "Country Series" examines the flow of more than 1,500 different products from the United States and its major exporting competitors into the major importing countries. These reports are a gold mine of information on what is in demand, how much the United States is supplying, and where the major competitors are located.

Because the information is given for a number of years, it also gives a good picture of whether the competitiveness of U.S. firms is improving or fading for a large number of manufactured products.

How To Narrow Your Choices

EXHIBIT 2.1

background notes

Thailand

United States Department of State
Bureau of Public Affairs

July 1985

**Official Name:
Kingdom of Thailand**

PROFILE

People

Nationality: *Noun and adjective*—Thai(s). **Population** (1984): 51 million. **Annual growth rate:** 2.0%. **Ethnic groups:** Thai 75%, Chinese 14%, other 11%. **Religions:** Buddhist 95.5%, Muslim 4%, other 0.5%. **Languages:** Thai, ethnic and regional dialects. **Education:** *Years Compulsory*—7. *Attendance*—83%. *Literacy*—84%. **Health:** *Infant mortality rate*—51.4/1,000. *Life expectancy*—62.7 yrs. **Work force:** 25 million. *Agriculture*—73%. *Industry and commerce*—11%. *Services*—10%. *Government*—6%.

Geography

Area: 514,000 sq. km. (198,500 sq. mi.): about the size of Texas. **Cities:** *Capital*—Bangkok (pop. 5.5 million). *Other cities*—Chiang Mai (115,000), Hat Yai (105,000), Nakon Ratchasima (98,000). **Terrain:** Four general regions—a densely populated central plain watered by the Chao Phraya River system; an eastern plateau bordered on the east by the Mekong River; a mountain range spanning the country in the west and separating the plain and plateau in east-central Thailand; and the southern isthmus joining the land mass with Malaysia. **Climate:** Tropical monsoon.

Government

Type: Constitutional monarchy. **Constitution:** December 1978. **Independence:** Never colonized.
Branches: *Executive*—king (chief of state), prime minister (head of government). *Legislative*—bicameral National Assembly. *Judicial*—three levels of courts.

Administrative subdivisions: 73 provinces, subdivided into 642 districts.
Political parties: Multiparty system; the Communist Party is prohibited. **Suffrage:** Universal over 20.
Central government budget: About $7.9 billion (213 billion baht).
Defense: 21% of budget.
Flag: Two red stripes at top and bottom, two white inner stripes, and wider blue band in middle. The blue represents royalty; the white, Buddhism; and the red, "Thailand," which means "land of the free."

Economy

GNP: $42 billion. **Annual growth rate:** 6%. **Per capita income:** $828. **Avg. inflation rate:** 8%.
Natural resources: Tin, rubber, natural gas, timber, fisheries products, tungsten.
Agriculture (20% of GNP): *Products*—rice, corn, sugarcane, tapioca. *Land*—24% agricultural.
Industry (18% of GNP): *Types*—textiles, agricultural processing, wood products, tin and tungsten mining.
Trade: *Exports*—$9.771 million: rice, rubber, tin, tapioca, shrimp, corn, sugar. *Major markets*—Japan, EC, US, Singapore, Hong Kong. *Imports*—$11,326 million: petroleum, machinery, food, capital equipment, fertilizer, chemicals. *Major sources*—Japan, EC, US.
Official exchange rate: 27.5 baht = US$1.

Membership in International Organizations

UN and some of its specialized agencies, including the World Bank Group and General Agreement on Tariffs and Trade (GATT); Association of South East Asian Nations (ASEAN); Asian Development Bank; INTELSAT.

EXHIBIT 2.2

Another useful report referred to as the FT Four Ten is put out by the Bureau of Census each month. The title speaks for itself: "Foreign Trade Report, FT 410: U.S. Exports—Commodity by Country." It shows the quantity, sales, and value of more than 4,500 U.S. products to most countries for the previous month and cumulatively for the year to date. An examination of the reports over a number of years will show the largest markets and the expanding markets for your product, your type of product, or your product group. A review of these reports and the "Market Share Reports" could very well indicate what markets are saturated, where the best growth areas are for your product, and where you are likely to be most competitive.

If you cannot get the information you need from these reports, you should contact your industry officer at the Department of Commerce. The major industrial groups such as industrial goods, construction, high technology, and financial and management services have specialists in each area. There are also "Export Statistics Profiles" put out by the Department of Commerce on specific industries, and yours may be included. They include information on the highest demand products, the best potential foreign markets, and your major foreign competitors. If you are interested in the export or production of agricultural commodities overseas, the Economic Research Service and the Foreign Agricultural Service of the Department of Agriculture issue a number of reports on production, exports, and trends in supply and demand worldwide. This is the kind of information that could be very useful if, for instance, you were interested in investing in food processing or supplying materials to that industry.

NARROWING YOUR CHOICES

At this stage you have focused your attention on a few attractive countries, and you want to take a closer look. Let's say one of those countries is Thailand and your product is in the telecommunications field. You will already have learned a lot about the Thai market from the "Market Share Reports," "Exports Statistics Profile," and the other aforementioned publications. But now you will see if the Department of Commerce has an "Overseas Business Report" on Thailand. These reports are designed to assist business people in finding new markets. They provide detailed marketing and commercial information on individual countries and are of great assistance in pursuing the steps necessary to narrow your choices. Of even greater interest because of their detail are

EXHIBIT 2.3

FT410/January 1984

Issued March 1984

U.S. EXPORTS

Schedule E Commodity by Country

Contents

Page

Explanation of Statistics 1

Abbreviations for Units of Quantity 6

Tables:
1. Value of Schedule E Groupings of Commodities—Domestic Merchandise 1-1
2. Schedule E Commodity by Country—Domestic Merchandise 2-1
3. Schedule E Commodity by Country—Foreign Merchandise 3-1

U.S. Department of Commerce
Malcolm Baldrige, Secretary
Clarence J. Brown, Deputy Secretary
Sidney Jones, Under Secretary for Economic Affairs

BUREAU OF THE CENSUS
John G. Keane,
Director

How To Narrow Your Choices

EXHIBIT 2.3 CONT'D.

International Marketing Information Series

Overseas Business Reports

December 1979   OBR 79-38

Marketing in Thailand

Prepared by Todd Burns
Office of Country Marketing

OBR

U.S. Department of Commerce
Industry and Trade Administration

EXHIBIT 2.3 CONT'D.

Contents

Page

Foreign Trade Outlook ....
  Best Export Prospects—Agribusiness Machinery and Equipment—Food Processing and Packaging Equipment—Mineral Prospecting and Processing Equipment—Hotel, Motel and Restaurant Equipment—Medical, Surgical and Hospital Equipment

Industry Trends ....
  GDP Movement—Growth Sectors—Business Climate—Government Role

Distribution and Sales Channels ....
  Import Marketing—Domestic Trade Channels—Market Characteristics and Preferences—Purchasers' Power

Transportation and Utilities ....
  Water Transport—Air Transport—Rail Transport—Road Transport—Electricity

Advertising and Research ....
  Advertising Agencies—Media—Market Research

Credit ....
  Capital Availability—Regulation of Supply—Financing Sources

Trade Regulations ....
  Documentation and Procedures—Taxation of Imports—
  Marking and Labeling Requirements

Investment in Thailand ....
  U.S. Investment—U.S.-Thailand Agreements—Forms of Business Organization—Foreign Investment Policy and Regulations—Labor Relations

Guidance for Business Travelers Abroad ....
  Entrance Requirements—Pertinent Treaties and Regulations—Foreign Exchange—Language—Holidays

Information Sources ....
  Government Representation—Publications

Market Profile ....

the "International Market Research Surveys" and the "Country Market Surveys" also produced by the Department of Commerce. The former are in-depth market studies, and even if they do not specifically cover your product in Thailand they may provide information on end users, potential buyers, and government purchasing requirements for other related products that could be of great interest to you. The "Country Market Surveys" summarize the market-research surveys by selected industrial groups, including communications equipment.

Certain countries on your short list may also be regarded as strategic countries by the U.S. government for foreign-policy reasons, and other agencies of the government may have specific programs to assist you. The Caribbean Basin and Egypt, for example, are areas that are getting the special attention of several government agencies. But getting back to Thailand, you would find that the Agency for International Development of the State Department has contracted management and consulting firms to provide assistance and information to U.S. companies interested in doing business in Thailand. Thailand is on the priority list of the Overseas Private Investment Corporation (OPIC) that has in the past organized investment missions to Thailand where small- and medium-sized U.S. firms are put in contact with potential partners, potential customers, and the relevant government officials.

As I mentioned earlier, many firms enter a foreign market for the first time by responding to an unsolicited request. But, as you systematically investigate markets or if you want to test the waters, you need not wait for someone to come to you because once again the Department of Commerce can provide you with many leads and help you to follow them up.

The "Commerce Business Daily" provides a daily list of U.S. government procurement invitations as well as foreign business opportunities. Most of the projects financed by the Agency for International Development (USAID) are advertised here. Many of the contracts are for consulting services and technical assistance, but often there is a large commodities component that must be supplied by U.S. firms under the loan or grant agreement. Commodities required under this funding are advertised in the "Export Opportunity Bulletin" of the USAID office of Business Relations. The agency sets aside certain components to be supplied by small businesses and also gives advice on how they can provide the equipment and materials required by USAID projects overseas. Responding to such a request funded by U.S. dollars out of Washington may be a rather painless first step into a market, such as Thailand, that you wish to develop.

How To Narrow Your Choices

How To Narrow Your Choices

EXHIBIT 2.4 CONT'D.

THAILAND INVESTMENT MISSION

JULY 10-17, 1982

Sponsored by
Overseas Private Investment Corporation
with the full cooperation of the
United States Department of State and the
Department of Commerce

OVERSEAS PRIVATE INVESTMENT CORPORATION

OPIC, a self-sustaining U.S. Government agency, assists U.S. investors in identifying and undertaking long-term private investments in some 100 friendly less-developed countries and areas in Latin America, Asia, Africa, Europe and the Middle East. OPIC programs offer qualified U.S. investors direct financial assistance to help establish commercial projects in the developing countries as well as insurance to protect investments against political risks.

OPIC programs are available for new ventures or for the expansion of existing projects which will contribute to host country development and help to strengthen the U.S. economy as well.

Insurance Program: OPIC's insurance program provides coverage against losses due to: inconvertibility of local currency earnings and return of capital; expropriation; war, revolution or insurrection, and certain types of civil strife.

Finance Program: OPIC's finance program is designed to promote and finance commercially viable projects for U.S. companies in the developing world. The three principal incentives are: feasibility study assistance, all-risk loan guarantees, and direct long-term loans for small businesses and cooperatives.

THAILAND INVESTMENT MISSION OBJECTIVES

- To enable mission participants to gain insights and information on the investment climate and the economic and political outlook for Thailand from the highest and most knowledgeable levels.

- To assist mission members on an individual basis, in the identification and evaluation of appropriate investment opportunities in the industry sectors of particular interest to them.

- To introduce mission members to the Thai business leaders and U.S. executives based in Thailand in related industries.

THE MISSION SCHEDULE

The Thailand Investment Mission objectives will be accomplished through the following activities:

Briefings
U.S. Embassy: U.S. Ambassador John Gunther Dean and key members of his staff will provide a background briefing on major political, economic, commercial, social and cultural trends in Thailand.

Business Briefings: Key business groups in Thailand will discuss in detail the decision making process towards establishing operations and investing in Thailand.

OPIC Officers: Throughout the mission, and at the pre-mission briefing in San Francisco, OPIC Insurance and Finance officers will brief mission members on the procedures for initiating or expanding an investment in Thailand.

Individual Business Appointments:
OPIC officers will travel to Bangkok in advance of the mission to arrange private business appointments for each mission member. These meetings, with prospective joint venture partners, Thai and American business leaders, and other appropriate persons, will comply with the objectives outlined by each company to OPIC.

Official Meetings
Chief of State or his Deputy: This meeting will provide insights into trends and possible changes in government policy.

Cabinet Ministers: Mission members will meet as a group with the Cabinet Ministers whose responsibilities bear most directly on the concerns of U.S. investors. Subsequent private meetings, for individuals or smaller groups, will be arranged if necessary.

Cross Cultural Activities
Mission members will experience life in Thailand through various receptions and dinners given by our Thai hosts; a tour of Bangkok and surrounding temples and palaces; plus shopping and exploring expeditions during free time.

EXHIBIT 2.4 CONT'D.

AN OVERVIEW OF THAILAND

The Country and Its People
Thailand occupies the center of mainland Southeast Asia. Approximately the size of France, Thailand can be divided geographically into four areas: the fertile central plain, the mountainous North, the semi-arid Northeast and diverse South. With a population of approximately 48 million, Thailand has a literacy rate of 85% for the population above age 10. Buddhism is the national religion.

Thailand has been a constitutional monarchy since 1932; a permanent constitution took effect in 1978. Continuity of government policies is maintained by the permanent bureaucracy with the support of the essentially conservative armed forces.

The Thai Economy
Thailand's GDP grew at an average rate of 8.7% in real terms between 1975 and 1979. GDP in 1980 was U.S. $32.9 billion, with agriculture accounting for 26% of the total and manufacturing 20%. Present U.S. investment in Thailand approximates $750 million.

Agriculture remains the mainstay of the economy and still accounts for over two-thirds of goods exported and employment. Furthermore, the processing of agricultural products accounts for a large part of manufacturing production. In recent years, manufactured exports have become an increasingly important source of growth. Thailand's economic policies aim towards restructuring both agricultural and industrial production so as to reduce imports and increase exports.

During the Five Year Plan (1982-1986), exports are targeted to increase at an annual average rate of 21.8 percent. Export-oriented industries which are expected to show high growth rates during the period include animal feeds, sugar, processed foods, textiles, rubber and leather goods, plastic and metal products, metal parts and electrical appliances. In the case of industries manufacturing for local consumption, the following are expected to perform well: paper and pulp, chemical fertilizers, oil and natural gas and the manufacture of rubber, cement, steel, agricultural machinery and motor parts.

The restructuring program will emphasize development of medium and small industries, as well as non-energy-intensive industries. The government will also step up the pace of development of principal industries, namely natural gas, steel, fertilizer and soda ash. The fact that the country now has its own large natural gas deposits will help lessen the gravity of energy problems. The completion of the gas separation plant in 1983 will spawn a large number of other industries.

Thailand has 16 local commercial banks with extensive national networks, 14 foreign commerical banks, and 10 foreign representatives. The Bank of Thailand is the central bank.

Thailand's Foreign Trade
Thailand's trade is greatest with Japan, the EEC and the USA although there is extensive Thai-ASEAN trade. Products traded include primary agricultural products, processed foods, manufactured goods and petroleum products. Thailand's manufactured goods and primary industrial products go chiefly to the USA. Trends suggest that Thailand's extra-ASEAN foreign trade will increase at a high rate.

Investment Climate
Thailand's investment climate continues to be attractive to the U.S. investor. Thailand has granted a variety of promotional privileges to foreign investors since 1954. The Board of Investment (BOI) continues to encourage investment through the provision of promotional privileges. Thailand has 5 investment promotion zones, or industrial estates. Special benefits and incentives are extended to investors who invest in export-oriented industries, industrial enterprises in the provinces and investment promotion zones.

Among the attractions to the U.S. investor in Thailand are:
- an industrious and loyal work force
- a freely convertible currency
- no restrictions on repatriation of profits, dividends or capital
- one hundred percent foreign ownership permitted
- corporate tax exemptions
- no import duties or business taxes on imported machinery
- wage rates among the lowest in Asia
- benefits and protection from dumping through special tax barriers against imports of various products plus other guarantees in accordance with the Investment Promotion Act
- protection against double taxation through bilateral agreements between Thailand and foreign governments including the U.S.
- special incentives to businesses exporting 50% or more of their production
- a well developed infrastructure

Investment Potential
The most promising and profitable sectors for U.S. investment include: food processing, animal feeds, insecticides, mining, machine tools, industrial and agricultural machinery, tourism, electrical/electronics equipment manufacture, chemical fertilizers, and other labor intensive industries including leather products, wooden furniture and marble working.

Over 300 U.S. companies are operating in Thailand through wholly owned subsidiaries, joint ventures or subcontracting arrangements. The companies include: IBM, Union Oil, Firestone, Hyatt International Hotels, Johnson & Johnson, Star Feed Mill Co. and Carnation International.

(see reverse for schedule outline and application procedures)

How To Narrow Your Choices

EXHIBIT 2.4 CONT'D.

TENTATIVE SCHEDULE OUTLINE
OVERSEAS PRIVATE INVESTMENT CORPORATION
THAILAND INVESTMENT MISSION

Date	Time	Activity
July 10 Saturday + 24 hours (Crossing International Date Line)	10:30 a.m.	Briefing San Francisco Airport Hilton San Francisco International Airport (SFO)
	Noon	Depart Hilton Hotel for VIP Lounge (SFO)
	2:30 p.m.	Depart San Francisco via Pan Am Flight #5 to Hong Kong
July 11 Sunday	10:00 p.m.	Depart Hong Kong via Pan Am Flight #1 to Bangkok
	11:35 p.m.	Arrive Bangkok Transfer to the Oriental Hotel
July 12 Monday	9:00-10:00 a.m.	Briefing at U.S. Embassy by U.S. Ambassador John Gunther Dean and Embassy staff
	10:30-11:30 a.m.	Briefing by Thai Government ministers
	11:30 a.m.-7:00 p.m.	Individual business appointments
	7:00 p.m.	Reception at U.S. Ambassador Dean's residence
July 13 Tuesday	8:30 a.m.	Breakfast briefing hosted by the American Chamber of Commerce in Thailand
	10:00 a.m.	Optional tour of Investment Promotion Zones
	10:00 a.m.-6:00 p.m.	Individual business appointments
	6:00 p.m.	Sunset dinner cruise aboard Rice Barge Charter down the Chao Phraya River
July 14 Wednesday	9:00 a.m.	Optional tour of Thai Temples and Palaces
	Entire Day	Individual business appointments
	7:00 p.m.	Banquet hosted by the Thai Manufacturers Association
July 15 Thursday	Entire Day	Individual business appointments
	7:00 p.m.	No group dinner is scheduled however dinner will be available in the Oriental Hotel at OPIC's expense if desired
July 16 Friday	Entire Day	Individual business appointments
	7:00 p.m.	Gala Banquet hosted by OPIC for mission participants and Thai hosts at the Suan Pakkard Palace
July 17 Saturday - 24 hours (Crossing International Date Line)	8:30 a.m.	Depart Bangkok via JAL Flight #476 to Tokyo
	5:20 p.m.	Depart Tokyo via Pan Am Flight #12 to SFO
	10:30 a.m.	Arrive San Francisco

NOTE: Alternative travel arrangements may be made with the mission's travel agent either to remain in Thailand or to return to the U.S. on other flights, normally without additional charge for air fare, unless indirect routes are desired. The mission's travel agent is Dottie Spicer, American Express (202/457-1354). She will contact you upon receipt of final payment.

Briefing Materials
A Thailand briefing book will be sent to each mission member upon receipt of final payment for the mission. Each participant will also receive information on how to dress, flight and baggage information, U.S. government baggage tags, etc.

Payment and Application Procedures
The price for each participant of $4,400 is due no later than June 15. It includes clipper class air fare on Pan Am 747's, first class hotel accommodations with single occupancy at the Oriental Hotel, all meals except lunches, transportation to and from scheduled events, airport taxes, and sight-seeing and entertainment as specified. THE CLOSING DATE FOR RECEIPT OF APPLICATIONS AND FULL PAYMENT IS JUNE 15, 1982. Additional applications are available from OPIC.

For further information, contact:
Mary V. Cunningham
OPIC
1129 20th St. N.W.
Washington, D.C. 20527
202/653-2924 or
800/424-6742 toll-free

IT-2PAIDCLH

Business America, published twice a week, also gives information on trade opportunities as well as information on exhibitions and international trade fairs where you may wish to introduce or display your product.

The department also has an International Market Search Program where they select specific industries to be promoted worldwide for one year. In 1983 telecommunications was selected for promotion through the publication "Commercial News U.S.A.," and if your firm and product qualified for entry in this program, you could have been exposed to an estimated 200,000 business and government leaders worldwide. If your product is new, it could also qualify for inclusion in "Commercial News U.S.A.," so that foreign customers looking for your specific product can respond directly to your firm.

Another service of the Commerce Department is the Trade Opportunities Program (TOP). There is a weekly "TOP Bulletin," which is a synthesis of trade leads received and covers a broad range of products. The same information is supplied on computer tape in "TOP Datatape Service." But TOP also provides a more specialized service where you can list your product or product line and your short list of countries and TOP will attempt to match you with customers or representatives in the targeted countries who are looking for your product. You will receive a trade opportunity notice providing quite detailed information on the foreign buyer and their requirements.

The department also keeps an index of high potential foreign buyers called the Foreign Traders Index (FTI). It contains information from most countries and more than 150,000 potential firms, agents, importers, or users of your product. An attractive feature of the Index is that it can be retrieved on your own computer facility and is also available in booklet form for selected countries and products.

These are your main sources of information available from the U.S. government and required at this stage of your investigation. There is other valuable information available that you will need as you proceed to enter a foreign market, for example, on insurance, funding of feasibility studies, or export and import assistance. We will deal with this as we proceed. It comes as a great surprise to many business people that the government has so much information available and is willing to help them in so many ways to find a foreign market. The information is valuable; it costs a lot of money to assemble, and yet it is all available to you in your home office at a cost that would probably be less than one expensive overseas trip to one market. The homework to be done on this

How To Narrow Your Choices

SUMMARY OF FEDERAL GOVERNMENT INFORMATION AVAILABLE
FOR MARKET RESEARCH

---

1. Bureau of Census
2. "Background Notes"–Department of State
3. "Market Share Reports"
4. Foreign Trade Reports (FT 410)
5. "Export Statistics Profile"
6. "International Market Research Surveys"
7. "Country Market Surveys"
8. "Overseas Business Reports"
9. "Export Opportunity Bulletin"
10. Trade Opportunities Program (TOP)
11. "Commerce Business Daily"
12. "Business America"
13. "Commercial News U.S.A."
14. Foreign Traders Index
15. Foreign Agricultural Service

---

information is considerable and requires a disciplined approach, and it is so much more exciting to get out there and take a look oneself. In fact, a week spent in your home office will probably give you far more hard information on a country and a market than many weeks in the field trying to get the same information. The trip to the field comes at a later stage when you know where you should go and you have concrete goals to achieve. The difference is essentially one of taking a systematic and planned look at the international marketplace with a long-term perspective versus responding to immediate sales opportunities that may arise and look very attractive for the short run.

OTHER SOURCES OF INFORMATION

One of the great advantages of the information you get from most U.S. government agencies and particularly from the Commerce Department is that it is geared toward helping business people like yourself. In other words, it is already processed. But there may be gaps in it, or you may need more detail on, for example, production figures in a particular sector, or you may want to double check information with a second source. There are many sources of extra information, but we will concentrate here on three: the World Bank, the United Nations, and the host country itself. If between the U.S. government and the three sources just mentioned you cannot get the information you want, then you will have to turn to organizations that focus on the particular region or countries in which you are interested. Two such sources are of particular interest, namely, the European Economic Community (EEC), which has information centers in Washington and New York, (although most of its information is in Brussels) and the Organization for Economic Corporation and Development (OECD). This is an association of the industrialized nations and is a particularly good source of information on those countries. It is based in Switzerland but has a New York Office.

The World Bank

The World Bank is owned by the government of 46 countries and has as its central purpose the promotion of economic and social progress in the developing countries, a goal it achieves mainly by raising money in the financial markets of the developed countries and lending it to the less developed countries for a wide variety of projects. The World Bank lends money only after several detailed feasibility analyses have been conducted in the field. This provides it with a unique collection of information, a lot of which it is willing to make available to the public at a minimal cost.

Again, to get a handle on this mass of material, it is useful to break it down into two categories: world statistics and specific country information. At the world level, three publications are of particular use for scanning markets: (1) "World Tables," which contains the most up-to-date information on all the countries covered by the World Bank and includes countries of the Eastern bloc that may not be very well covered by U.S. government sources. The most recent edition is divided into two volumes. Volume 1 gives statistics on population, national accounts, balance of payments, external trade, external debt, central government finances, industrial statistics, trade in manufactures, and what may be of particular interest to you, the most recent conclusions on purchasing-power parities and real gross domestic product across different currencies. Volume 2 is very useful in determining some of the dynamics of a

How To Narrow Your Choices

EXHIBIT 2.5

MARKET SHARE REPORTS/COUNTRY SERIES

	NTIS Stock No.		NTIS Stock No.		NTIS Stock No.
Algeria	PB85-795001	Guatemala	PB85-795024	Pakistan†	PB85-795050
Argentina	5002	Haiti	5089	Panama	5051
Australia	5003	Honduras	5025	Peru*	5052
Austria	5004	Hong Kong	5026	Philippines	5053
Bangladesh	5083	Hungary	5080	Poland	5074
Belgium-Lux.	5005	India	5027	Portugal	5054
Bolivia	5006	**Indonesia**	5028	Qatar	5086
Brazil	5007	Iran	5029	Romania	5081
Bulgaria	5077	Iraq	5088	Saudi Arabia*	5055
Cameroon	5008	**Ireland**	5030	Singapore	5056
Canada	5009	Israel**	5031	South Africa*	5057
Chile	5010	Italy	5032	Spain	5058
China	5076	Ivory Coast**	5033	Sweden	5059
Colombia	5011	**Jamaica***	5034	Switzerland	5060
Costa Rica*	5013	Japan	5035	Taiwan	5061
Czechoslovakia	5078	Jordan*	5091	Tanzania	5062
Denmark	50114	Kenya*	5036	Thailand	5063
Dominican Rep.	5015	Korea	5037	Trinidad & Tobago	5064
Ecuador*	5016	Kuwait	5038	Tunisia	5065
Egypt	5068	Liberia	5040	Turkey	5066
El Salvador*	5017	Libya	5041	Uganda	5067
Ethiopia*	5018	**Malaysia***	5042	United Arab Emir.	5082
Finland	5019	Mexico	5043	U.S.S.R.	5075
France	5020	**Morocco***	5044	United Kingdom	5069
Gabon	5085	Netherlands	5045	Venezuela	5070
German Democratic Rep.	5079	New Zealand	5046	Yugoslavia	5072
		Nicaragua*	5047	Zaire	5012
Germany	5021	Nigeria	5048	Zambia	5073
Ghana	5022	Norway	5049	Zimbabwe	5087
Greece	5023	Oman	5091		

The Country Series gives import trends in 1,500 manufactured products. A 50 to 90-page report is available for each of 88 countries for 1980-83 except as noted (* 1980-82, **1981-83, and † 1982-83). Reports on countries in bold face are based on import data; other reports are based on export data from 14 major industrial nations.

Order your   Country Series of

MARKET SHARE REPORTS

with this special coupon

Name ....

Address ....

City, State, ZIP ....

COUNTRY REPORTS, $11.00 each ($22.00 foreign orders). Send check or money order payable to the U.S. Department of Commerce.

Please send me—
PB 85-79 ....
PB 85-79 ....
PB 85-79 ....
PB 85-79 ....
PB 85-79 ....
PB 85-79 ....
PB 85-79 ....
PB 85-79 ....
PB 85-79 ....
PB 85-79 ....

MAIL TO: National Technical Information Service, U.S. Department of Commerce, Springfield, Va. 22161

EXHIBIT 2.5 CONT'D.

ITA's New Market Share Reports Provide Data On Manufactures Exports To Foreign Markets

The International Trade Administration has again updated its Commodity series of Market Share Reports which compare the export performance of U.S. goods in foreign markets with those from the 13 other major supplier nations. The reports identify trends in the value of exports from each of those suppliers and the U.S. share of that trade for about 1,500 manufactured products sold in 100 country markets from 1980 through 1983. The new issue of the Commodity Reports continues a series designed for evaluating both short- and long-term trends in market performance.

The data in these reports, which cover nearly 80 percent of the world's exports of manufactured products, provide exporters with an efficient and economical method of obtaining market information. They help identify foreign market opportunities by showing:

—systematic overviews of import markets

—market trends for established products

—advance indicators of emerging markets

—shifts in supplier performance.

Individual companies are provided a basis for assessing the effectiveness of their own sales efforts with those of other U.S. suppliers. The data help pinpoint where these efforts should be strengthened. These reports will also aid market analysts in projecting future demand and market share potential.

These easy-to-read reports present products classified according to the widely used United Nations Standard International Trade Classification, Revision 2 (SITC).

The Commodity Reports, prepared by the Trade Statistics Division/Office of Trade and Investment Analysis/Trade Information and Analysis, are available for sale by the National Technical Information Service, U.S. Department of Commerce, Springfield, Va., 22161, at $7.50 each.

Prices and instructions for ordering sets of reports are given on the following page. The full list showing each separate report begins on page 32.

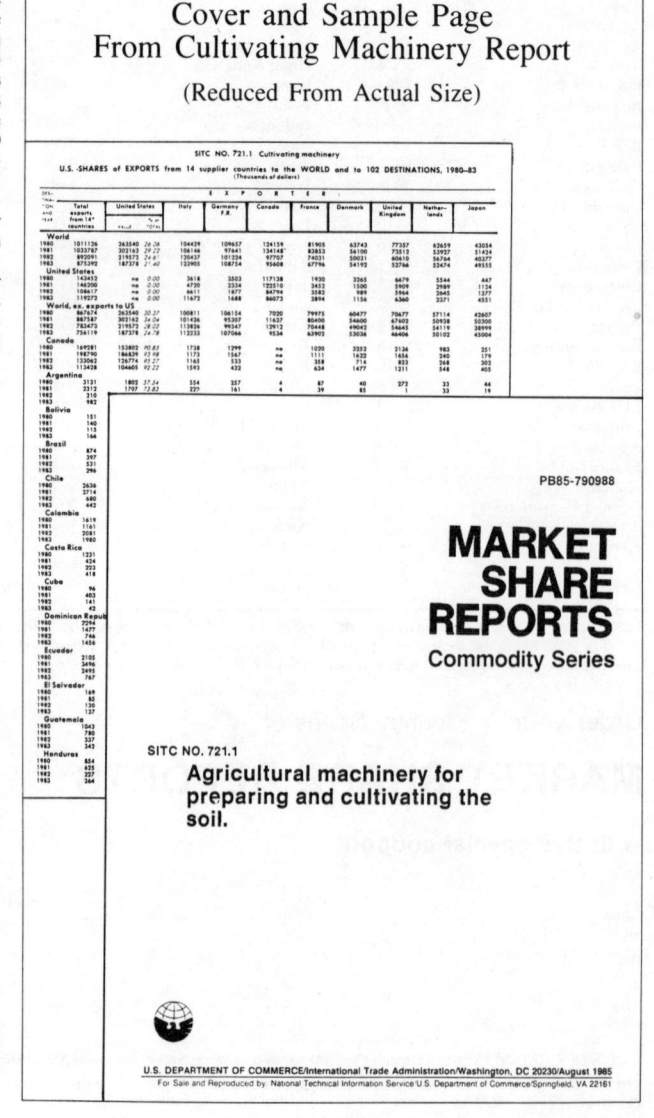

Cover and Sample Page From Cultivating Machinery Report
(Reduced From Actual Size)

particular market because it gives time-series information in such areas as population, employment, incomes, and consumption. (2) The "World Bank Atlas" presents figures on GNP, per capita GNP, annual growth rates, and population for 189 countries and territories. (3) The "World Development Report" is like an annual report on the condition of the planet, and it contains a statistical annex, called World Development Indicators that provides profiles of more than 120 countries.

The information on individual countries can be of great assistance as you try to narrow your choices and get detailed information on things like present consumption, production, or trade. This information can be quite detailed and consequently most useful. It is collected on the ground by professionals who are either hired by the Bank or are employees sent to the country to prepare, appraise and evaluate projects that the Bank plans to finance. Some of these reports require market studies or information that is relevant to your market study and is focused on particular sectors or subsectors. Sometimes the Bank collects a lot of this information in one book, but usually these are regarded as internal Bank documents, which can be gotten only after the loan is approved and then through the U.S. government representative in the Bank. If you want to know what projects or sectors the Bank is now studying in any or all countries, you can find out from the "World Bank Operational Summary." This is put out each month and gives a status report of each loan being planned in each country and what stage it is in in the project cycle. Getting back to our example of telecommunications in Thailand, you would see if the Bank were planning a loan in this area or whether it had conducted appraisals or feasibility studies in related areas that could supply you with a lot of the information you need.

The World Bank is by far the most significant multilateral lending agency, but there are other area-specific banks that may have information on specific sectors that you are interested in. These include the Asian Development Bank, the Inter-American Development Bank, the African Development Bank, and the Caribbean Development Bank. All conduct their own detailed studies before giving a loan or a grant and may just have information on an area, a sector, or a project that you need.

United Nations

The Commerce Department collects information to assist firms entering foreign markets; the World Bank collects information to prepare its loans, and some say the United Nations collects information just for the sake of collecting information. One way or the other it probably has the most information of all agencies but often in a form that you will have to process to draw the conclusions you need.

The *United Nations Statistical Yearbook* provides a vast amount of information about more than 200 countries. The economic commissions conduct studies in their respective areas and issue regular publications such as the "Economic Survey of Latin America" and "Economic and Social Survey of Asia and the Pacific." The International Monetary Fund (IMF) and the General Agreement on Tariffs and Trade (GATT), affiliated organizations, issue international financial statistics and data on world trade. Of particular interest to firms doing business overseas are the reports and information collected by the Specialized Agencies of the United Nations. The most relevant are the World Health Organization (WHO), the Food and Agriculture Organization (FAO), the International Labor Organization (ILO), and the United Nations Development Program (UNDP). Several of these procure millions of dollars worth of equipment, commodities, and supplies such as medical and agricultural equipment. But of greater use to most companies are their publications and reports that may contain information you need. For example, if you wanted to get information on labor conditions, labor costs, or levels of skills in a particular country the place to start looking would be the publications of the ILO. Or if you were in the food or food-processing industry, you would find that the WHO and FAO have a publication, "Current Food Additives Legislation."

NEED MORE INFORMATION? HAVE YOU CHECKED THESE SOURCES?

---

1. EEC offices in Washington, New York, Brussels
2. The Organization for Economic Corporation and Development (OECD)
3. The World Bank: A. World Tables
   B. World Bank Atlas
   C. The World Development Report
   D. World Bank Operational Summary
4. United Nations Statistical Yearbooks
5. The International Monetary Fund

Getting Information from the Host Country

This source of information is purposely placed last because it is likely to be the least rewarding and the most difficult to get, especially if you are trying to export there. You would start by approaching the commercial officer of the embassy or the consulate in the United States. Of course, their priority is to expand exports into this country rather than promote imports into theirs, so the type of information they have available or are willing to release will center around that goal. It might also be possible to get the information you need from a well-known or established distributor in the country or through another company or its distributor. The commercial attaché at the U.S. Embassy may also be able to root out specific information that you need and that is not generally available. The least rewarding source, especially at a distance, is to try and get the information directly from government sources themselves.

If you are thinking of investing in the market and the country is looking for foreign investment, however, the picture changes significantly, and all kinds of information may be made available from all the aforementioned sources. The country may even have an information office here in the United States with the specific purpose of helping you in this goal.

CAN YOU SUPPLY THE MARKET?

There comes a stage when you have learned as much as you can learn at your desk. The next step will be a visit to the country or countries that you have decided offer you the best opportunities. You have reviewed a massive amount of information on the global marketplace, you have seen certain trends that may have come as a surprise, and some of your short-listed countries may be ones you would never have considered without this systematic scanning. But what you have been looking at are mainly market factors, and on that basis you are zooming in on a few countries. You now need to take into account some other important factors that will confirm your choice of the target markets or assist you in narrowing your choice further. These factors include entry barriers, your time frame, and your capabilities.

Most barriers are presented by the host country. The most obvious one is a specific tariff that is designed to keep your product out or make it too expensive to compete. This may be imposed to protect a local producer or to give an advantage to a different supplier. Probably more common than the explicit tariff barrier is a non-tariff barrier (NTB), which is designed to make entry into the market difficult or impossible while still technically obeying the rules of international free trade. This can be achieved by making customs and entry procedures twice as difficult as they already are, or by imposing health or quality standards designed to keep imports out, or by subsidizing local production to make it the most competitive producer, or by requiring the importer to deposit a high percentage of the value of the imported product in a noninterest-bearing account in the central bank. For example, the French greatly slowed the import of Japanese video-recording machines by simply insisting that they all clear customs at a port with very few customs officials. Similarly, there has been a dramatic drop in U.S. exports to Mexico over the last few years because of the unavailability of foreign exchange to most importers.

In looking at these kinds of barriers, however, it is also important to look around them. Very often they are meant to target imports, but the government may be quite sympathetic to a different form of entry into the market; for instance, a form of entry that would create employment or generate exports out of the country or utilize abundant resources in the country. So although the normal progression for a foreign firm in entering a foreign market is first to export and later to invest, that need not necessarily be the case. If the market is attractive, you might decide to get in behind the barriers designed to affect only imports.

So the evaluation of the market potential is intimately connected with how you decide to enter the market, but to eliminate a market because of the difficulty of one entry method would be a wrong conclusion at this stage.

Home-Country Barriers

This applies mainly to exports of technical equipment or skills that could help an unfriendly foreign power. The U.S. government may also limit exports to achieve foreign policy goals like, for example, the limitation of trade with Poland. Similarly the U.S. government has regulations making it difficult for U.S. firms to comply with the Arab boycott of companies doing business with Israel. If you are in a high-technology area, these barriers could affect you. Also, if you intend to produce overseas you might come under pressure from the local government to export to countries that the U.S. government has embargoed.

Is your orientation to particular foreign markets for the long run, the short run or a mixture of both? If you are systematically evaluating different markets as previously outlined, you are almost certainly interested in a long-term penetration into your targeted markets. However, there may be markets on your short list that are attractive only

How To Narrow Your Choices

for the short term and that could generate a significant amount of sales over that period. In these situations the long-term economic or political outlooks are not so important.

If you are entering the market for the long term, the economic and political factors are going to have an impact on your effort, these subjects will be dealt with in detail in the next two chapters.

If you were looking at the Nigerian market when oil prices boomed in 1979, you might have decided to enter the market for immediate and profitable sales or contracts, but to hold off on the long-term commitment because of either balance of payments or political considerations.

In the short run you are not too interested in further analysis of the market beyond the fact that you can make immediate sales at a profit and get paid. If you decide to visit a country, it will be to promote that objective. But if you are interested in the long term, you are going to do much more research before visiting the country and you are going to look much more closely at channels into the country, channels within the country, and such concerns as product adaptation for the market in question.

Can I handle the market? As a firm begins to move into a foreign market a key question is how much effort can be put into developing, supplying or financing the market. If you are narrowing down your choices, your resources will determine how many markets you can afford to enter, at what level, and with what method of entry. What this involves is an inventory of your own capabilities and this can be systematically done by looking at your Personnel, Production and Financial resources.

Personnel: Two aspects are important here. First, how much time and effort can top managers spend on the development of international markets? This is very often the key to success because without the commitment of top management it will be extremely difficult to get the resources needed or to get products adapted and so on. If your firm has no international marketing involvement at all, the situation is likely to be more difficult, and this is where short-term sales or occasional exports may indicate to top management what can be achieved. Second, what personnel have international experience or what resources are available to bring some of that experience on board. This expertise is invaluable in planning and evaluating data on foreign markets and especially necessary when it comes to visiting the country, making contacts, or conducting negotiations with foreign governments or business contacts. This is probably more necessary now than in the traditional U.S. export markets of Europe and Canada. More trade moves East now to the Pacific than across the Atlantic, and these markets are more complex and unknown and more difficult to analyze.

Production: If you are just entering a foreign market for the first time, the key question is the capacity to supply it with existing facilities when and if it opens up. Related to this is your capacity to make any necessary changes in the product or its packaging or labeling if one or several of these require it. Finally, in the longer term, or if you are forced to invest in production facilities overseas, a big question is where you will locate your facilities, how one plant can be coordinated with others, and what advantage the location of your production facilities are likely to give you.

Financial: Last, but definitely not least, is your financial ability to make the move into a foreign market. Again, this will depend on the degree of involvement, the time frame, and the method of entry. It could range from the small expenditures used to research and export to a market to the cost of setting up a manufacturing facility on the inside if that is the only or the best way to supply the market.

REFERENCE

1. R. Moyer, *Journal of Marketing Research*, "International Market Analysis," 5 (1968):235.

3

A STEP-BY-STEP APPROACH TO EVALUATING FINANCIAL RISK

You had a nice arrangement with your distributor in Venezuela. All sales were invoiced in dollars, and as your relationship developed, you often allowed 60 or 90 days to pay after the date of export. There was never any problem. Then after a particularly large shipment and without warning, the Venezuelan government imposed exchange controls to halt the flight of capital out of the country. Your goods are in the country, but you cannot get your money out.

In 1979 the price of oil had gone over $30 a barrel. The British pound was very strong, and the experts predicted it would get stronger as the income from Britain's oil exports got higher. Facing a choice to finance your investment in England in either pounds or dollars, you chose dollars at an exchange rate of £1 = $2.00. You expected the pound to rise to $2.50 and because your revenues would be in pounds you would be paying off the loan in cheaper dollars. Six years later it is the pound that has dropped to £1 = $1.50 as the demand and price of oil dropped. Where you expected to be able to pay off your debt at the rate of $2.5 for every pound earned you can now pay off only $1.50 for every pound.

But it can also work the other way. You plan an expansion of your production in Mexico to be largely self-financed by your subsidiary there, using local equipment and machine tools. More than 50 percent of your output is exported to the United States and paid for in dollars. A sharp drop in the Mexican peso dramatically increases your income in pesos and makes financing of your plant so much easier.

The foregoing situations illustrate an area of financial risk unique to international business, namely, the risk associated with foreign currencies. All investments domestic or international involve risk, and the manager has to make a decision on a reasonable balance between the risks involved and the profits he or she hopes to achieve. The forces affecting the risk in foreign currencies are largely outside the control of the firm, but what is not outside its control is the firm's ability to foresee risk and to take steps that minimize the negative impact or even turn it into an advantage.

In the large multinational companies, tracking the pressures and movements of foreign currencies is the full time job of experts, but every manager needs to know the roots of the problem and the tools that are used to analyze it. Foremost among these tools is the ability to interpret the balance of payments of the countries where you do business.

WHAT YOU CAN LEARN FROM THE BALANCE OF PAYMENTS

The balance of payments is a set of statistics published on a regular basis by each country showing the transactions that have taken place between residents of the country and foreigners over the recording period. In other words every export, import, payment, or receipt of dividends and interest and investments into or out of the country, as well as the movement of gold and foreign exchange reserves are recorded by the government and published, usually on a yearly basis, although most industrial countries also publish quarterly and even monthly figures. When the amount of money or goods a country receives from foreigners equals the amount it pays to foreigners the economy is considered to be in equilibrium or in balance with the other economies of the world. Of course, within any particular period it is unlikely that the inflow of goods or currency will exactly equal the outflow. But if a country runs a longer term and serious surplus or a longer term and serious deficit, then the warning signals are beginning to flash red and corrective actions are likely to be taken by the government, actions that could have a profound effect on your business if you are not prepared. In order to be able to analyze what is happening it is necessary to know how the balance of payments is put together and what the important categories are within the balance of payments statement as a whole.

Double Entry

In putting together the balance of payments every transaction is regarded as an exchange of one thing for another and so is recorded twice. If you import a fancy Mercedes from Germany, the transaction is recorded as an import and also as an out-payment made to the German manufacturer. The import is regarded as a debit and the payment as a credit. The words "debit" and "credit" are simply bookkeeping terms that have no great significance in themselves. The important thing to remember is that every debit is matched by a credit, and under the rules of double entry bookkeeping an increase in assets is always listed as a debit and an increase in liabilities as a credit. The combination of the debits shows the country's claims against the rest of the world while the credits show the rest of the world's claims against the country. For example, when you buy that Mercedes, there is an increase in the claims of foreigners against you, a resident. When you pay in German marks from your bank, you are in effect reducing the claims of foreigners against you by that amount. Since every transaction is recorded twice, the end result is a balance where total debits equal total credits. This end result has no significance at all; what is significant is what is happening to the flow of goods in and out of the country and how they are being paid for. For example, if a Mexican firm wants to buy six trucks from Ford, it will have to buy dollars with its pesos, because obviously, Ford will want payment in dollars. When the Mexican firm gets the dollars, it is in effect reducing the ability of the Mexican economy to meet foreign claims against it by that amount. Of course, it is expected that at the same time Mexico is exporting oil or other goods and so is earning dollars to offset the outflow of dollars. If the outflow and the inflow are about equal, there is little effect on the official reserves of gold and foreign exchange. However, if Mexico has to dig into its official reserves to supply the foreign currency necessary to meet its import requirements and the claims of foreigners against it, and if it has to do this on a continuous basis, it means it will run out of foreign currency and not be able to meet its foreign obligations. It also means that the Mexican economy has been moving out of balance with the other economies of the world, and the steps it is likely to take to bring it back into balance could have a serious impact on your firm.

The Balance of Payments Format

The International Monetary Fund (IMF) has a standard presentation for the balance of payments, and the key to interpreting it is to know the significant sub-balances and what they are telling you about the economy. The IMF format is broken down into three different accounts, namely, the current, capital, and reserves accounts. In short, the current account covers imports, exports, services, interest, dividends, and payments such as royalties, rentals, and management fees. The capital account covers the movement of money into foreign investment, foreign portfolio investment, and foreign loans both long-term and short-term, private and official. The reserves account shows what the official monetary authority of the country has been doing with the reserves of foreign currencies, gold, and the reserves on deposit with the IMF. Within these three categories are the important sub-balances that show what is really happening to the economy vis-a-vis the rest of the world. These sub-balances are highlighted in Figure 3.1 in an abbreviated version of the IMF format.

Interpreting the Balances

Earlier we mentioned that the balance of payments always balances, and yet it is regularly stated of a country that it has a balance-of-payments "surplus" or "deficit." What is being referred to here is a surplus or deficit within the various sub-balances, and a surplus or deficit in these varies in significance from country to country. The root cause of most balance-of-payments problems lies in a continuous deficit in trade.

A country is like a household; in the long run it has to earn enough foreign exchange to pay its foreign obligations for imports, or loans, or other liabilities. If there is a persistent trend in the deficits, you know that the money to pay will have to come from other sources, or the country is using up its reserves. The government can take several steps singly or together to try to remedy the situation. (1) It may reduce imports by imposing a total ban, or tariffs or non-tariff barriers. If you are an exporter into this market, you are immediately affected. If you are producing inside the country but using imported components, you may not be able to get them or they may be much more expensive.

If your product is generating employment locally or is of a productive nature, there are likely to be fewer restrictions. If you are an exporter out of the country and the overall impact of your business is positive by

FIGURE 3.1

		Debits	Credits
I.	Current Account		
A.	Merchandise Trade	Imports	Exports

MERCHANDISE TRADE BALANCE

| B. | Services, including freight, insurance, travel, tourism, fees, royalties, construction services | Outpayments | Receipts |

GOODS AND SERVICES BALANCE

| C. | Investment income, profits from foreign investment including interest, dividends, and reinvested earnings | Profits Out | Profits In |

GOODS, SERVICES, AND INCOME BALANCE

| D. | Unilateral transfers, pensions, gifts, economic and military aid | Out | In |

CURRENT ACCOUNT BALANCE

II.	Capital Account		
E.	Direct investment	Out	In
F.	Portfolio investments	Increase	Decrease
G.	Long-term capital: loans by the government and private parties, loan repayments	Out	In
H.	Short-term capital: increase and decrease in assets held by foreigners or residents		

CAPITAL ACCOUNT BALANCE

III.	Office Reserves		
I.	Gold	Out	In
J.	Foreign Currencies	Out	In
K.	SDRs	Out	In
L.	Reserves in IMF	Decrease	Increase

OFFICIAL RESERVES BALANCE

increasing exports and limiting imports, you are likely to do better, although an across-the-board tariff could make you less competitive when you pass the cost on in other markets. (2) The government may decide to devalue the currency. By doing so it makes imports more expensive and makes exports cheaper because it now takes less of the foreign currency to buy the same amount of that country's goods. Going back to our British example when the pound was one for two, the cost of a $50,000 American computer would be £=25,000. At $1.50 to the pound the cost is more than £33,333. The opposite is true for British exports to the United States, so British exports will rise and U.S. exports will drop, and in this way Britain would hope to remedy its trade deficit. In the meantime, you can get whiplashed and your profits could be wiped out if, for example, you have reserves of cash or securities in the local currency or a lot of outstanding receivables or inventory whose price cannot be adjusted. On the other hand, if you have large loans in the local currency you can now pay the debt with less of your own currency. In 1982 the Mexican peso began to go down and eventually went from around 25 pesos to the dollar to close to 500 pesos to the dollar. If you had a million dollars sitting in pesos when that happened it would now be worth approximately $50,000. (3) The government may also impose exchange controls to prevent the movement of foreign exchange out of the country and to limit the purchase of imports. What this means is that certain outflows, including repatriation of interest, dividends, profits, and capital, would have to pass through a government agency or central bank. If the problem is serious, the amount you may take out may be rationed, or there may be different exchange rates imposed where a special rate is allowed for the importation of priority items while you may be forced to use a so-called "free market rate," that is higher for other cash flows, meaning you will get less dollars for the local currency. (4) Another step the government may take is to try and cut the internal costs of production that are making their products too expensive on the world markets. If inflation is growing faster in one country than in others and the exchange rate remains the same, it means the prices of goods in that country are growing that much faster than in others. The result is a drop in exports and balance-of-trade deficits. The government may limit the money supply, raise taxes, impose price controls, and generally slow down the rate of growth of the economy. Price controls may affect you, as could a loss of demand from either increased taxes or increasing unemployment. On the other hand, if the costs of production are coming down and you are exporting from that

Evaluating Financial Risk

country, your product may become increasingly more competitive in other markets.

FIGURE 3.2   HOW BALANCE OF PAYMENTS PROBLEMS COULD AFFECT YOU

Government Action	Impact on You
1. Ban imports, tariffs, or nontariff barriers	Limits or increases price of your exports. Cannot import inputs.
2. Devaluation of currency	Imports more expensive Exports cheaper
3. Exchange controls	Reduces or prevents repatriation of dividends, interest, profits
4. Internal deflation	Reduces demand and imports. Makes exports more competitive.

How To Read the Signs of Balance-of-Payments Problems

As we have seen, the consequences of policies to rectify balance-of-payments problems can be severe, but if you can anticipate these events you can protect your investment in several ways. Here are some of the most important signs you should monitor.

1. Has the country been importing more than it was exporting over a number of years, or is it just a short-term problem?
2. If it is a longer term trend, has it been getting worse rather than better? For example, the U.S. trade deficit has been getting worse over a number of years while that of other countries has been getting better.
3. If it is a trend, is it because exports are no longer competitive, or is it because there is an increased demand for imports, or is it part of both?
4. If exports are no longer competitive, what is the cause? It could be that local production is too costly or products are no longer in demand on the international market. For example, what has changed countries like Mexico and Nigeria from expanding markets for imports into countries with severe balance of payments problems is the fall in price and loss of demand for oil.
5. If imports are increasing, is it in the area of luxury consumer items or for inputs essential to local production? If you are an

exporter, you could be severely affected if consumer items are cut off. If you are in production inside the market, the most important thing for you is what happens to productive imports that you need, e.g., raw materials or components.

6. Is the country a member of the World Debt Crisis Club?
7. If so, what steps are they taking or likely to have to take to pay the interest and principal in the future?
8. What percentage of exports are used to service the debt and what percentage is available for essential imports?
9. What is happening to the country's reserves of gold and foreign currencies? If they are declining, there is probably trouble on the horizon.
10. Are banks and international agencies willing to lend money to the country? If so, it is a fairly good bet that they regard the country as having good long-term prospects.
11. Are investors still willing to invest in the country?
12. Are local citizens moving their assets out of the country? This is a bad sign because they are likely to know more of what is going on than anybody else.
13. Is there a high inflation rate? If so, the cost of local production is getting higher and the produce is getting less competitive on the world market, unless there is a continual adjustment of the exchange rate to balance out the domestic inflation rate. An adjustment of the exchange rate will make your imports of consumer goods or essential inputs more expensive.
14. Is the central bank propping up the local currency by buying on the open market? This means the foreign exchange specialists are selling. They may be wrong, but they are putting their money on it.
15. What are the foreign-exchange forecasters predicting? If there is widespread expectation of a decline in the currency, it may become a self-fulfilling prophecy.

Most of the data on these questions can be obtained from the balance of payments and other public statistics, but obviously many of the answers involve a degree of judgment, not least on what the government is likely to do to remedy the situation.

Looking at all these factors together, you will have to decide what kind of protection you need, for what time period, and at what cost.

Evaluating Financial Risk

Making the judgment is more an art than a science because there are so many forces, like the government itself, that can change direction overnight. Some research services, bankers and other business people, can assist in checking out your judgments. In general, the most painful steps for the domestic population, like deflation, increasing unemployment, or wage controls are the most difficult for most governments to take, while exchange controls, tariffs, or a devaluation are far easier to impose but are much more likely to have a negative impact on foreign firms who need to repatriate foreign exchange or use imported inputs in local production.

In a later chapter we will outline the steps you can take to protect yourself from financial loss. Basically, you can decide to try and modify risk, which will be a low cost activity, or you can use self-insurance, which means you yourself take on the cost or you pass the risk onto third parties in the form of options or other financial tools. One way or the other, you are going to be dealing with the currencies of different countries, a subject we will now turn to.

THE WORLD'S MONEY: AS IT WAS, AS IT IS, AND AS IT WILL BE

A Little History

When we hear of Sir Isaac Newton, we usually think of an apple falling on his head and the discovery of the law of gravity as well as a host of other brilliant discoveries in mechanics, optics, and calculus. But it was as Master of the Mint of the British Empire that in 1717 he decreed that one ounce of gold would henceforth be worth three pounds, seventeen shillings, and ten and half pence, and this amount of gold would be exchanged for the currency on request. The sun never set on the British Empire as it expanded around the world and moved the raw materials from the colonies while trading the new manufactured products of the Industrial Revolution. The British pound was the international trading currency, and close to 90 percent of world trade was financed out of London. Most other trading nations also tied their currency to gold, so there was little problem in exchanging currencies because both were related to the common denominator: gold. For example, there were 480 grains in a troy ounce of fine gold. The British pound contained 113 grains, while the dollar had 23.22 grains, so the fixed exchange rate between the pound and the dollar was 113 ÷ 23.22, or £1.00 = $4.8665.

Fundamental to the working of the system was the commitment to exchange gold for the currency. So if the United States imported more than it exported, dollars would begin to accumulate abroad and the traders could just trade them in at the Central Bank and claim their gold. There had to be gold to back up every dollar that existed, so as gold stocks were depleted by the claims of foreigners, the supply of money had to be cut because the gold was no longer there to back it. Then, as now, a contraction in the supply of money depressed the economy, which among other things would lead to lower costs of production and fewer imports. As products became cheaper, exports would expand and gold would begin to flow back, and equilibrium would be restored.

The British suspended the convertibility of the pound only twice in 200 years, first to fight Napolean and then to fight the First World War. The reason was simple: They needed more pounds than they had gold because wars are very costly to fight, and win. In the 1920s Britain attempted to go back on the gold standard and to maintain the value of the pound, but confidence in the pound had fallen and the government could not sustain the pressure of the domestic depression, especially as the world recession of the late twenties began.

The Germans also abandoned the gold standard to fight the war. Between the beginning of the war and its end prices doubled. By the mid-twenties, the German mark was devaluing so fast that workers demanded to be paid each day, and it took one trillion marks to buy a single U.S. dollar. The cash savings of the whole nation were wiped out, and the road was paved waiting for Hitler to arrive.

In 1931 Britain had given up any attempt to hold the value of the pound to gold; the pound was allowed to float, and its value from day to day was determined by what buyers and sellers agreed on. The Great Depression in Europe was a period of economic war that preceded the shooting war. Trade died as countries put up tariffs to protect domestic jobs, and there were devaluations and counter-devaluations as countries tried to export their unemployment and get an advantage with cheaper products on a shrinking world market. Needless to say, most of the major currencies lost their convertibility, and the curtain came down on an era of European trade and expansion.

The Dollar and the Gold Standard

After the destruction of the Second World War the U.S. economy dominated the world, and it was inevitable that the dollar would take over the dominant position formerly held by the pound. Meeting at Bretton Woods in New Hampshire in 1944, the finance ministers of the major powers set up the International Monetary Fund and tied the dollar to gold. One ounce of gold was to be worth $35; if you were the president of a foreign central bank and you presented the United States with $35.00, you would get one ounce of gold. All other major currencies were tied to the dollar and were under obligation to keep the value of their currencies within 1 percent above or below their dollar value. They would do this by selling foreign exchange or gold as necessary. If the currency became so weak that its value could not be held up by the central bank support, the country could devalue up to 10 percent. The goal was to establish a stable international monetary system where international trade and investment could flourish because exchange rates would be stable. Business people could sleep easy at night not fearing that they would wake up in the morning to find their currencies or profits wiped out by a wild fluctuation that occurred halfway around the world.

The System Breaks Down

By the mid-fifties trade was booming, all the major currencies were easily convertible and the dollar was literally as good as gold. The United States was producing almost half of the world's oil, automobiles, and manufactured goods, and the dollars that went out in military economic aid or in direct investment came back to purchase American goods. But there were clouds on the horizon. The European and Japanese economies were recovering and beginning to compete with U.S. exports. U.S. dollars continued to flow out and pile up overseas, and nations were willing to hold on to them because they had confidence in the dollar and it supplied the liquidity necessary for expanding world trade. But during the sixties, as the outflow picked up speed and confidence began to wane, the holders of dollars began to switch to gold. Between 1948 and 1971 the U.S. gold stock was cut in half and the U.S. treasury could cover only one dollar in four with gold. Foreign central banks together held close to $63 billion in dollar reserves. Obviously, the U.S. dollar was no longer as good as gold since the gold was not there to back it up. A request to exchange even a small portion of these reserves for gold would have emptied the U.S. treasury. Just such a request for 3 billion in gold from the British government is what is supposed to have forced the hand of the U.S. government. On August 13, 1971, the U.S. government announced it would no longer pay gold for dollars, and the shock waves closed the world money markets. When they reopened, the major currencies were in effect floating in a market where the laws of supply and demand determined the value of each currency. In practice, wide swings in exchange values were limited by the intervention of central banks often working together to keep a currency from rising or falling too fast or too much.

Paper Gold and the World's Currencies Today

The nearest thing to an international currency today are the Special Drawing Rights or SDR's of the International Monetary Fund. Referred to as "paper gold," SDR's are used for official transactions between countries, to get loans, or to pay a loan. Its value was linked to gold until the breakdown of the gold standard. Now its value is determined by a weighted daily average of the exchange rates of the dollar, the German mark, the yen, the British pound, and the French franc. Its value now ranges around 1 SDR = U.S.$1.20. Each country has a quota of SDR's on reserve in the IMF, and they can be used to support the currency or to assist in balance-of-payments problems.

The major currencies that determine the value of the SDR float fairly freely against each other, and most of the smaller economies have tied their currencies to one of these major currencies and go up and down with it. Many, especially in Latin America, are tied to the U.S. dollar; another large group are tied to the SDR; many ex-French colonies are tied to the franc and ex-British colonies to the pound. But within Europe where there is a common market, all members except Britain have joined in what is a fixed rate between their own currencies. Since half of their trade is with one another, this was important in order to promote stability and the expansion of trade. There is a new currency unit called the European Currency Unit, or ECU, which is the European equivalent of the SDR. Its value is determined by a weighted average of the currencies of the member countries, and the currency of any one country is allowed to float only within a certain range above or below the value of the ECU.

In Eastern Europe and Russia the currencies are not convertible, but that has not prevented a significant volume of trade between East and West as firms have successfully arranged barter deals, payment for technology in the form of output from the plant, and "switch trading" where a third party sells the goods from the Eastern bloc and pays the western exporter.

MANAGING FOREIGN EXCHANGE

Since the breakdown of the gold standard, the management of foreign exchange has become a critical part of the management of overseas business. What makes it increasingly important and more difficult is the growing numbers of participants trading in currencies. These include commercial and investment banks, brokerage houses, commodity firms, large institutions and, of course, rich speculators. It is estimated that $250 billion is traded daily in the major foreign-exchange markets in New York, Europe, Tokyo, and Hong Kong. Almost all of this trading is in the dollar, the pound, the German mark and the Swiss franc because these are the countries that allow anyone to buy or sell their currencies. Most countries have some restrictions, but, of course, even if they are not trading, their value is going up or down with the major currency they are tied to.

The fundamental fact about a currency-rate change is that there is always a winner and a loser. Most international managers, especially in smaller companies, have relatively modest goals; namely, they do not want to belong to the latter category. A later chapter will give the details of the tools you can use to avoid a foreign-exchange loss no matter what your degree of involvement in international markets. Here we will concentrate on how the market works, who are the main actors, and how they forecast exchange-rate changes.

How the Market Works

When you go into a bank and buy traveler's checks or pounds to spend on your vacation in England, you are making a transaction at the spot or present rate of the currencies. In other words, you are trading dollars for pounds for immediate delivery. If a British firm agrees to pay you an advance of $15,000 on an export shipment, it will go into a London bank and if the exchange rate £1.00 = $1.50, it will pay its bank £10,000 and they will cable their correspondent bank in the United States to credit your account with $15,000.

In the forward market, you are buying or selling for delivery at a future date, usually within one year. The significant thing is that although you won't give or take delivery until six or nine months down the road, the exchange rate is locked in now, no matter what happens to the currencies in the meantime. Most major newspapers publish the foreign-exchange rates for the major trading currencies every day (see

EXHIBIT 3.1

FOREIGN EXCHANGE

Tuesday, May 27, 1986

The New York foreign exchange selling rates below apply to trading among banks in amounts of $1 million and more, as quoted at 3 p.m. Eastern time by Bankers Trust Co. Retail transactions provide fewer units of foreign currency per dollar.

Country	U.S. $ equiv. Tues.	U.S. $ equiv. Fri.	Currency per U.S. $ Tues.	Currency per U.S. $ Fri.
Argentina (Austral)	1.2484	1.1751	.801	.851
Australia (Dollar)	.7203	.7183	1.3883	1.3922
Austria (Schilling)	.06226	.0625	16.06	16.00
Belgium (Franc)				
Commercial rate	.02154	.02157	46.43	46.35
Financial rate	.02149	.02146	46.73	46.60
Brazil (Cruzado)	.07225	.07215	13.84	13.86
Britain (Pound)	1.5075	1.4950	.6633	.6689
30-Day Forward	1.5035	1.4908	.6651	.6708
90-Day Forward	1.4968	1.4842	.6681	.6738
180-Day Forward	1.4887	1.4761	.6717	.6775
Canada (Dollar)	.7276	.7315	1.3743	1.3670
30-Day Forward	.7267	.7307	1.3761	1.3686
90-Day Forward	.7251	.7291	1.3791	1.3716
180-Day Forward	.7227	.7267	1.3837	1.3760
Chile (Official rate)	.005278	.005296	189.46	188.82
China (Yuan)	.3127	.3018	3.198	3.3135
Colombia (Peso)	.005324	.005351	187.83	186.87
Denmark (Krone)	.1189	.1190	8.4050	8.4000
Ecuador (Sucre)				
Official rate	.009153	.009153	109.25	109.25
Floating rate	.006329	.006390	158.00	156.50
Finland (Markka)	.1904	.1910	5.2525	5.2350
France (Franc)	.1382	.1381	7.2355	7.2395
30-Day Forward	.1380	.1381	7.2585	7.2400
90-Day Forward	.1377	.1381	7.2625	7.2410
180-Day Forward	.1375	.1381	7.2700	7.2430
Greece (Drachma)	.007005	.007042	142.75	142.00
Hong Kong (Dollar)	.1281	.1279	7.8115	7.8135
India (Rupee)	.07893	.07924	12.67	12.62
Indonesia (Rupiah)	.0008865	.0008897	1128.00	1124.00
Ireland (Punt)	1.3360	1.3335	.7485	.7499
Israel (Shekel)	.6743	.6798	1.483	1.471
Italy (Lira)	.0006423	.0006414	1557.00	1559.00
Japan (Yen)	.005921	.005893	168.90	169.70
30-Day Forward	.005933	.005904	168.56	169.37
90-Day Forward	.005955	.005926	167.94	168.76
180-Day Forward	.005989	.005958	166.96	167.84
Jordan (Dinar)	2.9833	3.0093	.3352	.3323
Kuwait (Dinar)	3.3807	3.4578	.2958	.2892
Lebanon (Pound)	.03720	.03720	26.88	26.88
Malaysia (Ringgit)	.3797	.3820	2.6340	2.6175
Malta (Lira)	2.5773	2.5773	.3880	.3880
Netherland (Guilder)	.3911	.3914	2.5570	2.5550
New Zealand (Dollar)	.5520	.5530	1.8116	1.8083
Norway (Krone)	.1299	.1300	7.7700	7.6900
Pakistan (Rupee)	.06078	.06079	16.45	16.45
Peru (Inti)	.07173	.07174	13.94	13.94
Philippines (Peso)	.04876	.04880	20.51	20.49
Portugal (Escudo)	.006568	.006633	152.25	150.75
Saudi Arabia (Riyal)	.2740	.2740	3.6500	3.6500
Singapore (Dollar)	.4492	.4494	2.2260	2.2250
South Africa (Rand)				
Commercial rate	.4285	.4390	2.3337	2.2779
Financial rate	.2663	.2813	3.7551	3.5549
South Korea (Won)	.001127	.001129	887.60	885.60
Spain (Peseta)	.006887	.006935	145.20	144.20
Sweden (Krona)	.1378	.1380	7.2550	7.2450
Switzerland (Franc)	.5316	.5305	1.8810	1.8850
30-Day Forward	.5328	.5316	1.8770	1.8811
90-Day Forward	.5348	.5337	1.8697	1.8736
180-Day Forward	.5385	.5375	1.8570	1.8604
Taiwan (Dollar)	.02608	.02603	38.33	38.41
Thailand (Baht)	.03798	.03807	26.33	26.27
Turkey (Lira)	.001468	.001491	681.03	670.62
United Arab (Dirham)	.2724	.2723	3.6715	3.673
Uruguay (New Peso)				
Financial	.006885	.006957	145.25	143.75
Venezuela (Bolivar)				
Official rate	.1333	.1333	7.50	7.50
Floating rate	.05038	.04998	19.85	20.01
W. Germany (Mark)	.4398	.4399	2.2740	2.2730
30-Day Forward	.4407	.4409	2.2690	2.2680
90-Day Forward	.4424	.4427	2.2602	2.2590
180-Day Forward	.4449	.4453	2.2478	2.2458
SDR	1.15083	1.15369	0.868938	0.866787
ECU	0.941244	0.943512		

Special Drawing Rights are based on exchange rates for the U.S., West German, British, French and Japanese currencies. Source: International Monetary Fund.

ECU is based on a basket of community currencies. Source: European Community Commission.

z-Not quoted.

Source: *Wall Street Journal.*

Exhibit 3.1). In the United States the exchange rates are quoted in terms of the dollar value of each unit of foreign currency and also in terms of the units of value of the foreign currency to the dollar. If you need the rate of exchange between two currencies such as the Canadian dollar and the Swiss franc, you can easily get it by relating both to the U.S. dollar. For example, in the foreign exchange table given above for May 27, 1986, the dollar was worth 1.3743 Canadian dollars and the Swiss franc was 1.8810. The price of the Canadian dollar in terms of the Swiss franc is C$/S franc = 1.3743/1.8810 = 0.7306 Swiss francs. The price of the franc in terms of Canadian dollars is 1.8810/1.3743 = 1.3687C$. If you are making an export to England and you want to buy a forward contract to protect yourself against the possibility of a devaluation in the 60 days before you get paid, you can see from the tables that the difference between the spot rate and the 60-day future rate is $1.3510 and $1.3574 respectively. This means the market expects the pound to appreciate slightly in that period, so if you were being paid a million pounds in 60 days and you did nothing and the spot rate matched the future rate, then you would collect $1,357,400 instead of $1,351,000. But the exchange rates could go the other way, if, for example, Britain were hit by severe strikes or there were an unexpected change of government or economic policy. You don't want to be exposed to that risk, so you can ensure you get the $1,351,400 by entering into a forward contract with a bank so that in 60 days for every pound you get $1.3574. The bank makes its profit by the margin between the buying and the selling rates, and it protects its own exposure by matching one transaction against another from the other currency. This presumes that the supply and demand for foreign currency will exactly coincide, or coincide for the exact period of time that protection is needed. As an exporter, you are shifting your risk in buying a forward contract, and the bank that covers it also has to be covered. Moreover, there is an active exchange market only in the major currencies. In some developing countries there are multiple exchange rates. For example, looking again at the table we will see Venezuela has a controlled or official rate of 7.5 bolivars to the dollar, while the floating rate is 19.85. The official rate usually applies to imports that are critical to the economy or employment or that generate exports. The floating rate could be used to discourage the import of certain luxury items or to give an incentive to exporters who earn dollars by allowing them to exchange the dollars at the floating rate.

The Actors

In the foreign-exchange markets there are those who need the market, those who make the market, and those who speculate in the market. The importer or exporter uses the foreign-exchange market to get paid or to protect his or her accounts payable or receivable in the event there is a change in the value of the currencies. The major companies operating in dozens of countries use the markets to transact day-to-day business, to protect assets held in foreign currencies, and to hedge flows of money in the future such as profits or dividends. With their sizeable resources in different foreign currencies, they will also use the foreign exchange markets to maximize returns on their available funds.

In normal circumstances differences in interest rates should balance out the discount or premium between the spot rates and the forward rate of a currency. That is not always the case, however, and money will move into the higher rate currency, increasing the demand, and closing the gap. For example, let's presume you are sitting on £1 million that you want to invest safely for the short term. If British and U.S. government securities for 90 days were yielding 14 percent and 15 percent respectively, the difference should be made up in the exchange rates so that whether you put the money in pounds or dollars you get the same at the end of 90 days. In other words, the difference of 1 percent in the interest rate should be matched by a 1 percent premium for the pound on an annual basis. But if it is less, then it would pay the financial manager to buy dollars and invest them at 15 percent for the 90 days and then seek protection from the foreign-exchange exposure by buying £1 million plus interest 90 days forward.

The major international commercial banks make the market in foreign exchange. They perform a variety of functions: extending credit, moving money across borders, and providing protection against risk for international business firms. The foreign-exchange market is a vast network of communication links between the international departments of commercial banks, buying and selling foreign exchange both domestically and with banks in all the major financial cities of the world, such as London, Frankfurt, and Hong Kong.

The central banks of the major industrialized countries enter the foreign-exchange markets usually to try and stabilize rates and to prevent a key currency rising or falling too rapidly. A central bank can act on its own or together with the other major central banks. The U.S. dollar plays a key role in international trade and also as a reserve currency. A sharp, quick decline resulting, for example, from a political crisis would lead to such an intervention, but it could also be a longer-term strategy as, for example, when the central banks cooperated in 1980 to prevent a further decline in the Japanese yen, a decline that was making Japanese exports even cheaper on world markets.

Last, but not least, are those who use the foreign-exchange markets to speculate. Most foreign-exchange transactions are used in trade and investments and to avoid risk, but currencies can be traded like any commodity. This can be done through the commercial banks or through the markets specifically used for trading in foreign-exchange futures such as the New York Futures Exchange. The futures market allows speculators to trade on margin. If the foreign currency is expected to appreciate, the speculator will want to purchase; if it is expected to decline the speculator will want to sell short. Sometimes speculators can have a significant impact on the markets as, for example, with the French franc when a socialist president was elected. From the point of view of the international business person, it increases the necessity of shifting risk or having protection in case an unforeseen event leads to large-scale speculation.

Forecasting the Exchange Rates

The nice thing about a long-range forecast is that it takes a long time for anyone to find out you were right or wrong. In the high-speed world of currencies, three months is a long time and three hours is long enough to make or lose a lot of money. Some experts claim that the foreign-exchange market is an efficient market with all the hopes and expectations and information built into the futures rate. Any new information or change in circumstances, such as a rise in interest rates or a major strike, is likely to be responded to rapidly with little room for speculation; or, in other words, the forecasted rate will quickly become the actual rate. In forecasting exchange rates, projections are made based on balance of payments, gross national product, political factors such as upcoming elections, and even psychological factors likely to influence speculators. One of the big uncertainties is that the market is not really a free market because there is always the uncertainty about how the government will react to various things happening in the economy, especially the balance of payments difficulties. The independent forecasting services and the forecasting services of the major banks, using econometric models and technical analysis, claim to be able to beat the forward rate. The record is mixed. The consensus, for instance, in 1983–1984 was for a big drop in the dollar while, in fact, it hit new highs. It was only a concerted intervention by the major industrial powers that eventually forced the dollar down in 1986. Some companies have now dropped their technical analysis altogether and automatically hedge everything.

The core of the difficulty is the fact that there are so many non-economic factors like politics, union relationships, and psychology that can affect rates, especially in the short run. So, a forecaster may be able to decide what the rate *should* be from an analysis of a host of economic factors, but forecasting what it *will* be presumes an ability to forecast what politicians and bureaucrats may decide to do. If anyone could forecast that, there wouldn't be any problem in the exchange rates in the first place.

CONCLUSION

In evaluating financial risk, we have concentrated on the risks associated with the balance of payments and the dangers of devaluation and other controls that follow. We have not dealt here with the risk associated with making the investment at all in terms of what the return on investment will be. That is because that kind of analysis will be very similar to a ROI analysis for a domestic investment. Also, projections on inflation levels, interest rates, taxes, or the regulatory environment are part of an evaluation of the financial risks, but again they are also part of the risk in a domestic environment. What is distinctive is the role that inflation may play in causing balance-of-payments problems or the possibility that taxes may be used to lower imports or to cut a spending deficit in order to ease balance-of-payments problems. So, in operating in an international market, there is a whole new area of risk to be evaluated, but an area in which there are a lot of actors and a lot of information helping you to forecast what is likely to happen to exchange rates or what a government is likely to do to rectify a balance-of-payments deficit. It is essential to know the risk and the reason for the risk in order to be able to balance the degree of risk with the protection required because, as we will see, all protection costs money.

4

POLITICAL RISK: WHETHER THE CAT IS BLACK OR WHITE MAKES NO DIFFERENCE AS LONG AS HE CATCHES MICE

Political risk conjures up images of bearded revolutionaries and massive losses of American assets overseas. More than 25 years ago one such revolutionary descended from the Cuban hills and took over almost all American foreign investment. A few years ago another bearded leader, this time in his 80s and with a completely different ideology, arrived in a jumbo jet in Iran, and American investors faced potential losses of over $1 billion. The result is that political risk has become a growth industry. Large multinationals have built up staff units to deal with it, universities are teaching courses in it, and private consultants, former intelligence agents, and even former secretaries of state are making money out of it. Yet, there is hardly any area of international business where there is greater confusion. Most managers have been well trained in economics and finance, but few have had much exposure to the real advances that have been made in understanding international politics over the last few decades.

The result has been many missed opportunities because the risk was perceived to be too high. Surveys have shown that investors have eliminated countries and indeed whole regions from their consideration. What was simply unfamiliar or different was often equated with being hostile. Meanwhile, several other companies have been quite successful in the same areas.

The first principle for the international manager should be "The world is my marketplace, and I can do business anyplace." Or, in the words of the old Chinese proverb "Whether the cat is black or white makes no difference as long as he catches mice." In the past, U.S. business people concentrated on the familiar markets of Europe and Canada. But the mass of potential consumers and the new opportunities lie elsewhere. Companies like Coke, Continental Grain, and American Motors have set up operations in China; there are numerous successful joint ventures with the Communist state of Yugoslavia while the Pacific Rim countries and the Middle East are the fastest growing areas in the world.

The second principle is that you yourself are the best judge of foreign risk. Of course, there are services and consultants who can assist, but ultimately it is your product, your company, and your money that is involved. To make no decision because of unfamiliarity is a no-go decision and in the long run may turn out to be just as costly as another "go" decision that failed.

To clear away some of the confusion in the area, it is first necessary to destroy several myths about political risks so that the remainder of the discussion can be focused on the central issues. One central issue is how to prevent risk arising for you rather than how to cure it when it does. This is a matter of structuring and packaging your investment in the best possible way. It is also important not only to assess risk before going in, but also to monitor it continuously so that you can change your strategies with changing conditions. If risk is growing, there are several ways to minimize it so that your business can continue to prosper even as conditions change. Throughout this chapter we talk about risk to the direct foreign investor, but most of what is discussed applies, but to a lesser degree, to the other forms of entry to a foreign market.

FOUR MYTHS ABOUT POLITICAL RISK

Myth No. 1: The real danger is confiscation of your investment. This myth developed because of the communist takeover of property in Eastern Europe after the war and the so called "resource nationalism" of the newly independent countries, which was an effort by these countries in the sixties to gain ownership of their natural resources. But, in fact, there have been very few confiscations of manufacturing industries in the last 20 years. There is a danger of underestimating the risk by overnarrowing its definition. The real losses and costs you may face will not involve anything so dramatic as a takeover, but rather a shifting of forces or a series of small changes that could add up to a significant cost to the company and could change the calculations on which the original decision to invest was made. For example, a new or increased tax rate, imposition of tariffs or quotas on your essential imports, exchange controls on your profits or dividends, a new labor law—any one of these could be quite costly, and they make up the main areas of political risk.

Brazil has a very large public sector with vast purchasing power. The government ordered all public agencies to purchase their telecommunications equipment only from majority-owned Brazilian companies. The result could have been a large cut in market share for all foreign-owned companies in that business.

Political risk, therefore, is a much broader concern than simply forecasting the possibility of confiscation. The risks are much broader and involve any change that will incur a new cost to the company or affect it to its disadvantage.

Myth No. 2: Frequent changes of government by elections, power struggles, or coups indicate high levels of political risk. This is not automatically true in itself and may not be true for your business or project. I managed a project in the Yemen Arab Republic between 1975 and 1977. During that period there were three presidents. Two were assassinated. Meanwhile, the whole government, including the prime minister and ministers, remained the same and business carried on as before. Italy has had more than 40 governments since 1945, and very little has changed for the operation of foreign business. What is much more important than change of government is the continuity of a set of rules or code of behavior that continues no matter what government is in power. Ironically, it may be where there are few changes of government that real swings in policy and real costs to foreign business occur. This happened in France with the election of the socialist government of François Mitterand. Jamaica is considered a high-risk country although changes of government occur at fairly predictable intervals and by an election process. The reason is that the two major parties have significantly different attitudes toward foreign business, and when the government changes a new set of rules apply. What you need is a certain continuity or stability in the rules over time. This is where the reality is much more important than the political rhetoric. Even some of the most capitalist countries classify themselves as socialist, and in many developing countries the rhetoric is simply designed to prevent another politician or party from co-opting your position, especially on the left. The reality may be that you get the same cooperation and do business the same way as before. Unfortunately, in many cases political speeches that raise the political temperature become self-fulfilling prophecies.

In Ghana, one of the poorest countries in Africa, Kaiser Aluminum have watched governments come and go over the last 20 years. Most were military, a few were civilian; they have had ideologies of the left, the right, and the center. Kaiser has not only survived it all, but have made handsome profits. They are a large employer, the third largest earner of foreign exchange for the country and probably the largest single taxpayer. Not every company has such leverage, but in general you can do business under any form of government if the investment is worthwhile to the country as well. What is much more important than musical chairs at the top of the civilian or military leadership is the stability of policies and your ability to adjust as they change over the long run.

Myth No. 3: Risk is the same for everyone, everywhere. In fact, risk is not the same for everyone, everywhere. Major upheavals such as those that occurred in Cuba or China obviously affect all foreign business. But the much more frequent type of risk is one that may be directed at your industry or your product or your project. Moreover, this type of risk will differ from country to country and over time in the same country. That is why you are your own best judge of risk. Overall indices may be positive for a country but may miss important factors that could be negative for you. This is why political-risk analysis or monitoring on an ongoing basis is so important so that you don't end up trying to close the door after the horse has bolted. For example, if local nationals are beginning to compete strongly in your area or you are in a sensitive or targeted industry, then the risk is specific to you. In the sixties and early seventies natural resource or extractive industries became particularly vulnerable. In recent years banking in France and the oil industry in Canada were singled out for special treatment. But if the investment is worthwhile and the management flexible enough, specific changes can also create new opportunities, or in other words, political change can be for better as well as for worse.

Myth No. 4: Regimes that strongly protect free enterprise and private property are the safest for foreign investors. This would seem to

Political Risk

> ### FOUR MYTHS ON POLITICAL RISK
>
> 1. The real danger is property confiscation
> 2. Frequent changes of government indicate high levels of political risk
> 3. Risk is the same for everyone, everywhere
> 4. Self-proclaimed protectors of free enterprise are the safest for foreign investors

be a fairly obvious conclusion since almost all foreign investment is private. However, it can be wrong on two counts. The government may have one set of rules for domestic business and another for you because they need your investment. Second, countries that give large incentives to foreign investors and loudly proclaim their defense of free enterprise may in fact be provoking much greater unrest in the future and may be much riskier than countries that have strict property-control laws. In this latter case, they have gone through their revolution, property has been redistributed, and the likelihood of any radical change is lessened. The safest place in the world today for your investment could well be a socialist or socialist-type state. You know exactly where you stand before you enter. In contrast, the military or military-type regimes of Central and South America or the Philippines that are all for private enterprise and private property are often protecting a privileged propertied elite and hiding great inequalities of income. To put this another way, the rhetoric of free enterprise is really concealing, at least temporarily, what is in fact a much higher level of risk. Of course, a company can decide to enter such a market to make a quick kill, to rapidly recapture its investment and maximize returns over the short term. This is a vicious circle because the political risk has led to the short-term outlook and the short-term outlook increases the political risk. On the other hand, you can set up your investment for the long haul with a longer-term vision with smaller immediate returns, independent of any political system. Then even sudden political change may not affect you because your investment is also a contribution to the country.

IMPORTANT STEPS IN PACKAGING YOUR PROGRAM

There is some latent hostility to foreign investors in most countries. In the United States it may be against rich Arabs buying up land and real estate. In the Philippines, the Japanese control so much investment that nationalists say they might as well have won the war. In South America, it is aimed primarily at the large American multinationals. The hostility is natural because the investor has not been elected or appointed, and yet controls capital, technology, essential goods, employment, and revenues that the investor can decide to locate or relocate in one country or another. From the country's point of view there are costs and benefits to foreign investment, and it is only because the benefits outweigh the costs that the investment is acceptable. In other words, the country for one reason or another believes it needs you just as you need the market and resources it can give.

Since there are costs and benefits, there will almost certainly be arguments and propaganda for and against by local interests. Many companies spend a lot of time and money trying to assess and forecast such factors in the political environment, whereas the real challenge is to so structure and package your project that what it contributes to the country is clear even to those who do not wish to see it.

Packaging your project correctly is really the power of positive thinking. Instead of concentrating on what might go wrong, the emphasis is on what both sides may achieve. The goal of the investor is profits, the goal of the country is that the investment add in some way to the economic social, or human development of the country. These goals are not mutually exclusive, but the onus is on the investor to identify the country's goals and show how the project will help the country reach those goals. Many countries require that you meet certain criteria to enter, but whether they do or not, you should make clear in your package what you are contributing in these five basic areas.

Balance of Payments. Show the net positive impact you are having on increasing exports and cutting down imports. Many countries are in serious balance-of-payments trouble because of large outpayments for oil and the foreign exchange they must earn to pay back and service foreign debts. Your enterprise will also have a negative impact, first of all by sending home profits, dividends, or fees, which is the reason you are there in the first place; and second, if your project requires imported goods, parts, or services. These negatives need to be outweighed by the imports you save by supplying necessary goods to the local market and second, by the goods you export either to other parts of your own company or to other markets. It is doubtful if you are welcome in many countries today if the overall impact on the balance of payments is negative.

Use of Local Resources. Set up your project so that you use local materials and local producers and suppliers to the fullest extent possible. In this way your investment acts like a missing link or an engine of growth that stimulates other areas of production and the use of previously underutilized materials. Obviously, no company will do this if local materials are more costly than imports, but it is amazing to see, for example, the import of prefabricated building materials or office furniture like steel desks when alternative building materials and locally made mahogany furniture are available at low cost. But the real payoff is if local suppliers are contributing something to the process on a continuing basis. From the point of view of your firm, it creates a local interest group that wants you to succeed. Firestone did this very effectively in Liberia with its rubber-growers-assistance program. It provided the farmers with improved trees and technical advice. It supplied materials and equipment at cost and with interest-free credit whenever they were needed. It also assisted in marketing and transport. The result was a stimulus to the local rubber-growing industry, while at the same time Firestone was protecting itself from any negative moves by the government against its investment.

Transfer of capital, technology, and scarce skills. This is the reason the country needs you. If a country had the capital and could buy the technology, it would prefer to do so. But in both the rich and poorer countries capital is a scarce commodity and in high demand in many areas. In the poorer nations a shortage of capital is the most serious obstacle they face because many of them do not have the foreign exchange to acquire even standardized technology or the management and technical skills required to produce even essential goods. Highlight what you are transferring in capital, technology, and skills.

Employment created. Every country in the world has an unemployment problem. Your package should highlight not only the immediate direct employment you are creating, but also the stimulus to employment in the backward links your project has to other producers, as in the Firestone case, and forward links if outsiders are involved in packaging, transporting, or selling the product. A delicate balance has to be maintained here by, on the one hand, having the most advanced state-of-the-art technology that produces the goods at the least cost and often with the least labor and at the same time creating local jobs. Both can be reconciled in some cases by having the most advanced technology at the core of the production process and sacrificing automation to manual handling in the steps leading into and out of the production process.

FIGURE 4.1

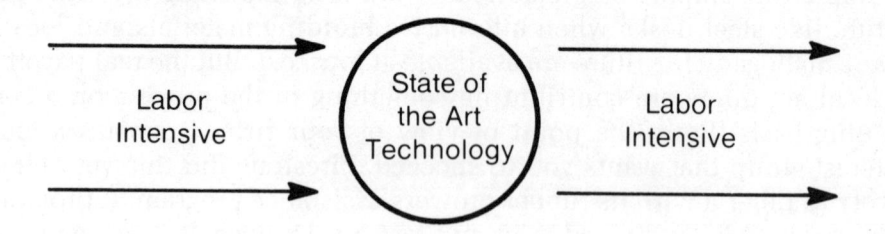

```
Labor            State of           Labor
Intensive    → the Art    →      Intensive
                 Technology
```

Another thing to watch out for is that if management or technical skills are scarce, you don't antagonize local producers by attracting away their brightest. It is not going to help you a lot if you seduce the irreplacable permanent secretary to the minister of finance to leave his post at three times his present salary. At the beginning expatriate technical and management experts will be needed, and that can greatly improve your package if combined with a training program designed to replace them with newly trained local staff within a definite period.

Taxes contributed or saved. Unless you are getting some kind of tax holiday or tax break, it is in your interest to pay the taxes locally up to the U.S. rate because the United States gives you a tax credit up to the total amount paid. In a small economy this may be a significant contribution and should improve your overall position with the government. But the impact is not limited to direct taxes you pay. It includes the taxes your workers pay as well as sales tax paid on the goods produced or the tariffs on goods imported. Finally, there is the costs saved the government, if you are providing new infrastructure such as roads or water supplies, housing for workers, or health or educational services for their dependents.

One final point: if it is possible set up your investment so that you are an intermediary or in other words only part of a larger product or service. This has a few advantages. Since you are not making or selling the final product, you will be able to keep a low profile and not be identified with high consumer prices. Second, since you are not the sole user of imports or other inputs, your source of supply is less vulnerable. Examples of intermediate production include equipment or supplies for food processing; engines that have multiple usages in pumps, agriculture machinery, or construction; or materials or services necessary in the distribution of the product from the manufacturer to the consumer. The intermediary has the advantage of being necessary for the final product and yet is responsible for only part of the total cost. An excellent opportunity right now for a foreign intermediary that stimulates local production, increases employment, and stimulates exports is the food-processing business in Thailand and other countries of the Pacific Rim.

HOW TO ASSESS LEVELS OF RISK

Any political system is like an extended family. There is a clan leader, several husbands, many wives, numerous children, and dozens of cousins. The resources of the family may be large or small, but are nevertheless limited. There is a hierarchy in the family and pressures and conflicts because of power, prestige, wealth, and position. The family develops a capacity to adjust to these pressures, to keep them at a manageable level so that it does not break up or end up in civil war. If the pressures get too great, there may be fundamental changes in the type of government the family has and the way its resources are distributed. But usually the family has an adjustment mechanism that enables it to respond to such pressures. In the family, leadership may be passed on from father to son or elected or grabbed by force; but it will only survive if it contains the different pressures from different groups. The art of assessing political risk lies in knowing the levels of pressure within the extended family, which is the nation, and the political system's ability to cope with it. The management of political risk is the ability to change your strategy as alliances or attitudes change in that system.

Two Pitfalls to Avoid

I refer to the first pitfall as the "six-o'clock-news syndrome," where wars and the rumors of wars and those bearded revolutionaries appear on a regular basis. The result is a country not even considered as a market because the pressures are perceived to be bubbling over, or the political risk discount figure becomes so high that nobody would dream of investing there. Often the larger-than-life news event may in no way affect the business climate. American companies have been quietly operating at normal levels in El Salvador and Northern Ireland through the violence of the last several years.

The second pitfall can be called the "old-hands syndrome," or those who claim to know because they are living or have lived there. The classic example was the "old China hands," mainly missionaries and businessmen, who never believed Mao Tse-tung could take over China. But Mao and his peasant followers were not exactly regular guests at the tea parties in Shanghai or Peking where such judgments were often formed. Moreover, many "old hands" do not want to believe that what is going to happen will happen, and indeed they will probably have less knowledge of what is happening at the grass roots than somebody systematically tracking events at headquarters.

Steps to Follow

"Systematically" is the key word in the last sentence. *Have a system* because even if your system is bad, it should still indicate when change is taking place, and supply enough of a warning to look closer.

Step 1: Learn as much as possible about the country from sources readily available to your home office. You can start with country handbooks put out by the U.S. Commerce Department, literature put out by the host governments, reference books, and business information services. Going a bit deeper you can get systematically collected economic and social data assembled by international organizations like the IMF, the U.N., the World Bank, and OECD. Finally, there may be some data on public opinion, interest groups, and legislators' opinions published by individual scholars. Already at this stage you should have a good feel for the political system, its history, its economy, its pressures, and its form of leadership. Moreover, the exercise can break down some misperceptions and explain some things that look like conundrums to us, as for instance, how democratic a single-party system can be in some African countries or how even a monarchy or military regime can be representative and responsive.

Step 2: Identify the areas of risk you need to watch out for when you are deciding to go in and that you need to monitor when you get in.

Political Risk

These are of two kinds: general risks that could affect all foreign investors and risks specific to your company. There are six areas that are fairly inclusive of general risk: (1) expropriation, (2) exchange controls, (3) destruction of your plant, (4) taxes, (5) import or export restrictions, and (6) labor costs. Obviously, specific risks will depend on your product, service, or company, but a few areas of risk could include: (1) ownership restrictions, (2) local content requirements, and (3) export targets to be met.

Step 3: Identify the possible sources of the general risks within the political system. These are the pressures and conflicts we talked about earlier in the context of the extended family. Countries have different pressures with different levels of intensity, and they all interact among themselves and other social, economic, or cultural aspects of the society. Reverting again to the image of the extended family, a conflict over wealth may well be associated with the marriage status of that person within the group. But, despite the complexity, we can identify six important sources of risk that include the major pressures in the society and that could have an impact on the six risks outlined in Step Two. These are (1) distribution of wealth or income, (2) strength of political parties or movements that blame poverty, lack of growth, or inequality on private ownership and/or foreign investment, (3) balance-of-payments position, (4) levels of government spending, (5) unemployment levels, and (6) levels of extra-legal opposition.

Step 4: Identify possible sources of risk specific to your product or company. These could include (1) local competitors, (2) alternative sources of technology or skills, or (3) selective price controls.

Step 5: Combine the types of risks and the sources of risk both general and specific into a matrix, as in Figure 4.2. You can now rank the possibility of any of the risks materializing on a scale of, say, 0–10, with 10 being a high probability and 0 being nonexistent. You can make this judgment by examining each one of the sources of risk and evaluating its likely impact on each one of the risks. For instance, if the country is importing far more than it is exporting or its reserves are being run down, then the balance of payments indicator will be bad and the levels in risk number 2 and number 3 will be high.

At this stage you face a choice on how deeply in you want to go. You can simply rate each source of risk on a three-level scale of good, medium, or bad and rank the level of each risk accordingly. If you want a

FIGURE 4.2 SOURCES AND TYPES OF RISK IN FOREIGN BUSINESS

	Income Distribution	Anti-Bus Parties	Balance of Payments	Government Spending	Levels of Unemploy.	Extra-Legal Opposition	Local Competitors	Alternative Technologies	Price Control
Types Risk (0–10)									
Expropriation									
Exchange Controls									
Destruction Of Plant									
Taxes									
Import/Export Restrictions									
Labor Costs									
Ownership Limits									
Local Content									
Export Targets									

(General / Specific)

Political Risk

more quantifiable and precise result and if you can get the information, you can continue the following steps that are somewhat more convoluted and will be given only in outline.

Step 6: Identify one or several indicators that accurately reflect each source of risk. For instance, distribution of wealth or income could be measured by the amount of wealth held by each percentile of the population, and the more it is skewed the higher the risk. Or, again, in extralegal opposition you could measure it by indicators like number of acts of political violence, kidnappings, bombings, and so forth. All of the sources of risk can be quantified, but it is important that the indicators accurately measure the source of risk in question and that you don't fall into the fallacy of trying to quantify the unquantifiable or leave out an important indicator because it is not easily quantifiable.

Step 7: By now, by having one indicator or combining several, you have a measure for each source of risk, and you can now decide what level of impact each will have on the various risks on the left side of the matrix. As the source of risk increases or decreases, as the pressures build up or fade, the level of risk can be adjusted accordingly.

Step 8: You can also compare one country with another by drawing out a complete matrix for each country, or simpler still, you could give a certain weight to each source of risk and rank each source on a scale of 0–10. By multiplying the weight by the rank and adding them up you could come up with a single score for each country. For illustration purposes let's say we give the sources of risk percentage weightings as per Figure 4.3. In the case of Brazil if your indicators show inequality is at a high level of 8, then you multiply 8 by 0.2 because you have given inequality a 20% weight in the overall scale and so on along the line. When you add the total, you can come up with a country score for Brazil. The higher the score the higher the risk and vice versa.

The value of this method is that you have a systematic way of comparing countries before you enter and also of monitoring changes as they occur to determine their impact on your business. In early 1983 a service company was able to speed up payments out of Venezuela because two of the sources of risk indicated the possibility of exchange controls. Delay in payments, especially for service contracts, are common in Latin America and the pressure brought on the client to pay has to be delicately reconciled with the goal of maintaining the contract. But in tracking imports and exports and the fall in reserves as well as levels

FIGURE 4.3 COMPARING LEVELS OF RISK FOR DIFFERENT COUNTRIES

(Weighting X level of risk)

	20%	15%	25%	10%	15%	15%	
	Income Distrib.	Anti-bus parties	Balance of pays.	Govt. Spending	Levels of Unemploy.	Extra Legal Opposition	Country Score
Brazil	1.6	0.6	1.4	0.8	1.2	0.15	5.25
France							
Kenya							
Greece							

of government spending, the likelihood of exchange controls was rapidly increasing. Most of the money was out before exchange controls were actually imposed later in the year.

Another attractive aspect of the system is that you can do it yourself with limited resources to whatever degree of information you need now, or you can expand it to a greater degree of complexity as your needs require it. You can also modify the risks or sources of risk to make them more adaptable to your needs or to the countries you are interested in.

As you can see, there is a large amount of subjective judgment involved in ranking levels of risk, selecting sources of risk and indicators, giving weights to the different areas, and so on. The art of political-risk assessment lags far behind economic or financial analysis in the objectivity of technique, but to my mind this is inevitable because you are dealing with human and unpredictable behavior and factors that cannot be easily quantified or measured. The main thing is have a system.

The subjectivity can be lessened by having others in your company do the exercise and combine the results so that the best judgments of several analysts are combined. This is the essence of the so-called Delphi method. You can also cross-check your conclusions with outside services that analyze your country such as, for instance, the Business Environment Risk Index (BERI) or with independent country experts. There are also political forecasting models developed using sophisticated statistical techniques such as multivariate analysis. But in the end there remains a lot of subjective judgment, and the limits of these techniques can be judged from the pre-1978 predictions for Iran based on the political-risk models. Only 2 out of 10 gave any kind of accurate forecast of what actually happened.[1]

Very large companies have the resources to track a very wide range of factors. One major petro-chemical company examines close to 400 factors each day in all its overseas markets, and changes are analyzed by panels of experts. But at the end of the day there remain distinctive events that even the best monitoring could not immediately detect. For example, some experts say that the critical turning point in Iran was when the merchants in the Teheran bazaars turned against the Shah. It is very difficult to see how that could have been monitored in time to determine an appropriate response. We cannot accurately predict the future, but the manager can detect trends and see the warning signals in time to enable him or her to take the steps necessary to minimize the risk.

WAYS TO MINIMIZE THE RISK

You have packaged and structured your project in the best way possible, you are continually monitoring the risk, but what do you do if things start going wrong? There are several ways to minimize the risk as it develops:

Political Insurance. Most countries provide investment guarantees to foreign investors. For U.S. investors the Overseas Private Investment Corporation (OPIC) offers insurance against expropriation; nonconvertibility of currency; and losses due to war, insurrection, or civil disorder. The coverage is restricted because the rates are subsidized by the government to achieve foreign policy goals. It is heavily concentrated in low-income countries and toward small businesses. This insurance saved a lot of skins in Iran, and in many cases getting it is the difference between a bankable and a nonbankable project. It can be complemented by the private insurance market organized around Lloyds of London although at higher rates. Insurance is essential in today's world. It is hard to believe now that not a single U.S. firm bothered to take out a U.S. government guarantee against expropriation prior to the Cuban revolution. There are three things to watch out for, however: You cannot insure against import controls or tariffs, so for instance, if you had set up in Chile expecting also to deliver to Argentina, you would have been cut off several times as relations deteriorated between those two countries. Second, remember that if you take out casualty or other insurance in a host country with a nonconvertible currency, it is not much use to you if your plant or equipment has to be replaced with hard-currency expenditure. Finally, even if you have insurance it will cover the basic value or replacement value of the plant, but this may be far less than its real value to you.

Involve local groups in your investment so that they also stand to lose if any of the risks materialize. This could involve giving local investors a share in ownership, borrowing from local banks, subcontracting to local manufacturers, getting more materials from local suppliers. Your very best constituency may be a well treated and loyal workforce.

Structure your investment so that it is dependent on outside affiliates for components or markets. When others were being nationalized around them, Chrysler held on to its plant in Peru because 50 percent of its components came from other Chrysler plants in Brazil, Argentina, and the United States. The same applies if the output of the plant is

Political Risk

EXHIBIT 4.1

"We're thinking about expanding our overseas operations. How can we be sure our earnings can be converted into U.S. dollars?"
TALK TO OPIC BEFORE YOU EXPAND.

"If we go ahead with the overseas project, what would happen in the event of confiscation by a foreign government? Would we lose everything?"
TALK TO OPIC BEFORE YOU INVEST.

"We're planning to build new sites abroad in the next few years. If we do, how can we protect ourselves against potentially unstable political conditions?"
TALK TO OPIC BEFORE YOU MAKE A MOVE.

POLITICAL RISK INSURANCE MEANS GREATER INVESTMENT OPPORTUNITY ...AND LESS WORRY.

Though we can't predict your profit margin from new overseas investment or expansion, we *can* insure against the political risks that could drastically affect it. The Overseas Private Investment Corporation's political risk insurance is specifically designed to assist U.S. business in 100 of the world's developing nations.

OPIC's political risk insurance gives you peace of mind in three major risk areas. Our inconvertibility coverage protects against the inability to convert into U.S. dollars the local currency you receive as earnings, loan payments, or return of capital. Expropriation coverage protects against confiscation or nationalization of your investment without fair

WE CAN HELP.

compensation. What's more, OPIC protects against losses due to war, revolution, insurrection, or civil strife. To take advantage of our insurance, get in touch with OPIC *before* you make your investment commitment.

OPIC is a self-sustaining federal government agency that helps U.S. business create new outlets for goods and services in the world's developing countries. In addition to our political risk insurance, we also offer a wide range of financing services. If you're thinking about overseas investment or expansion, contact us soon.

Write us or phone 202-457-7010 and ask for our free brochure about OPIC's political risk insurance.

Overseas Private Investment Corporation

OPIC

Political Risk Insurance • Investment Missions • Financing • Information Services

☐ Please send me your free brochure describing OPIC's Political Risk Insurance.

Mail to:
Overseas Private Investment Corporation
1615 M Street, N.W.
Washington, D.C. 20527

NAME_____
TITLE_____
COMPANY_____
ADDRESS_____
CITY_____ STATE___ ZIP_____
TELEPHONE (___)_____

E 3/22/86

being sold as components to an affiliated assembly plant or you control distribution to other markets.

Negotiate special agreements with the host governments such as, for instance, the concession agreements in the extractive industries. A more recent technique is to make an agreement with the government where an increase in political risk will result in lower taxes so that the firm will meet its minimum rates of ROI. The danger with such agreements is that being associated with a particular government they can easily be repudiated and used by new regimes to show how a company was pulling the wool over the old government's eyes.

Move your resources into different areas of production or services. This applies in particular if your industry or product is specifically targeted for takeover and if the compensation is in local inconvertible currency, or you are forced to reinvest. It was under these circumstances that ITT shifted its assets in Peru into electronics and hotels. Smaller companies may not have that flexibility.

Finally, in a mature industry, when a company has lost most of its leverage because it is no longer transferring new technology or skills, and local capital and competition is emerging, it may be best to divest ownership and back off to a licensing or service status with the new owners. In this way, you may lose ownership but what is important is that you can maintain the cash flow, and after all, that is the bottom line.

SUMMARY

The following guidelines make up the essence of what you need to know and do in political risk analysis.

— Don't eliminate any market anyplace without a systematic look at it.
— Package and present your project so that the benefits to the country are easily seen by all.
— Remember in most cases you don't have to worry about confiscation or destruction but rather the smaller changes that make doing business more costly.
— Remember the pressures in a political system are always changing, which means you have continually to monitor sources of risk.
— Know why they may be picking on you, your product, or your

services, or in other words know *your* specific sources of risk.
— Don't be a passive observer. You can influence the outcome of the pressures and minimize the risks in several ways.
— Be flexible. As they say in the East, when the wind blows north the bamboo bends northward; when the wind blows south, the bamboo bends southward. And the bamboo survives a long time.

REFERENCE

1. For further reading on Political Risk consult "How Multinationals Analyse Political Risk" by R. J. Rummel and David A. Heenan in the *Harvard Business Review*, Jan.–Feb. 1978; "Rating Investment Risks Aboard" by F. T. Haner, *Business Horizons*, April 1979; "Political Risk Assessment for Foreign Direct Investment Decisions: Better Methods for Better Results," *Columbia Journal of World Business*, Spring 1981. For further information on the Iranian case see Working Paper No. 81–10 "Multinational Corporations, Political Risk Models and the Iranian Revolution" by Charles R. Kennedy, Jr., College of Business, University of Texas, Austin, April 1981.

5

VISITING THE COUNTRY

You are already an expert on the country you intend to visit. Now the time spent in the country is focused on very definite goals that can be achieved only by visiting the country. The last thing you want to do is spend that time seeking out information that is probably more easily available here in the United States. For example, if you need the production figures, or the source and size of imports of a certain product into Saudi Arabia, it is, of course, possible to get them in the appropriate ministry in Riyadh. But in many countries like Saudi, there may be an unwillingness to give out any government information, or when you get it the information is in Arabic, or it is scattered over several agencies of the government. Meanwhile, someone has already done all that work for you, especially in the most important trading nations. If they have not, you will almost certainly be able to piece the information together yourself from sources available to you. Of course, there is certain information you will be able to get only on the ground in the country; information like, for instance, what local bankers think of a potential joint-venture partner or how difficult it is, from ministry to ministry, to get approvals for your enterprise or how much obstruction or bribery is present.

Visiting a country is expensive in terms of time, air fares, accommodation, and all the other associated expenses. It is just good business practice to set goals to be achieved by the trip and to allow a realistic amount of time to achieve them. The amount of time required will usually be considerably more than a similar trip at home especially if the country is a developing one. No matter how fast you are going, things are going to move at the same traditional pace around you, and mainly it is you who has to adapt to that pace. The meeting you arrive for at 8:30 A.M. begins at 11, or the information that was going to be available for the afternoon's meeting will now not be available until tomorrow because the only photocopying machine in the office has broken down. What you don't want is to have tied yourself into such a tight schedule that you have to move on before achieving what you set out to do. A few years ago a major U.S. company was bidding for a very large contract with a Saudi government agency. The company sent one of their top officers to Saudi to seal the deal, which required the approval of the key members of the royal family. He waited several days to be summoned to the meeting, and when it was not coming, he left briefly for another pressing meeting in Europe. You don't do that to the royal family of the House of Saud. A European company got the contract involving hundreds of millions of dollars.

The goals you set yourself will obviously depend on how much you already know, how close you are to making a decision, how you intend to enter the market, and how much more detail you need if you intend to make a large commitment of resources over the long term. So, your goals could be one or all of the following:

YOUR GOALS FOR YOUR OVERSEAS TRIP

To corroborate information uncovered at the home office
To introduce yourself to prospective partners or government officials
To evaluate the competition first hand
To select an agent or distributor
To introduce your product at a trade fair
To sell so many units of the product now
To determine the cost and availability of support services such as service facilities, advertising, and so forth
To get approvals a, b, and c from the government
To finalize an agent agreement
To supervise research in the local market
To conduct a detailed feasibility study

HOMEWORK COMPLETED

You have already collected a mass of information on the country. You have related this information to your product and plans. To do this effectively you have organized the material in some kind of country report for your own use, where the information is organized around your plans for your product, taking into account your resources.

SUMMARY OF THE INFORMATION YOU NEED

A. Population:	Size and important segments such as age, rural/urban, density, occupation
B. Topography:	Rivers, mountains, transport problems, and climatic factors that affect your product
C. Income Levels:	Size of the economy, per capita income, income distribution, local purchasing power
D. Product Suitability:	Whether they want what you have, or whether you have what they want
E. Competition:	Foreign or domestic, their advantages and yours in this particular market
F. Consumer Demand:	A check to see if you narrowed your choices with the best available secondary market data
G. Agents, Distributers and Joint-Venture Partners:	Identification of what is available and whom you are going to negotiate with
H. Financial Risks for the Country:	Balance of payments and other distinctive sources of risk
I. Political Risk:	Determining your entry decision, long term, or short term

BUSINESS ADVICE

Before going on an overseas trip and especially if you want to fill out gaps in the published sources, it will be useful to talk to the country specialists in the departments of Commerce and State. They will often be able to give background on things like the investment climate, political risk, overseas marketing research firms, and contacts with the commercial people in the U.S. embassies overseas as well as with U.S. business people already active in the country. Getting some of this information means a trip to Washington, but the place to start is the nearest Department of Commerce District Office. These offices, located all over the United States, have trade specialists as well as the department's most up-to-date reports and statistics. Through these offices you can get specific advice or information on a particular country for a modest fee. The district office will contact the commercial office in the U.S. embassy for you and request the information you need or will provide help in planning your trip in that country. For example, if there was a recent change in the foreign exchange regulations that could affect the demand for your product, you could request clarification and advice on the likely impact on your plans.

Another source of advice may be your own state. The state agencies that promote exports usually work closely with the Department of Commerce District Office, but they may also give you, as a resident of the state, some specific help. For example, the Department of Commerce of New Jersey provides a range of services paralleling the Federal Department of Commerce, but focused particularly on New Jersey businesses interested in exporting. Exhibit 5.1 outlines the extent of the services offered. Many other states offer similar services.

Trade Fairs, Trade Exhibitions, and Trade Missions

If you are trying to introduce your product into the country, or to make contacts, the impact of your trip can be multiplied several times over by linking it to international trade fairs or exhibitions. These fairs and exhibitions occur at various international locations on a regular basis, while others are sponsored by the Department of Commerce itself.

In planning the overseas trip you may decide to build around such a fair or exhibition especially if the Commerce Department is promoting one in your product area in a country or region in which you are interested. The department provides this information in its "Overseas Export Promotion Calendar." The department will arrange exhibit space for you, provide advice on such matters as exhibit design and market conditions and on all the details of getting your products there and displaying them. This service may also be supplied by your state. See

EXHIBIT 5.1

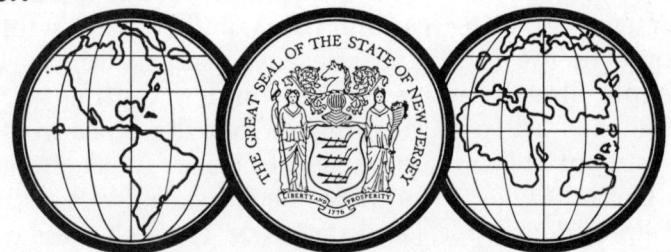

EXHIBIT I
State of New Jersey
Dept. of Commerce & Economic Development
Division of International Trade

TRADE PROMOTION & INFORMATION SERVICES

THE DIVISION OF INTERNATIONAL TRADE OFFERS FREE ASSISTANCE TO EVERY NEW JERSEY COMPANY INTERESTED IN DEVELOPING ITS EXPORT BUSINESS. IT IS RESPONSIBILE FOR EDUCATING AND INFORMING NEW JERSEY BUSINESSES OF OPPORTUNITIES IN THE INTERNATIONAL FIELD, A COMPREHENSIVE PROGRAM EXISTS AND PRESENTLY BEING EXPANDED TO PROVIDE THESE SERVICES:

MARKETING INFORMATION AND EDUCATION

1. DIRECT REFERRAL OF EXPORT OPPORTUNITIES

2. IN-PLANT CONSULTATIONS WITH BASIC MARKETING INFORMATION FOR NEW-TO-EXPORT COMPANIES

3. COMMUNITY EXPORT SEMINARS THROUGHOUT NEW JERSEY

4. PUBLISH EXPORTERS' ASSISTANCE GUIDE

5. PROVIDE SOURCES OF INFORMATION FOR MARKETING DATA ON SPECIFIC PRODUCTS WHEREVER PER-REQUEST

6. FILES-BY COUNTRY FOR USE BY FIRMS

7. ARRANGE CONSULTATIONS BY COUNTRIES FOR NEW JERSEY BUSINESSES VENTURING ABROAD FOR TRADE

TECHNICAL CONSULTATION/REFERRAL

1. SOURCE OF INFORMATION ON FOREIGN TRADE PROGRAMS IN NEW JERSEY

2. ACT AS CENTRAL REFERRAL AGENCY TO ASSIST EXPORTERS IN SOLVING TECHNICAL PROBLEMS IN MARKETING, SHIPPING AND FINANCE

PROMOTIONAL ACTIVITIES

1. REPRESENT THE STATE OF NEW JERSEY ABROAD AND HOST VISITING FOREIGN BUSINESS REPRESENTATIVES AND DIGNITARIES

2. PROVIDE OFFICIAL WELCOME

EXHIBIT 5.1 CONT'D.

3. ARRANGE APPROPRIATE CONTACTS AND MEETINGS WITH BUSINESS REPRESENTATIVES

4. SPONSOR AND PARTICIPATE IN TRADE SHOWS AND TRADE MISSIONS TO EXHIBIT NEW JERSEY PRODUCTS

5. PUBLISH AND DISTRIBUTE ABROAD AND IN THE U.S. THE NEW JERSEY INTERNATIONAL TRADE DIRECTORY, LISTING EXPORTERS BY PRODUCTS

LIAISON

1. WORK WITH ALL INTERNATIONAL GROUPS IN NEW JERSEY AND PROVIDE A CHANNEL FOR NEW JERSEYANS TO GET THEIR VIEWS ON INTERNATIONAL ISSUES BEFORE THE STATE GOVERNMENT

2. SERVE AS AN ASSOCIATE OFFICE OF THE U.S. DEPARTMENT OF COMMERCE

3. INVOLVE THE STATE OF NEW JERSEY IN OTHER STATES' INTERNATIONAL PROGRAMS

DIRECT INVESTMENT FROM ABROAD

1. PROMOTE NEW JERSEY INVESTMENT POTENTIAL ABROAD THROUGH:

   A. DIRECT MAIL
   B. ADVERTISING
   C. "HOW-TO-DO-BUSINESS IN NEW JERSEY SEMINARS"
   D. CONFERENCE PARTICIPATION
   E. SPECIALIZED INDUSTRY CALLS, COORDINATE INVESTMENT MISSIONS AND SIMILAR ACTIVITIES ABROAD AND IN THE U.S.
   F. PROVIDE TECHNICAL INFORMATION AND ASSISTANCE TO FOREIGN FIRMS SEEKING TO INVEST IN NEW JERSEY
   G. IDENTIFY NEW JERSEY COMPANIES INTERESTED IN JOINT VENTURES OR LICENSING ARRANGEMENTS WITH FOREIGN FIRMS IN NEW JERSEY

FOREIGN TRADE ZONES

1. THE DIVISION IS RESPONSIBLE FOR COORDINATING AND ADMINISTRATING ALL EFFORTS AS RELATES TO THE DEVELOPMENT AND/OR EXPANSION OF FOREIGN TRADE ZONE ACTIVITY WITHIN THE STATE

   A. ASSISTS IN THE INITIAL STAGES OF LICENSE (GRANT) DEVELOPMENT
   B. COORDINATES AS A TIE-IN TO OUR FOREIGN INVESTMENT EFFORTS
   C. PROVIDES LEADS AND SIMILAR HELPFUL INFORMATION TO ZONE DEVELOPMENT GROUPS
   D. SERVES AS A CATALYST WORKING WITH FEDERAL AGENCIES, IN PARTICULAR THE U.S. FOREIGN TRADE ZONES BOARD AND THE U.S. CUSTOMS

* *

Exhibit 5.2 for the State of New Jersey's schedule for the period January 1984 to June 1984.

Probably the most significant aspect of the trade fair or exhibition is the number of customers, agents, distributors you are exposed to and the presence of professionals from the Department of Commerce and your state to assist you.

Trade missions supported by the Department of Commerce are designed to promote the sale of U.S. goods and services overseas. Some are organized by industry groups and get the assistance of the department; others are organized by the department and supervised by it. A typical mission may involve visiting several countries in a region to promote a particular sector. One of the big advantages is that the Commerce Department, through its contacts, will be able to arrange meetings with local business people and high government officials that may be difficult for you to arrange on an individual basis.

The Overseas Private Investment Corporation (OPIC) promotes similar investment missions to certain developing countries. Again, as an agency of the United States Government, OPIC can arrange contacts with both private investors and government officials at the highest level. It also facilitates meetings on a face-to-face basis with local business people who are interested in investing or becoming joint venture partners. OPIC has arranged several such missions to large markets such as India and Egypt. An example of what you could get out of such a mission is clear from the mission schedule to Belize (Exhibit 5.3). These missions are well prepared and have the specific purpose of assisting mission members in the identification and evaluation of investment opportunities of particular interest to them. A lot of the work is done for you. Taking the Belize example, OPIC officers traveled ahead to set up appointments for mission members with prospective business partners. Meetings were arranged with high government officials you would never be able to reach on your own. The primary focus of the visit was individual business appointments, which is the primary purpose of your overseas trip. Last and not least is that all of this is arranged at a very reasonable cost.

FINDING OUT WHO'S WHO

One of the secrets of success of an overseas trip is knowing beforehand whom you want to see and, if possible, having the meeting already set up before you leave home. This is true whether you are going alone or as

EXHIBIT 5.2

**New Jersey Division of International Trade
EXHIBIT SCHEDULE
JANUARY 1984 THROUGH JUNE 1984**

March 27–31	SIBEX 84–US PAVILION Building & Construction Equipment (2 booths)–8 Spaces Available	Singapore
March 28–31	INVEST IN AMERICA'S CITIES '84 Investment Conference Open to Municipalities and Their Agencies	Hong Kong
April 4–11	CEBIT '84–(US PAVILION) Computer & Office Equipment (2 booths)–8 Spaces Available	Hanover, West Germany
May 8–10	EUROPE SOFTWARE '84 Computer Software Products & Services (2 booths)–8 Spaces Available	Utrecht, The Netherlands
June 12–22	SIAL '84–SEA FOOD USA International Food Show (2 booths)–8 Spaces Available	Paris, France

a member of a trade or investment mission. A lot of the work will be done for you in the latter case, but you will get the most value out of the trip when you know specifically whom you want to see, and the organizers of the mission can help you arrange the meetings.

Agents, Distributors, or Joint-Venture Partners

The reason you are making the trip to a particular country is that you already are very interested in entering that market, and your first step will probably be through export. To efficiently penetrate the market you will need an agent or distributor and, even if you could make some short term direct sales, the local government may insist you have a local agent. How do you select him or her? Again, the Department of Commerce can give you a lot of assistance before you leave so that before arriving in the

EXHIBIT 5.3

SPONSORED BY OPIC (Overseas Private Investment Corporation)

FEBRUARY 23-28, 1986

BELIZE INVESTMENT MISSION

Visiting the Country

EXHIBIT 5.3 CONT'D.

BELIZE INVESTMENT MISSION

FEBRUARY 23-28, 1986
Sponsored by the
Overseas Private Investment Corporation

OVERSEAS PRIVATE INVESTMENT CORPORATION

The Overseas Private Investment Corporation (OPIC) is the U.S. government agency responsible for encouraging investment in some 100 nations. OPIC programs offer qualified U.S. investors direct financial assistance to help establish commercial projects in the developing countries and insurance to protect investments against various political risks.

OPIC programs are available for new ventures or for the expansion of existing projects which will contribute to host country development and not be detrimental to the U.S. economy.

INVESTMENT MISSION OBJECTIVES

To generate new investments in Belize by private U.S. firms, mission participants will be provided with:

- Insights into the country's investment, economic and political outlook from the highest and most knowledgeable levels.
- Information on specific investment projects proposed by Belizean entrepreneurs seeking U.S. partners, and other investment opportunities.
- Prearranged schedules of private business appointments tailored to meet individual needs.
- Advice from Belizean and U.S. businessmen with successful experience in doing business in Belize.
- Access to highest levels of government officials and to decision makers in Belizean commerce.

THE MISSION SCHEDULE

Private Business Appointments

Group meetings are limited to key briefings which will take place at the beginning of the mission. The major portion of the mission will consist of individual business appointments arranged in advance to correspond with the particular needs and interests of each mission participant. Private appointments may be scheduled with:

- prospective Belizean joint-venture partners
- U.S. executives established in Belize
- U.S. and Belizean Government officials
- representatives of financial institutions, and law and accounting firms

Briefings

The U.S. Embassy: The U.S. Ambassador and key members of his staff will brief mission participants on the major political and economic trends in Belize.

Government of Belize: Representatives from the Ministry of Foreign Affairs and Economic Development and other key ministries will brief mission participants and answer questions about the procedures involved in establishing and operating businesses in Belize.

Businessmen: Separate briefings on doing business in Belize with question-and-answer sessions will be given by a group of U.S. businessmen residing in Belize and by a group of Belizean businessmen.

Official Meetings

Belizean Government Officials: The mission group will meet with cabinet ministers who are most able to respond to questions and concerns of U.S. investors. Subsequent private meetings, for individuals or smaller groups, will also be arranged if desired.

EXHIBIT 5.3 CONT'D.

INVESTMENT OPPORTUNITIES

TENTATIVE MISSION SCHEDULE

The following are brief descriptions of project proposals submitted to OPIC by Belizean firms seeking U.S. joint ventures.

Additional project proposals are expected to be submitted soon. Firms which are interested in participating in the mission, but do not find suitable projects listed below, should contact OPIC to determine if arrangements can be made to pursue their interests during the mission.

Agribusiness
- fruit processing
- tomato canning & packing
- honey production
- aloe vera production & processing
- coconut milk processing
- horticulture
- cocoa production

Fishing
- fresh water shrimp hatchery
- shrimp larvae hatchery
- shark fishing/processing
- lobster fishing

Manufacturing
- prefab homes
- glass windows
- wooden doors

Tourism
- hotels

Sunday, February 23

2:20 p.m.	Depart Miami via TACA Flight #311
3:30 p.m.	Arrive Belize City
Evening	Reception hosted by U.S. Ambassador

Monday, February 24

9:00 a.m.	Briefing by OPIC Staff
9:30 a.m.	Briefing by U.S. Embassy Staff
10:00 a.m.	"Doing Business In Belize" panel discussion with U.S. businessmen residing in Belize
11:00 a.m.	"Doing Business in Belize" panel discussion with Belizean businessmen
Noon	Briefings by Belizean government officials
Afternoon	Individual business appointments

Tuesday, February 25 through Wednesday, February 26

Individual business appointments & trips to project sites.

Thursday, February 27

Individual business appointments and trips to project sites.

5:00 p.m.	Final meeting with Government of Belize and U.S. Embassy officials

Friday, February 28

10:10 a.m.	Depart Belize City via TACA Flight #310
1:10 p.m.	Arrive Miami

OPIC
Overseas Private Investment Corporation

country you have a short list that you can contact, and you might even conclude an agreement with one of them. You would probably start with the Foreign Traders Index (FTI), mentioned earlier, that shows firms who import from the United States and are interested in representing U.S. firms. This information is available by industrial sector, product, and country, so you can easily begin to focus in on a few firms, depending on your needs. If you want specific information on a company or companies overseas, the "World Traders Data Report" will be prepared for you for a fee by the Department of Commerce. This will give you important information about size, reputation, product lines, owners, and managers, as well as bank and trade references.

The report also gives an evaluation of the company by the U.S. official who conducted the investigation.

The foreign commercial officials at the U.S. embassies overseas will go one step further and search for a foreign representative specifically interested in your product line. Your needs are matched with the interests of several interested foreign firms and you are supplied with the name, address, and telephone or telex number of the key persons to contact. To obtain this service, you have to complete an Agent/Distributor Service application and submit it to your local district office. You should have a reply within a few weeks. A side advantage of this service is that the foreign commercial official who has conducted these investigations for you in the country will be familiar with your needs and will have made several preliminary contacts for you before you visit the country. By the time you get there you know the agents that you want to talk to first hand; you know the warehousing, distributing, or service facilities they can provide, and you have a general idea of their financial and business performance.

U.S. Overseas Officials

As mentioned previously, the first person you should contact is the commercial officer in the embassy, especially if that officer has already worked on your project. But there are several other people to talk to that may corroborate, correct, or supply some extra information. The political officer in the embassy will be following trends in regulations and laws as well as the general political environment that may affect your investment. Often things can be said face to face that cannot be included in an official report. It can be a painful experience to spend months cultivating a good relationship and understanding with a prominent member of the government whose approval you need, to find out that one month before the signing of your document he is "promoted" to the Ministry of Fine Arts.

There are other officials in agencies outside the embassy that can supply useful information. Officers in the Agency for International Development (AID) will often have a better first-hand knowledge of rural conditions than anybody else. They will have the information you need on the goods and services being procured under the AID programs. In some countries like Egypt, Peru, and Central America this can be quite sizeable and cover a wide selection of products and services. Of particular interest, and gaining more importance, is the Bureau of Private Enterprise of USAID, which has targeted the promotion of the private sector in several developing countries. They plan to do this by assisting local firms with technical assistance, financing, and joint ventures with U.S. firms. The names and telephone numbers of all these officers are easily available from the State Department, USAID, and the Department of Commerce in Washington.

Other U.S. Firms

In general much more information is exchanged between firms in a foreign market than domestically. This is not competitive information, but rather more general information on the local market, operational difficulties, and the general environment for doing business. The managers of U.S. banks, accounting firms, and other service companies overseas may be very helpful. Whether they are American or foreign, they probably have a good small-town knowledge of the firms that interest you. Since they are doing business with large multinational companies, they often collect a lot of information on trade possibilities and markets as a service to their clients, and this information can be made available to you since you are now a potential future customer of theirs as well. The accounting firm can provide the information you need on financial, legal, and tax questions. These firms also produce some very valuable information in a published form to firms doing business in a particular country, for example, "Doing Business in Saudi Arabia," by Price Waterhouse.

Foreign Government Officials

In many cases the success of your venture will depend on the cooperation of government officials and your ability to get documents approved or signed and in the way you are perceived by the host government. One of the advantages of making the trip as part of a U.S.-government-sponsored mission is that you get to see the important people at the ministerial level early on. That personal contact can be invaluable later. But, one way or the other, a basic rule is that you aim for the top at the beginning and try to see the top official involved. Of course, the Minister of Planning is not going to see every businessperson who passes through, and he probably is not familiar with the details of your program anyway. But when he passes you on to the appropriate lower officer, the directive has come from the top down, and this may be an important plus in your discussion. The names of the people you need to see will be available from the commercial attachés or other officials of their embassies in Washington. The embassies may also have a lot of information on the country that could be useful. There are certain countries that are trying to speed up their industrial development and create employment by attracting foreign capital. They make entry easier, give tax holidays, and allow liberal repatriation of profits. They are likely to have promotions officers in the United States and if you are planning an investment in such a country, either in the short or long term, they can be of great assistance not only on information, but also in setting up meetings with the key officials you need to see when you visit.

ON-SITE RESEARCH OR FEASIBILITY STUDY

Your first trip to a country is likely to have limited goals such as getting the extra information you need, or selecting an agent or distributor, or getting the approvals you need to proceed to enter the market. In the case of smaller companies the usual procedure is to begin by exporting and after gaining experience in the market, to proceed to other, usually more profitable methods of supplying the market, for example, by direct investment inside the country itself. But for several reasons this gradual approach may not be a feasible way of entering the market because, for example, the country is trying to keep imports at a minimum or is protecting a local producer. The market may still be very attractive but will require a much larger commitment of funds on your part if you are required to assemble or produce your product within the market. So import entry barriers do not mean that a market is eliminated. The country that does not want you to import may be willing to give you a good welcome if you are producing within the country, creating employment, and supplying goods that otherwise would be imported. If this is the case, you will need to do a more detailed investigation before making such a large commitment. In your first trip you may be conducting what is in fact a preliminary or reconnaissance-level study, which is basically the first step in determining whether to proceed with a detailed feasibility study. Or your homework may already have brought you far enough to make the decision that a full-scale feasibility study is warranted, and you set about getting the necessary information on the first trip. In this case you are likely to have several specialists with you covering different technical aspects of the proposed project.

The Feasibility Study: Steps to Follow

Whether yours will be a preliminary or a more detailed study you can structure it around the following main sections with, of course, the adaptations suitable to your product or firm or the different conditions in different countries. For example, if you are looking at the service sector, the "production plan" section would have to be changed accordingly. If you are looking for a loan or grant from OPIC or other government agencies, you will be required to give a preliminary feasibility study that could be built around this outline.

A preliminary feasibility study would look at most or all of these elements but using secondary information and probably applying results from similar situations. A more detailed study requires considerably more expertise and more time in the country and will cover many of the major decision areas that will be covered in Sections 2 and 3 of this book. For example, the decision to go into a joint venture will have an impact on the financial, legal, and management aspects of the plan.

On-Site Market Research

The small- or medium-sized firm that is likely to enter the market by exporting will probably not need or be able to conduct a real market-research study. This is particularly true in less developed countries where this type of research faces several almost insurmountable difficulties. But, once again, if the investment is going to be large, or at least large in proportion to the resources of the firm, you may need certain information that only some kind of direct market research can give you. But the key question is "What information do I need?" That, in turn, determines how you set about getting it. It may be possible to get the information from an informal survey of distributors or retailers, or you might use your trip to the country to talk to representative or knowl-

FEASIBILITY STUDY OUTLINE

(i)	Project Description:	—Proposed Name —Proposed Ownership —Proposed Management —Source of Funds
(ii)	Financing Requirements:	—Total Costs (Broken Down) —Source of Funds —Anticipated Cost of Funds

(iii)	Production Plan:	—Technology—What Kind
		—Levels of Management and Technical Skills
		—Training Requirements
		—Supplies—Source of Raw Materials
		   Labor Availability
		   Labor Conditions

(iv)	Location:	—In Relation to Markets —In Relation to Suppliers
(v)	Marketing Plan:	—Product Positioning —Market Segments —Transportation and Distribution —Pricing —Packaging —Promotion and Advertising
(vi)	Financial Plan:	—Projected Pro Forma Income —Statement and Balance Sheet for Five or Ten Years —Projected Cash Flow or Rate of Return
(vi)	Legal Situations:	—Foreign-Exchange Regulations on Repatriation of Profits, Dividends, Capital, or Interest —Ownership Legislation —Immigration Laws —Tax, Rates, and Kinds —Import/Export Tariffs —Stability of Legal Environment
(vii)	Management Plan:	—Organization —Relation to Home Base
(viii)	Implementation Schedule:	Detail critical path schedule for each phase of the project

edgeable figures who might know the consumption patterns in the particular area in which you are interested.

For example, doctors in urban or rural clinics could give you information on over-the-counter medicines bought by their patients, or agricultural extension agents would have information on what fertilizers or pesticides or machinery the farmers use and why.

However, if you were investing in an industrialized country with a large market and facing a lot of competition, you would probably need a more formal research study using the types of techniques familar in the home market. This would be especially true if you were in the consumer-goods area. In a developing country it is unlikely that you can use all of these techniques, but it may be possible to use one or two you have found useful elsewhere to get the information you need. Anyway, you may not need the kind of detail that market research generates if your use of secondary data and selective interviewing of key people show you that it is a seller's market, that the need is there, and that you will at least sell the minimum to justify going in.

The difficulties you face in conducting market research can be summarized under language, family structure, and logistics. These are present to a greater or lesser degree in every country, though the logistics problem will be found to a much lesser degree in other industrialized countries.

Language: The single most important difficulty is language. Research will have to be conducted in the language of the country. This involves translation of questionnaires and/or the availability of people who can speak the language. The problem is compounded by the fact that within one country there may be many languages or dialects. Then, of course, there is the cost and difficulty of translation. Inevitably, in translation words change their meaning, and small but significant changes in meaning can distort the results. There is a problem of literacy levels in many countries where a written questionnaire will be almost useless, or your sample will be very slanted by the very group that can read and write.

Family Structure: Other problems relate to the family structure and who the decision makers are in the purchase of certain goods. In the United States the nuclear family is a separate purchasing unit, with the woman playing a very large role in purchasing decisions. In other countries the family unit may be much larger including aunts, uncles, and cousins, and it it may be very difficult to determine from where the purchasing decision comes. If the housewife is interviewed in a country where the man makes the buying decision or does the shopping, the information may be misleading. This is particularly true in the purchase of consumer goods, but even in industrial products the key decision may be made by somebody who does not even show up on the organization chart of a firm. In several countries in the Middle East you could easily find yourself talking to a manager who officially is in charge, but all the key decisions may be made by a family member who does not even have an office in the building. Another factor to be alert to in this area is that in many cultures you will be told what you want to hear because it is a high cultural priority to please the questioner who has honored the family by the visit. Closely related to this is the danger of being given downright false information because there is a suspicion that the data will be used for taxation purposes. This is particularly true of countries with a tradition of colonialism, landlords, and the assessment of rent or taxes based on assumptions about income or consumption.

Logistical Problems: These problems can range from the unavailability of a reliable postal service to the fact that many streets may have no names and houses may have no numbers. Even in some countries in Europe telephone access is less than 50 percent.

Even if a telephone survey were feasible because you are interested in the upper-income market segment, the way the system works, even in urban areas, may make an effective survey impossible.

A small contractor installing water pipes on a construction site knocked out the phone service of a large section of Riyadh with one dig of his excavation shovel. It took weeks to repair. Mail delivery in developing economies can take weeks, and there may be a lot of it lost altogether. But this is not confined to developing countries. In Italy it can take weeks to get a letter from one city to another.

In light of all these difficulties, the market would need to be quite large and lucrative to justify the effort and expense involved in on-site research. But, increasingly, in many countries there are good research organizations that you can call on. Brazil has at least 15 firms in marketing research, and of course, there are many such agencies in Europe and Japan.

In many of the other markets, if it is at all possible, the best way to get a feel for the market is to begin by exporting and seeing what happens. As we will see later, exporting is the least costly way of entering a market, and it involves very little exposure to loss. In a short time, and particularly if you have a good agent or distributor, you are going to get a lot of feedback on your product and your firm, information that may be much more accurate than information gained beforehand from a market-research study. But, of course, if you cannot export and you want to enter the market, you need the information, and one of the ways of getting it is to contract a local research organization and go there and supervise them while the information is being gathered.

Financing the Trip or Feasibility Study

If you join a trade or investment mission sponsored by the Department of Commerce or OPIC, the usual arrangement is that you pay your own costs and some contribution to the mission expenses. The latter expense has no relation to the real value the mission may be to you in opening doors, getting introductions, and making contacts. In certain cases OPIC will provide funds to smaller companies for reconnaissance trips to developing countries to investigate specific projects. On a selective basis, OPIC will share the cost to investigate the feasibility of an opportunity that you yourself have identified in a foreign market. Small businesses are eligible for assistance in all the countries in which OPIC operates. The study has to be carried out by the executives and employees of the firm, and in order to qualify for assistance you will have to submit a preliminary type of feasibility study as outlined earlier to indicate that you have already done your homework and that the project appears to be economically and financially feasible.

The Bureau for Private Enterprise within USAID will provide 50 percent of the total cost of some feasibility studies. The goal is to promote joint ventures in priority areas in selected countries. The main limitation here is that the investment has to be a joint venture with local investors although in certain situations this may be exactly what you want. USAID also provides funding for feasibility studies for specific countries like Egypt or the Caribbean area that have a particular strategic importance for U.S. foreign policy. Finally, look to the host country itself. If you are forming a joint venture or if you will be making a significant contribution to employment or exports, the host country itself may be willing to assist you. This help is unlikely to apply to any direct costs of your trip, but could include support services, transport in-country, and technical assistance in judging the feasibility of an enterprise. Several countries are building their industrial strategies on attracting scarce foreign capital into their economies. This usually takes the form of tax breaks, supply of manufacturing facilities, and training grants, but in some cases could also lead to help in the advance stages. To a large degree, in looking at financing for your trip and/or your feasibility study, you are looking at special situations where your goals and the goals of agencies like USAID and OPIC or the host country coincide.

There is another problem, that many firms are pursuing this funding. In one recent year OPIC's budget for feasibility studies was already exhausted by May. But these agencies are increasing in importance and there is increased emphasis being given to combinations of foreign and local private capital. Because of the cost of overseas trips, feasibility studies, and even elementary market research, it clearly makes sense to investigate financing for your trip.

THE BASICS OF NEGOTIATION

For some cultures negotiation is a sport, for others it is an unattractive necessity, and for the British it is something that gentlemen do not engage in, except, of course, that we all have to. To negotiate is to strike a balance that will persevere between the demands and expectations of the makers of the deal. Negotiation is an art, not a science, and like a lot of arts it can be learned and improved on and depends for its effectiveness on good preparation. Once you get involved in international business you are going to be involved in negotiations on a variety of issues in many different countries. This will certainly involve negotiations with the local government as well as a host of other interests including suppliers, agents, distributors, and possible partners. In different countries negotiating methods will differ, and in many the other party will have highly developed negotiating skills. This is because bargaining for them is a way of life. From the bazaar to the taxi driver the price is negotiable; in Italy you even negotiate your taxes. But the important thing is to arrive at a fair balance. Whatever the differences in ways of negotiating, the goal is always the same, namely to reach the balance acceptable to both. In different cultural contexts the roads will be different, but it helps to visualize the goals and the process.

The fact that negotiations take place at all usually means that both parties have common goals, unless, of course, it is purely a public-relations exercise. The fact that negotiations are needed means there are conflicting interests. Negotiating is the process of resolving the differences. How you actually go about achieving an agreement within the negotiating range will differ, but it should be possible to have a good idea of the range. This is the ability to put yourself into the others' moccasins and to realistically assess what the others' position is, the

FIGURE 5.1
Negotiating is the Process of Resolving the Differences

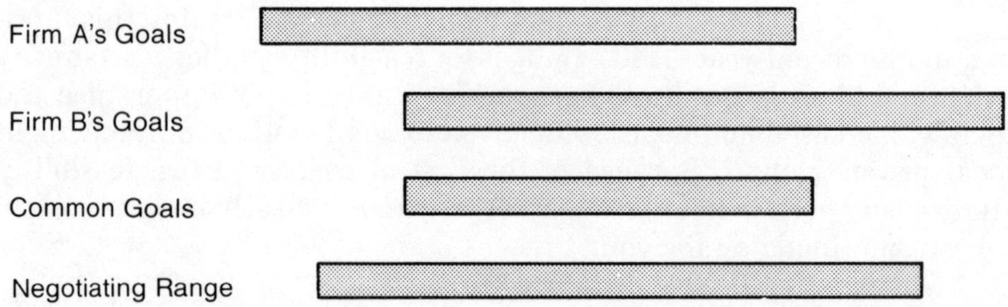

Firm A's Goals

Firm B's Goals

Common Goals

Negotiating Range

pressures the other is under, and the limits to which that person can go. You also know, of course, the limits to which you yourself can go.

Some Practical Guidelines

1. Define your fallback positions and have a clear idea of what you will require in return for yielding ground. If an agent is demanding a higher percentage of sales than you are prepared to give, you could meet the agent halfway if he or she covers the cost of warehousing and customs clearance.
2. Beware of the "ratchet effect" or, in other words, giving in piece by piece on a number of small items that when put together amount to a considerable dilution of your original goal. A manager of a U.S. service company negotiating with a Turkish government official found himself in this position. A detailed line item budget was taken line by line and a bit cut from each until it was so lean that the contract had little attraction to the firm and would also be difficult to effectively implement within the new budget constraints. Obviously, a contract has to be negotiated a piece at a time, but not at the price of the whole. Otherwise, you will find yourself outside your negotiating range.
3. Set no deadlines. The enemy of a favorable negotiation is time, and since you are in the host country staying in an expensive hotel with home-office matters clamoring for attention, you are at a disadvantage. This disadvantage can be readily perceived by the other party and this person may sit it out to see whether he or she gets what is wished. You don't have to finalize all details

now; if you are in general agreement the remainder could be settled at a distance by cable, telex, or letter. Many foreigners know the impatience of American negotiators, so they sit them out, get unwarranted concessions, and sign an agreement only at the very last moment.
4. Don't try to get the best deal possible for you. What you are trying to reach is a *balance* so that you can have a good long-term relationship that will hold up and not be reneged upon by either party. The best deal possible may have short-term advantages, but will likely lead to a lot of operational problems later.
5. Have a built-in delaying tactic. This is particularly important if the areas of disagreement are important and there is a danger of breakdown or you need time to come up with alternative positions. Such a delaying tactic would be the necessity to refer back to the home office or consult with other managers or technical experts. This may also allow informal negotiations to continue to see if the gap can be breached, and it is particularly useful if these can be conducted between specialists in their own areas, for example, accountants talking to accountants, lawyers to lawyers, engineers to engineers with a view to coming up with a solution.
6. Save face. Only masochists want to lose face, but some cultures put a much greater priority on saving face than others. This is a delicate procedure and requires great sensitivity to the culture. In the Eastern cultures it is a very strong value. In negotiations ground has to be yielded on both sides, but there may be a great need to cover up that fact. For example, make a purely cosmetic face-saving counter concession, but above all, make sure that the other party is not forced to yield under pressure or exposed to criticism by his or her peers. In our cultures rejection of a person's idea does not necessarily mean rejection of him or her as a person. That is not true in other cultures.

Examples of Nuances in Negotiations

Saudia Arabia: In most Western, industrial societies a business agreement is largely depersonalized. It is something worked out in the abstract, independent of personalities and can be negotiated by representatives who don't know one another or may not even like one an-

> **BASIC TIPS ON NEGOTIATING**
>
> 1. Have a fallback position.
> 2. Beware of the "ratchet effect."
> 3. Set no deadlines.
> 4. Don't try to get the best deal possible.
> 5. Have a built-in delaying tactic.
> 6. Save face.

other. The agreement stands on its own, with all loopholes closed and covered, and very little left to any mutual understanding or personal relationship between the negotiators. After all, very soon they may be gone, promoted, demoted, or working elsewhere, but the agreement stands. In a Saudi situation the agreement can be very personalized and based on mutual trust. The Saudi businessman you are dealing with probably owns, or is part of a family that owns, the business. He has a long-term perspective and wants to build a long-term relationship. The foundation is mutual trust that will take time to establish and requires on-site individual contact. Any kind of written agreement is secondary to the trust built between partners. History is one of oral contracts, and the effort to legalistically pin down every aspect of an agreement in writing is viewed as lack of trust. Details need to be nailed down, but this is at a very late stage in negotiations and may be done by subordinates while the main partners keep the high ground. Although a lot is based on trust, the Saudi is a superior negotiator with centuries of experience in merchandise transactions. But having achieved the main goals of negotiation, the Saudi may tend to brush over some of the smaller details that can become major irritants later on. So, it is important that all details be covered. I have seen Middle Eastern business people and officials read with surprise, an agreement they signed, apparently with very little awareness that they agreed to some details that now had become important.

China: Negotiations in China take a long time. Most U.S. companies that have gained access to the market have done so after months or even years of discussions. One of the main reasons for the slow pace is the nature of the political and economic system. The foreign businessperson is not negotiating with another businessperson, but rather with a bureaucracy. That's because most major production facilities are state owned, and licensing agreements or joint ventures are almost always with state companies. So any major decison on the Chinese side is a committee decision built on consensus. The Chinese, therefore, negotiate as a team, and they prefer to negotiate with a team of counterpart experts than with one strong entrepreneur who feels he or she can cut through the red tape.

But if negotiations are with a bureaucracy, that does not mean a lack of technical ability on the Chinese side. On the contrary, the Chinese are very well prepared and highly competent, and it would be a mistake for you to assume you know more about your product or process than your Chinese counterpart.

Negotiations can be speeded up somewhat by providing complete and full background information before visiting the country. However, the main issues have to be negotiated person to person because like other Eastern countries, the Chinese put great emphasis on smooth personal relations and on working out differences in a pleasant, nonconfrontational way.

Japan: In the East generally, and in Japan in particular, the biggest enemy of the U.S. negotiator is his or her own attitude toward time. This may cause him or her to initiate negotiations too rapidly with the attitude that, "I'm here to do business," while the Japanese host has an elaborate welcoming ritual to perform and must create a cultural atmosphere for negotiations. The Japanese will take all the time in the world to determine whether agreement is possible along broad guidelines and whether the two parties are in tune with one another. The U.S. negotiator will make a mistake if this delay leads him or her to present the negotiating position too early, in too much detail, or to start to yield on certain points to get the negotiations moving. Closely related to the attitude toward time is the attitude toward talk or saying "no". In many cultures it is neither a strain nor an insult to sit together in silence even for a prolonged period. In negotiations there may be a period of reflection or silent consensus forming. It does not mean rejection of the proposed agreement and does not require a response. When a point is being rejected, it may be in a very oblique way. The Japanese have more than a dozen ways of saying "no," without saying "no." Smooth interpersonal relations are a very high priority, and the rejection of your ideas or requests are seen as a rejection of you and so must be done in a way that saves face all around.

CONCLUSION

Once you have decided to visit the country you have gone a long way in deciding to enter a foreign market. The success of your trip will largely depend on how well you are prepared and whom you will be able to see. There is a lot of help the federal and state governments can give you in both areas, as we have seen over the last few chapters. If you are able to join a trade or investment mission that coincides with goals you already have, it is likely to multiply the advantages of your trip several times over. If you have done your homework well and you intend to export or enter by licensing, you may even be able to negotiate a deal on this first trip. One way or the other, you need to be adequately prepared, know how negotiating is carried on, what is and is not acceptable, what is the negotiating range, what you want to achieve, and how much you are willing to give. The art of negotiating is the art of compromising, of being able to strike a balance that will be rewarding to you and your partner over the long term.

6

HOW TO ENTER THE MARKET: THE COSTS AND THE BENEFITS

You have scanned world markets and made your selection of the areas with the greatest potential for your product or product line. You know the risks involved but you also see the increased rewards. You may realize that, whether you like it or not, you have little choice. Barring a return to the kind of economic warfare that characterized the thirties, you know you are in a world market even without going overseas because the competition will come to challenge you even if you don't go out to challenge it. In facing the competition and in exploiting the high potential markets you have identified, a decision of the greatest significance is how you decide to enter the market. This is not a problem or a choice you face at all in the domestic market. You are already where your customers are. If you are responding to on-and-off sales opportunities overseas, it is not a big problem either. If you have decided to enter only one market at this time and particularly with only one product, the decision is not very complex. But if you are thinking of many products in several different markets, the choice is more complicated. The assumption is that you have made a long-term commitment to international markets and that you are willing to commit the time and resources necessary to find the best way to enter to get the best long-term results. Now you are facing a decision on several products in several markets where it may be better to have a different form of entry for different products in the same market, or different forms of entry in different markets. So you might decide to export one product from your home base to Brazil while producing another product under license, also in Brazil. Or you might decide to enter a joint venture in Indonesia to lower your exposure but decide to go for a wholly owned subsidiary in West Germany because the rewards are likely to be greater in the access you get to all the countries of the European Common Market. What you are, in fact, doing is putting together a global market entry plan that is made up of piecemeal plans to enter individual markets. But you are not doing this in isolation. For example, if you are looking at the lucrative Saudi Arabian market, the most likely method of entry is by export. But if you are also looking at a European market, the best form of entry may be direct investment, in which case the best way to supply the Saudi market may be export from Europe and not from the United States because of high transport costs. In practice, many smaller or medium-size companies are likely to probe foreign markets first by exporting, and as they gain experience, they consider other methods of entering. However, even at an early stage, the attraction of alternative entry methods becomes apparent, and then the best entry for all markets has to be planned.

WHAT ARE YOUR CHOICES?

For our purposes the different choices open to you can be broken down into: (a) exporting, (b) licensing and contracting, (c) joint ventures, and (d) wholly owned subsidiaries. Within each major category there are subdivisions, which, as we will see, enable you to respond in the best way to individual markets.

Exporting

You can decide to handle exports in two ways: Do it yourself or get somebody else to do it for you. The latter way is the very minimal form of entry because basically it is a form of indirect exporting. You are using people and agencies in your own country without really having much contact or feedback from the market itself. It is a way of responding to an unsolicited request or of testing your product on a foreign market without making any significant commitment of time or resources to that market. In fact, there is little difference between indirect exporting and domestic sales. For example, if the buyer for a foreign

---

HOW TO ENTER A FOREIGN MARKET

1. Export $\begin{cases} \text{Direct} \\ \text{Indirect} \end{cases}$

2. Licensing or contracting
3. Joint ventures $\begin{cases} \text{Local firm} \\ \text{Other} \end{cases}$
4. Own your own plant

---

retail or wholesale chain likes a particular product of yours, or if one of your domestic customers makes a purchase for use in their foreign operations, then you are technically exporting your product although you have very little to do with it. These types of sales are sporadic and give you little control but are often the beginning of a stream of unsolicited orders or the stimulus that makes the firm look at foreign-market potential.

A more advanced form of indirect exporting that gives you more experience, market information, and control is the use of an Export Management Company (EMC). This is a company that does the exporting for several firms and saves you the cost of setting up your own export department, especially at the beginning of your entry into foreign markets. The EMC will negotiate for you, accept foreign credit responsibility, and since they are paid on a commission basis, they have an incentive to expand the exposure and sales of your product. It's also a low-cost way of exporting, as the export overhead costs are spread among several firms and shipping costs can be reduced by combining the shipments of several firms. Perhaps the greatest advantage of an EMC for the firm planning a longer-term commitment to a foreign market is the feedback and know-how it gets in the process, while developing its own export skills.

There are two conflicts built into the EMC relationship: While they may wish to increase your sales and increase their commissions, they may also fear that as your sales increase it makes much more sense for you to take over the export function yourself. Moreover, it will be contrary to the interest of the EMC to allow other forms of entry, such as a joint venture, although this may be the best way for you to supply the market in the long run. To protect themselves, some EMC's sell under their own names, purchase outright for resale, or have alternative suppliers available. There are close to 1,000 EMC's in the United States, and they vary in size, resources, and market coverage, factors that need to be taken into account when you decide to export through one of them.

Two other methods of indirect exporting are worth mentioning: piggyback exporting and the Webb-Pomerene Associations. In piggyback exporting there is a carrier and a rider. The carrier already has an export department, access to foreign markets, and a distribution network within the foreign market. The rider does not have these advantages or is not able to use them effectively, or they would cost too much to develop at existing sales expectations. The rider uses the facilities of the carrier, but there has to be something in it for the carrier. It may sell on a commission basis, or it may buy the product and sell it in a way similar to an independent distributor. Your product may complement their own products or may fully employ underutilized existing skills and resources that the company possesses and has to pay for anyway to market its own product. In certain markets, and for certain products, it may be very useful for a small firm to enter a market as a rider with a large brand-name firm. To do so, it will probably need a complementary product. For example, a small software computer firm could ride with one of the bigger computer manufacturers, or the manufacturer of a specialized piece of machinery could ride with one of the large machine-tool names.

The other method of indirect exporting is the Webb-Pomerene Associations. These associations were allowed under the Export Trading Act of 1918. Competing firms that would face antitrust charges in the domestic market were allowed to cooperate and share information and resources in foreign markets. The idea was to enable smaller U.S. firms to compete with foreign trading companies that had more lenient antitrust laws. Strangely, the legislation has not been taken advantage of to any great degree, except by agricultural and commodity groups. As international competition becomes more severe, and as massive surpluses of imports over exports into the United States in the eighties continue, the role of these associations could expand. They offer several advantages like combined market research, cooperation in pricing, sales and negotiations, name recognition—if the association is well known—and lower shipping and handling costs.

These associations are a far cry from the large general trading companies of Europe and Japan, which have a worldwide trading network. The best known are Japanese, Mitsubishi, and Mitsui. A new form of collaboration for smaller U.S. firms is to enter into an agreement with one of the large Japanese companies to gain access to their international trading network. Their resources and range of services are vast, including first-hand familiarity with the most important markets, on-site representation in many countries, the ability to provide credit and financing, and a worldwide network of wholesalers. The European Trading Companies are more focused on their ex-colonial territories like, for example, the United Africa Company, which is the largest trader in Africa.

DIRECT EXPORTING

The step from indirect to direct exporting is a large one but one that can be learned gradually through the process of indirect exporting. Direct exporting requires a set of specialized skills that includes knowledge about export documentation, selection of carriers, packaging and marketing, insurance, foreign-exchange regulations, and export financing. The cost is also high, but so are the rewards in higher sales, greater control, direct market information and familiarity with operations in the international marketplace. The change from indirect to direct exporting need not be abrupt or total. The need for direct contact with the market, increasing volume of sales, or cost considerations will push the firm toward direct exporting. But you can still use skills and expertise that are readily available from other firms until you master all of the tasks yourself. Or you may decide to use some of them all of the time, depending on the cost of doing it yourself.

The single greatest tariff barrier for exporters is the amount of documentation required. It makes no difference whether the shipment is large or small, worth $20 or two million, it will require close to 50 pieces of paper with 100s of copies to get it out and through the port on the far side. But, actually, all of this becomes quite routine after some initial skills are learned. Freight forwarders are experts at handling it, if you want to contract it out at the beginning. Your bank can assist in the financial aspects, your insurance company with insurance, and there are even firms that will do the packaging and labeling for you. In practice, the real challenge of direct exporting is after your product reaches the other side, in the effectiveness of your marketing plan and the agent or distributors who play such a key role in getting your product to the final consumer.

LICENSING AND CONTRACTING

In a broad sense this means of entry involves the sale of knowledge or skills to foreign buyers for use in their production. Usually referred to as "intangible property rights," they include know-how, patents, trade secrets, trademarks, or a company name. For a smaller firm that does not have a famous brand name, what is usually involved is a transfer of know-how, often accompanied by a technical assistance or management contract to ensure proper use of the technology and quality control.

Licensing as such is not a very complex entry method and does not give you the knowledge or experience in the market that you gain from direct exporting. For you, however, it may be the preferred way of entry into all, or one, of several markets. It gives you extra income with little risk, and if you do not have the financial or managerial resources to go another entry route, it may be a first step until you do. Alternatively, if your product is not suitable for export, or if you provide a service, it may be the only route to go. For example, a large-volume product may make shipping costs prohibitive, or opening a foreign office to provide your service may be too costly. The most common reason for using licensing as a means of entry to a market, however, is because imports are not allowed or are made extremely expensive by import duties. The only other way to enter would be through a direct investment, and that is a big first step that may be beyond your means, or it may involve too much of a risk. Technical assistance or management contracts associated with licensing can be a good source of income and have the advantage of giving the firm exposure to the working conditions or market in the country.

JOINT VENTURES

In a sense, both direct exporting and licensing are joint ventures involving, as they do, a relationship with an agent or distributor or the licensee. But as a method of entry into a foreign market, a joint venture means a share in ownership and management, which involves a significantly larger involvement in that market. Usually the joint venture is between the U.S. firm and a local firm, but there are other possibilities that have been used such as a joint venture with a state-owned firm, a joint venture with another U.S. firm in a foreign country or a joint venture with a firm from a foreign country in a third country. Some interesting possibilities are also beginning to emerge for joint ventures with Third World multinationals from countries like India, the Philippines, or Brazil that already have investments in other countries and need new resources or products to expand. For the smaller firm making its first ownership move into a foreign market that it already knows from exporting, a joint venture has a lot of advantages. The return on production and sales is likely to be larger, risk is shared, and if the partner is a local firm it will have management, marketing, and operational experience that could be a great asset in the host country. There will be inevitable limitations on the freedom of operation of even a majority partner in a joint venture, but there will also be a lot of protection because the local partner may represent several local interests and is likely to have a lot of contacts at the political decision-making level as well as with banks and important people in the local market. Finally, the joint venture may allow you to produce in two or more markets with your existing resources, where otherwise you might be confined to one location if you had to make the complete investment yourself.

WHOLLY OWNED SUBSIDIARY

For reasons of planning, management, and control most companies would prefer to completely own their production plants in foreign markets. So, for large companies this is by far the most preferred method of entry. They have the resources and the ability to assume a greater degree of risk. For them, each location is a link in a global chain of production and marketing. By having a high degree of control they can source their raw materials, use the cheapest labor available, and combine their plants, to supply their global markets in the cheapest way possible. But, even smaller companies may decide to set up a wholly owned subsidiary abroad. Many companies in the electronic and computer areas have set up assembly plants in Asia to avail themselves of cheap labor because it is only in this way that they can compete against foreign firms at home and overseas. This is often like double exporting, in which a company sends out most of the components to an offshore location for assembly and then imports them again to the U.S. market or exports them to other markets. If U.S. production costs remain high compared to other countries, it may be increasingly difficult for U.S. companies to compete by the export-entry method, and they may find their export sales eroding unless they go into full-scale foreign production. In practice, this is the sequence of events for most companies. They move overseas to reduce production and shipping costs, and to avoid tariffs. But, as can be expected, the risks are greater because a large investment has been sunk in a plant outside the jurisdiction of their own government.

Although most companies that have the resources move from exporting toward a wholly owned subsidiary and complete control, this is not necessarily the sequence for all markets or all products. A specialty-type product, for instance, may warrant only one production plant, or a market that is attractive as an export possibility may be altogether too small for a local production facility. So, all of the entry methods are options for different markets, and in certain cases, you may have to reverse the normal sequence of events to get into the market at all. For example, the only way to get into the Eastern European or Chinese market may be to form a joint venture right away because exporting is impossible. So, each situation will have to be judged on its own circumstances, and a decision made on the best entry method for each product for each market at this time.

HOW DO YOU DECIDE?

How you decide to enter a particular foreign market may be fairly straightforward, especially if you are doing so for the first time. You may not have the resources to take on anything more complex than exporting, or you may not be willing to take on the increased risks of a large investment. If you are planning a long-term involvement, or if you are planning to enter several different markets, a more systematic look at the costs and benefits of the different entry methods is required. The value of such a systematic approach is that it forces you to look at all aspects together, and it is likely to improve your profits in the long term. The crux of the matter is whether you are entering the market in the best possible way for you. Are you getting the best possible return on the resources you are committing to the market? You might be getting very satisfactory returns by exporting directly to several different countries, but there may be some of these markets where a joint venture or a wholly owned facility would greatly increase your returns. Moreover, a careful examination of your choices may lead you to take steps now to prevent a market from being closed off in the future. For example, if you are exporting to Brazil, which is a large and expanding market, you may be excluded in the long term if depreciation of the cruzeiro or severe balance-of-trade problems leads to a cutback in your exports. A direct investment or a joint venture or an assembly plant could ensure your

How To Enter the Market

continuing presence and even open up possibilities in other markets in South America.

But, deciding on the best entry method is a complicated task because of the number of different factors influencing the decision. In conducting your market research and in examining the political and financial risks, you have already accumulated a large amount of information that is available to apply to the decision on the best entry method. By combining this information with what you know about your product, your company's resources, and the market, you can get a pretty clear indication of what is the best way to go. But, like all decisions where you are trading off risks and returns, it ultimately comes down to a question of judgment. After looking systematically at the options, it will be an informed judgment even if no clear-cut, conclusive answer comes automatically from your analysis. You are making projections for a set future period on costs, sales, revenues, profits and larger economic and political issues such as the likelihood of depreciation of the currency or a change in the political climate. To over-quantify some factors to get a conclusive result will incur the danger of substituting figures for judgment because so many factors are unforeseeable or unquantifiable. However, to assist in the organization of all the factors involved and to provide yourself with a "picture" that clarifies your judgment, it is helpful to set up a simple matrix combining the different entry choices with the key factors that influence each choice.

The key factors influencing the decision can be combined under five main categories: (1) the characteristics of the market; (2) foreign environment; (3) product type; (4) investment of companies' resources; (5) expected returns.

Characteristics of the Market: Some of the characteristics that influence the entry decision are the market size, competition, location, and the marketing infrastructure in the foreign country. Obviously, if the market is small a low-cost entry method like exporting or licensing will be indicated. If transportation costs to the market are high, this may make your product too expensive and you might have to produce locally. This may be the best way to go if now, or in the future, the location of the market enables you to enter other markets or places you inside a regional market with preferential trading arrangements. For example, if you were deciding a few years ago to enter the Spanish market by either exporting or direct investment, a relevant judgment would be the likelihood of Spain getting into the EEC within a few years.

FIGURE 6.1 ENTRY METHOD

KEY FACTORS	EXPORT	LICENCING	JOINT VENTURE	DIRECT INVESTMENT
Market Characteristics				
Foreign Environment				
Product Type				
Resources Required				
Expected Returns				

The volume of sales and your market share may well depend on the competition, either local or foreign, and again depending on your circumstances, one form of entry may give you an advantage. By exporting, for example, you may gain the advantage of the economies of scale associated with centralized production for several markets. On the other hand, a move by a competitor inside the market may give him an advantage in lower transportation costs, lower tariffs, and possibly lower labor or raw materials costs. A final important factor is the marketing infrastructure inside the country. If it is well developed and there is a good network of agents or distributors, exporting is an option open to you. If it is underdeveloped and there are few qualified agents or distributors, or if they are already tied to the competition, you may have to make an investment in the country in the form of a joint venture or a marketing subsidiary.

Although we are classifying all of these factors under "characteristics of the market," they won't all necessarily point in the same direction. For example, the smallness of the market may exclude any large-scale investment in production inside the country, but at the same time the transportation costs may make exports less competitive. Nevertheless, when everything is taken together this factor should indicate a preferred entry method, a method that may be either reinforced or qualified by the other factors on the left-hand side of the matrix.

Foreign Environment: We have already examined the areas of political and financial risk. The conclusions and projections you have made in these areas will have a substantial impact on your choice of entry method. If the political climate is very unstable or there is hostility toward direct foreign investment, then you are unlikely to make a large investment of capital in the country even if several of the other indicators are pointing in that direction. You also have analyzed the balance-of-payments situation and what the future is likely to bring in exchange rates, tariffs, availability of foreign exchange, and the costs of production within the country. Here again, you may run into conflicting cross currents. Future trends may point to tariffs, quotas, or import controls, which indicate that you should try and produce inside the market, but at the same time the government may be lukewarm toward joint ventures or wholly owned production. Your problem is that if you remain dependent on exporting, the market you have spent a lot of resources developing may be closed down overnight. This has happened to many of the countries that experienced serious debt-servicing and balance-of-payments problems in the early eighties, for instance, Venezuela and Nigeria.

There are other factors in the foreign environment that influence the decision. Those include the growth rate of the economy, the logistical problems at ports, and the labor and regulatory environment. If the economy is growing rapidly and incomes and demand for your product are likely to rise, you may decide to take a longer-term view and invest more at the beginning than if you were looking only five years down the road. The condition of the ports and custom clearance is very important for exporters. Long delays, endemic corruption, or pilferage can be costly, and finished consumer products are the most vulnerable.

On the other hand, if the labor or regulatory environments are unfavorable, they may foreclose the possibility of production inside the country itself.

Product Type: Three aspects of the product or product line are important in determining the entry method. The first is whether the product is suitable for all entry possibilities. For example, consumer-type products can be exported or produced locally by a joint venture or a wholly owned subsidiary. Unless there is a valuable trademark or trade secret, however, it will be doubtful if the technology can be licensed because it is not exclusive, intensive, or very complex. The licensee could probably purchase the technology outright if he or she wanted to. However, in the knowledge-intensive industries of high technology or in specialized industrial products, licensing is a possibility. If you deliver a service, then obviously the choice of entry will be different than for material goods. A technical-assistance or management firm could operate on a contract basis, or a company could operate under a franchise as happens with the fast-food chains throughout the world. A service company could also set up a branch or a joint venture, a method of entry that could make them far more competitive by using locally available skills and expertise. For example, in the middle East you can use highly trained Egyptian engineers at a much lower cost than those from the United States and in the Philippines you can hire accountants or economists trained in the same United States tradition at a fraction of the U.S. cost. It costs a U.S. firm more than $100,000 to keep a middle-level manager in an Asian country for a year, while the corresponding cost for a Filipino firm could be less than half that amount.

A second important aspect is the degree to which the product has to be adapted for use in the foreign market. Generally speaking, consumer products, and especially the less basic or high-style consumer products, are very sensitive to differences in market tastes. Industrial products are less so, and they can be adapted, for example, to run on different electrical voltages. These types of products can be produced in one location to be exported worldwide, if necessary. Or they can be produced in a few foreign locations for several different markets. If the product has to be adapted for sale in several different markets, it probably would not be economical to try and do this in one location. Rather, you would need to locate near the markets and produce or adapt the product there. There is a movement toward the development of "world brands" that can be marketed around the world in the same way and that can use any method of entry into a foreign market. Examples are given of the success in the consumer area of products like Coca Cola and Marlboro. But "world brands" are far from being a reality. Examples abound of the need to adapt. General Foods tried to make Tang, its powdered orange drink, into a world brand but the Germans didn't like the name and the British didn't like the taste. Even industrial goods like, for instance, telecommunications equipment, have to be adapted to local systems. The trend may indicate a mix of entry strategies where common components are exported and assembled with local adaptations in an assembly plant in the foreign market, a procedure used in the production of the world car by both Ford and General Motors.

Finally, a lot depends on whether you have a distinctive product that is clearly differentiated from competitors or whether you are competing mainly on price. In the first case, you can afford to export and pay transportation and tariffs because the consumer is likely to be willing to pay a higher price. But if price competition is severe, other forms of entry are preferable if they lower production costs. Moreover, at some future date a mature nondifferentiated product may well be duplicated in the local market by a local producer, and you are unlikely to be able to compete with lower costs of labor and raw materials. In this case you may start with export with the intention of moving into local production later. A lot will depend on the competition and how it supplies the market.

Investment of Companies' Resources: You can decide to enter a foreign market with hardly any incremental investment of company resources in indirect exporting or you can make a large commitment of capital, technology, production management, and marketing skills by building, owning, and controlling your own overseas plant.

A lot depends on the resources you have available and the number of countries you want to enter. A large company with vast resources can decide the best entry method for each market based on the merits and conditions in each case. Where direct investment is too risky they can export or license; where exporting is ruled out they can enter a joint venture or acquire or build their own plant. A smaller company may not have the resources to make a direct investment or may not have the confidence or the management to enter production in a different economic, social, or cultural system. It may also have to forego exports into several markets while entering one market in a very costly manner. That is why a careful analysis of the likely returns on the different entry methods is so important and is the factor most likely to influence the final decision.

Expected Returns: If all other things were equal, you obviously would choose the entry method that gives you the largest profit. Let's say you choose export as the best entry method to Brazil, and you are able to sell $3 million worth of your product with a 20 percent profit margin, your profits amount to $600,000. However, if you directly invested, you could have a sales income of $8 million with a profit margin of only 15 percent, but it still comes to $1.5 million. Of course the payout comes much faster from exports than from a direct investment, and the size of the investment is smaller. So profits have to be related to costs and calculated for a similar period of time. Basically this is the same type of analysis as any investment decision.

To compare the profit contribution of each entry method all the costs and benefits of each entry method need to be calculated. For example, an investment in an overseas assembly plant can also generate exports of components as well as revenues from sales in the new market. But an investment in production can also eliminate a smaller export market you had previously, so that is a cost.

In looking at a particular situation, you will not need to examine the costs and revenues for all entry options, which would be quite a task, because you will have probably eliminated several entry methods on other grounds. In comparing costs, you take into account all start-up and operating costs over the period you are looking at, usually 5 or 10 years. Several of these costs will overlap in the different methods. For example, market research, management time, and new personnel will be needed in exporting as well as in direct investment, although to a greater degree in the latter case. Having calculated the costs, you estimate your revenues, after taxes, of each of the entry methods you are considering so as to get the profit yielded by each method for each year. Finally, you discount each year's revenue by the expected annual rate of return, which could be the same as that expected from a domestic investment or higher if you add a premium for increased foreign risk. Now you have the net present value of the future cash flow.

As an example, let's assume a firm is trying to decide between licensing and a wholly-owned plant in Indonesia because transport and tariffs rule out other options. By calculating expected revenues and costs over the ten-year planning period, they show $263 million profit for licensing and $4,192 million for direct investment. These figures have to be discounted to get net present values. In Indonesia licensing has a much lower risk level than investment, so you would have a higher-risk premium for the investment method. If your expected rate of return in the domestic market is 14 percent, you allow a full percentage point as a risk premium on licensing but 4 percent on investment. Getting the net present values for these figures you end up with the results in Table 6.1. From this analysis, looking only at net profits, it appears that the investment entry method is best. However, if capital is scarce or you wanted to enter a second market at the same time, you might prefer to look at the return on each dollar invested, which in the case of licensing is $107.87 \div 15 = 7.19$, while in investment it is 3.79, which would indicate a priority for licensing.

There are several other ways of looking at these figures and drawing other conclusions. These will be dealt with in the chapter on financial management and capital budgeting. For our purposes here, the priority is on the best profit entry method.

TABLE 6.1 PROFITS FROM LICENSING AND DIRECT INVESTMENT DISCOUNTED AT 15% FOR LICENSING AND 18% FOR INVESTMENT

		($000,000)		
Year	Licensing	Discounted	Investment	Discounted
0	(15)		(375)	
1	10	8.7	75	63.5
2	12	9.0	100	71.8
3	15	9.9	190	115.71
4	18	10.3	320	165.0
5	20	10.0	450	196.65
6	26	11.23	492	182.04
7	32	12.03	540	169.56
8	38	12.43	600	159.60
9	42	11.93	675	152.55
10	50	12.35	750	143.25
TOTALS	263	107.87	4,192	1,419.66

CONCLUSION

This chapter has examined the different methods of entering a foreign market and the costs and benefits of each. As mentioned earlier, the progression up the scale of greater direct involvement is usually an evolutionary one, as companies respond to export opportunities and only later make larger commitments in the form of joint ventures or wholly owned subsidiaries. But this situation is changing. In a very competitive international environment, this evolutionary approach may be a luxury even smaller companies can no longer afford. In other words, exporting as a first step may no longer be a possibility. This is why a carefully chosen entry method is important. The alternatives to export usually involve a much greater commitment of resources and a larger risk. But by completing the analysis required in the matrix on page 124 and by detailing the expected returns of the two or three realistic possibilities, you will have gone through the steps necessary to make an informed judgment, a judgment that will not be scientifically conclusive but which is the best you can make with the facts available at the moment.

7

THE OLDEST PROFESSION IN THE WORLD: TRADING

In the bazaars of the Middle East and Asia Minor trading is a sport, a sport with a long tradition that dates back thousands of years B.C. But trading was far from just being a sport; it was also a highly competitive business, conducted with great expertise for profit. For hundreds of years the Arabs kept the secret of the trade winds that blew their dhows laden with goods to the ports of East Africa. Rich civilizations lay on the path of the spice trade from India to Egypt and Europe. The Roman Empire was the forerunner of the common market, covering most of Europe, North Africa, and the Middle East with free movement of goods priced in one currency. We are late arrivals on the scene and in dealing with many of the traditional traders, it is easy to underestimate the shrewd business sense and the wisdom of the centuries that face you across a bargaining table.

As countries have replaced empires, strong national interests have tended to interfere with trade and even bring it to a halt at times of great tension like the thirties. Since the Second World War, however, trade has opened up with the effort to stabilize currencies, lower tariffs, and increase international commerce. American exporters had a boom period after the war as the European and Asian economies were rebuilt and because of the amount of cooperation and economic assistance geared to this effort. To a certain degree this was a captive market. But things have changed. The former importing countries have now become efficient exporting countries, and some of the formerly poor countries, like Korea, are now challenging the world in products as diverse as cars, steel, shipbuilding, construction, and electronics. In the global marketplace an advantage that many of these countries have is a network of family or ethnic relationships that can act as agents or distributors in many of the target countries. This is true of the Chinese in the Philippines, the Indians in Malaysia or East Africa or London, and the Koreans in the United States. The American exporter has no such ready-for-use contacts or relationships simply because this has been a country of immigration, not emigration. But if an American company is going to compete or operate effectively in a new market, particularly in the expanding economies, it is going to need at least an equally efficient and loyal network of agents and/or distributors. Moreover, even if you could do without them, in many countries you have no choice because the local government may insist that you have an agent if you are going to do business in that country.

FINDING THE RIGHT AGENT OR DISTRIBUTOR

Although we deal with agents and distributors together in this section, there are important differences between a foreign agent and a foreign distributor. An agent is an independent sales representative equivalent to a manufacturer's representative here in the United States. His or her primary purpose is to sell your product to wholesalers, retailers, or the final customers. The agent accepts very little risk or responsibility because he or she does not buy the goods or extend credit to customers. The agent is paid a commission on sales, and the commission may depend on the responsibilities he or she assumes under the agent agreement.

In contrast, the foreign distributor is usually a merchant who buys the goods from you at the best possible price and sells them at the greatest possible profit, either directly to the customer or to other middlemen. The distributor's risks and responsibilities are much greater than those of the agent. He or she takes title to the goods and may have to extend credit to his or her customers, as well as provide spare parts and service. As you decide between an agent and a distributor, you are essentially deciding how much responsibility you want to hold on to or delegate in the target market. With an agent you have greater control of price, promotion, service, and in-country transport and handling. The commission is likely to be much less than the discount you will have to give to the distributor to handle all of these functions, which of course you then have little or no control over. The importance of the agreement is that you don't lock yourself into a situation that limits your options later on.

In choosing an agent, particularly in a country where they are required, the one thing you have to avoid are the so-called "five percenters" who have little interest in really selling your product and may even be promoting a competitive line. In your efforts to locate a good agent or distributor, the first place to start is, again, the Department of Commerce. In particular, they have an Agent/Distributor Service to help U.S. companies find agents or distributors who are likely to be interested in your products. When you request this service, the U.S. foreign commercial specialists will usually supply information on up to six representatives who have indicated interest in your product and are willing to follow the matter further. The information supplied to you in a fairly short period at a low fee will include the name and address of the firm and the people to contact, as well as the telephone, cable, and telex numbers and a brief commentary on each firm.

You may also decide to contact other U.S. firms working in the country who have a first-hand knowledge of the local situation. Since you are unlikely to be competing with large companies in these markets, they will be willing to share their information with you. The biggest challenge here is to find the contact most likely to help you. Of particular interest are the international banks, especially if they have branches in the country. Or, even if they don't, they can obtain a lot of information for you through their correspondent banks. Remember, they are not just doing you a favor; you are a potential new customer. Two other sources of information worth checking out are freight carriers and American Chambers of Commerce, which have offices and contacts throughout the world.

If you come up with a short list of possible representatives on your own, the Department of Commerce will then help you check them out through their "World Trade Data Report." You submit the name and address of the company or companies to a U.S. commercial officer in the field who will then check them out for you. Information supplied will include general reputation, financial and trade references, product lines handled, and territory covered. The comment of the foreign commercial officer may be particularly useful if corroborated by information from banks or other sources.

PROFILE OF THE AGENT OR DISTRIBUTOR

The information you have collected on the market and the goals you have set for yourself should provide you with a set of minimum requirements you expect from an agent or distributor. Your needs will vary according to the size of the market, the areas you intend to penetrate, the competition, and the levels of responsibility and risk you expect the agent or distributor to assume. As you begin your search, it is extremely useful to have a profile of the kind of representative you need. The following six questions are useful starting points in narrowing the choice to a few agents or distributors:

1. Will the representative be able to cover the sales territory in which I am interested?
2. Do I need a firm with experience in introducing new or similar-type products?
3. What resources do I require, for example, physical, personnel, financial?
4. Do I need a representative with strong local contacts with government, banks, and key customers?
5. How important is knowledge of the product line and knowledge of the method of business overseas?
6. Do I need someone who speaks my language and with whom I can communicate directly?

It takes two to tangle and your representative as well as you must see the benefits of a future relationship. In well-developed markets the representative will be choosing you as well as you choosing him or her. He or she may have many lines and many manufacturers who would like to use him or her. It is probably this kind of representative your screening has highlighted in the first place. Having short-listed a few candidates, you might decide it is worth talking face to face with them if you are already planning to visit the country. Alternatively, you can make the approach in the form of a letter/proposal to the principal of the firm in which you are interested. The letter has to be short enough to ensure it will be read and long enough to "sell" yourself, your company, and your product. It is an indication of your seriousness to show you have checked the firm out, and it is a compliment that they have passed the test. The letter should be in the language of the person you are trying to influence or who will make the decision even if you expect to be dealing with somebody else at a later date. It is very important to include brochures, sales documents, and other material that will demonstrate your product and show its potential in this new market. This is one case where a picture is worth a thousand words. You might also include information that will help them check you out, for example, other U.S. firms in their country or banks or other companies they deal with in the United States. In the long run a relationship based on this type of information is likely to lead to the best results and to the avoidance of problems under the agreement. The replies to your letter should indicate the degree of interest of each firm in selling your product. Non-responses speak for themselves and are part of the screening process. Having received the expression of interest, you might decide to screen further by requesting information on discounts expected, outlines of a marketing plan, and expected sales volume, but this may be expecting too much at this stage and may be best left to be worked out in face-to-face meetings or in the negotiation of the agreement. In some of the developing economies, a firm may have neither the expertise nor the resources to answer these questions, at least in a formal way, but it may nevertheless be a good representative for you.

AVOIDING FUTURE PROBLEMS—THE DETAILS OF THE AGREEMENT

In many countries a good personal relationship is the foundation of a good business relationship. In the more developed economies and especially in the United States, business relationships are less personalized and depend less on the principals involved to cement a deal together. The basis of a business relationship is a carefully drawn up, legally binding, agreement that is a kind of objective guide, independent of personal relations. In places like Saudi Arabia, in contrast, the written agreement is secondary to a good working arrangement, and in some cases it may even be a delicate task to include in an agreement the kind of detail you need to protect yourself for the future. Covering this type of detail may be perceived by the other party as a lack of trust. So, timing is essential because if a move is made to finalize a legal agreement too early, it may kill the deal altogether.

In this type of situation the representative has one very big advantage: *time*. The U.S. business person always has a schedule, always has a deadline, always has another country to visit, or always has to be back in the office by a certain date. In certain circumstances you may be much better off spending the time you have in the country building a good working relationship and working out the agreement by telex or correspondence.

On one occasion in the Middle East after several meetings I thought everything was set up to conclude a deal, and I pulled a draft agreement out of my briefcase, at which time the party with whom I was negotiating announced that it was time to go to midday prayers. My timing set back the agreement for months, but then, having agreed verbally on everything of importance, the agreement was signed without the other party ever reading it. It was this level of trust I had missed in the first place.

But you need the agreement, and you have to get it. You will have to decide on the degree of detail you need and how to present it, but it is the formal agreement that can protect you from a lot of problems in the future. Ironically, it is the written agreement that can preserve the working business relationship if problems arise because the dispute need not be personalized.

Another important point to remember is that an agreement cannot force a good performance by the agent or distributor. For that you need a reconciliation of interests, where there are worthwhile margins, good support services, and good communication. The agreement is not trying to nail down the best deal for you, but the best deal for both of you because you both have the same goal, namely, expanding sales and profits, and what is good for one is good for the other. Some manufacturers, in dealing with weaker partners, drive such a hard bargain and surround the agent/distributor with so many limits that the partnership is stillborn. In establishing a relationship with a representative, a short-term gain can be a long-term loss. At the same time, you have to be realistic and include in your agreement the basic points that protect you from problems in the future.

OUTLINE OF THE AGREEMENT

In outline the agreement can be structured around the following broad format with clauses 1 to 8 being fundamental to any agreement while clauses 9 to 13 cover greater detail that will vary from case to case.

1. Identify the precise parties to the agreement. Having completed your screening of potential representatives, you will be able to identify exactly the legal entity you are contracting with

and what its assets and capabilities are. The danger you are trying to avoid here is you are not simply dealing with a paper company that does not have the resources you require and you are not contracting with one entity while thinking you are contracting with another. From your point of view, your firm will be the other contracting party, but you also need to consider whether there are any tax, management, or control advantages for you in establishing a subsidiary, or an offshore firm, as a partner for this agreement.

2. Specify the exact period of time that the agreement will cover. It may be desirable to keep this period short the first time around. It is easy to renew a good agreement. It is much more difficult to get out of a bad one, especially in a country where agents or distributors are few or have political links that may make continual operation in that country difficult for you. A small American firm designated a Saudi businessman and his firm as their agent simply by writing a letter to that effect to the firm. The relationship never worked, but the firm found it impossible to appoint a new agent without antagonizing the old one, so in effect, he had a veto power over the firm's operations in the kingdom. It was a situation of not being able to live with him and not being able to live without him.

3. Clearly identify the territory to be covered. This is another way of limiting the relationship and thereby limiting the damage if things go wrong. It is very easy to expand the territory later, but much more difficult to restrict it. In the Saudi case just mentioned, it would have been much easier to solve the problem if the agent in question had been designated for the Riyadh area. The U.S. firm would have been free to appoint another agent in Jeddah.

4. Specify the products or services covered by the agreement. It is in your interest to limit this initially to the products or services that your market research has determined you can sell in this country. There is no point in including a whole product line if you do not plan to sell all of them there.

5. In the case of the agent specify the commission you will pay, or in the case of the distributor, the discount terms to which you have agreed. In the case of the distributor you might also try to keep some kind of control of the retail price of your products even after you have given up title to them. This will probably be

difficult even if it is important in your efforts to expand within the market.

6. Define the responsibilities of both parties. This clause will cover sales activities, advertising, levels of sales expected, sales and technical support, and inland transport. Two items are of particular importance, and you may decide to single them out for special attention in separate clauses. They are responsibility for tariffs or taxes and responsibility for custom clearance. A misunderstanding on either one of these issues could be quite costly and could cause the destruction of your agreement.

7. Determine the method of payment. This clause is so important that a special section will be devoted to it later in this chapter.

8. Establish sole and exclusive rights. You do not want your agent or distributor selling or promoting competitive products. In countries where agents are required by law this may be a particular danger as there may be few qualified agents or distributors, and they are being pursued by companies from all over the world. Agents in particular have nothing to lose by signing up with several companies, especially if the company itself is doing most of the selling. And this is exactly what happened in the oil-rich markets of the Middle East, Indonesia, and elsewhere. One American company selling a line of electric water pumps for which there was great demand was being shown around its representatives' display rooms in Saudi after the agreement was signed only to find a competing French line prominently displayed.

9. Reserve the right to enter the market by direct investment, a joint venture, or other means sometime in the future. The time limit you put on your agreement may be adequate to handle this, but it may forestall ill will or future difficulties if it is made explicit at this stage.

10. Reserve the right to sell directly or at reduced price or commissions to certain buyers. For example, if you are supplying a firm here in the domestic market, you may want to supply it directly overseas as well, or if you are bidding for bulk orders by the government under international competitive bidding, you may want to lower prices or the commission and bid directly.

11. Clearly state the language and the legal system of the agreement to avoid disputes over translations or which laws of which country will govern the agreement.

12. Include a cancellation or termination clause that will allow a peaceful divorce after proper notice is given. This clause may also specify certain conditions under which the agreement is automatically cancelled, such as, for instance, bankruptcy, fraud, or the takeover of the firm. The clause is designed to give you a way out if the agreement is not working. It also, of course, gives the representative a way out if, for example, he or she wants to switch to what the representative considers a better line.
13. You might also include an arbitration clause that outlines a method of settling disputes in the event of a disagreement. In practice, arbitration is rarely feasible because it will probably occur under the laws of the foreign country, or if it is by the London Court of Arbitration or some other international institution, it will probably be too costly in time and money to be pursued.

The outline of the agreement given above serves your interests, but of course, the agent or distributor also has his or her own interests, and a lot of the details, for instance, responsibilities under Clause 6, will be negotiable. It is really in Clause 6 that you need the greatest degree of flexibility to achieve the kind of good working relationship that is your first priority. However, the flexible conditions of this working relationship should be hemmed in by the clauses that specify duration, territory covered, exclusive rights, and cancellation. If everything goes well, you can live with compromise on clause 6; if things go wrong, you need a way out. One final point: Always make sure you get the agreement checked out by legal counsel in the host country because there are restrictions in several countries in such areas as exclusive rights, termination clauses, and taxes. You can get a referral to a good local lawyer from other firms working in the country or from the U.S. commercial offices. Alternatively, you may seek a referral from a U.S. lawyer or legal firm. They often know lawyers in the other country who have gone to law school in the States, and you then have the added advantage of knowledge of both U.S. and the foreign country's legal systems.

EXHIBIT 7.1

<u>SAMPLE</u>

<u>AGENT's AGREEMENT</u>

This agreement, dated as of   by and between McMurphy and McNulty, a corporation duly organized and existing under the laws of the United States of America (hereinafter referred to as "M & M")

AND

Timbuktu Enterprises, a corporation duly organized and existing under the laws of Nigeria (herinafter referred to as "AGENT.")

WITNESSETH

1. APPOINTMENT OF AGENT AND PRODUCT LINE
M & M hereby appoints AGENT as non-exclusive sales agent in the Provinces in Nigeria listed on attached Schedule A (hereinafter referred to as "the Territory") for the M & M line of products listed on attached Schedule B (hereinafter referred to as the "Products.") While it is the intention of M & M that the full line of Products will be available for distribution, M & M reserves the right to delete or add Products to Schedule B. Likewise, M & M may unilaterally, on 30 days notice to AGENT prior to the annual anniversay date of this Agreement (based on the effective date set forth above), delete provinces from the list of provinces included in the Territory, as set forth on Schedule A.

2. DUTIES OF AGENT
   a) Agent shall actively promote sales of the Products in the Territory and shall solicit orders from third party purchasers on M & M's behalf. Upon receipt of an order for the Products, AGENT shall immediately transmit such order to M & M for acceptance or rejection by M & M as M & M sees fit. If M & M accepts such order, it shall execute the same by supplying the Products directly to the third party purchaser and by then billing the third party purchaser directly for the purchase price. While M & M will bill purchasers directly with respect to all orders, AGENT will assist M & M in obtaining prompt payment from purchasers with respect to such purchases and will vigorously assist with respect to debt collection, should this become necessary. To that effect AGENT will receive copies of collection reminder letters.
   b) AGENT shall assist M & M with respect to communications within the Territory and shall keep M & M advised of general market, economic, regulatory and other developments which may affect the sale of the Products in the Territory.
   c) Upon M & M's request, AGENT shall import samples, literature and other promotional material for use in the local promotion of the Products. Title to such material shall remain in M & M or its

affiliates at all times. Any expenses involved in the importation and clearance of the material shall be for the account of M & M.

    d)   AGENT shall do nothing which would jeopardize the goodwill of M & M or any of its affiliates or the reputation of the Products. The appointment of AGENT as a sales agent hereunder shall not create a joint venture, or an employer-employee relationship, and nothing hereunder shall be deeemed to authorize AGENT to act for, represent, or bind M & M other than stipulated hereunder.

3. SALES OF PRODUCTS AND TERMS

    a)   Sales of the Products by M & M shall be at the regular FOB (port of exit) prices, established by M & M in effect at the time of order. All orders shall be subject to acceptance by M & M and all sales shall be subject to the current terms and conditions of sale which will be provided in advance to AGENT in writing.

    b)   Once an order shall be accepted by M & M, shipments with respect thereto shall be made by M & M upon instructions received from AGENT, subject to the reasonable ability of M & M to do so. Such shipping instructions shall always be given with a view to minimizing the credit risk of M & M and its affiliates.

4. COMMISSION

    a)   With respect to orders in the Territory obtained as a result of the efforts of AGENT which M & M subsequently accepts and fills, M & M agrees to pay AGENT a commission of 15% of the net invoice price on all accepted orders for Products from those provinces listed on attached Schedule A. Net invoice price in all cases is defined as the gross amount of the order less (i) trade and quantity discounts, (ii) returns, credits and allowances, and (iii) less any freight charges that M & M incurs on such orders.

    b)   On tender orders or other orders transmitted by AGENT which are at prices lower than M & M's regular established FOB prices, the commission to be applied shall be adjusted downward by a percentage to be mutually agreed upon by M & M and AGENT prior to shipment.

    c)   Commission payments shall be due to AGENT with respect to a sale only after payment of the purchase price shall be received in full by M & M. In the case of the orders where Products are shipped in installments, no commission payments shall be due with respect to any installment until the purchase price of the final installment and all prior installments shall be received in full. Payment to AGENT of commissions under this Agreement shall be made to AGENT's address set forth in Paragraph 7 herein in accordance with AGENT's instructions which shall always be in accordance with all applicable laws and regulations.

5. TERMS AND TERMINATION
    a) This Agreement shall be effective as of the date set forth on the first page hereof and shall continue in full force and effect for a three (3) year period thereafter.
    b) If AGENT shall be or become insolvent, or a petition in bankruptcy shall be filed by or against AGENT, or AGENT shall make any assignment for the benefit of creditors, or a receiver of the property or a substantial portion thereof of AGENT shall be appointed, or AGENT shall take advantage of any other law or procedure for the protection of creditors, or if all or substantially all of the assets or control of AGENT shall be acquired by any other entity, either governmental or private, then, in any such event, M & M may terminate this Agreement immediately by sending AGENT written or telegraphic notice of such termination.
    c) If AGENT shall default in the performance of any of its obligations hereunder, then M & M shall have the right to terminate this Agreement immediately upon written notice of such termination to AGENT.
    d) Upon any termination of this Agreement, AGENT agrees to make no claim or request compensation of any kind because of such termination. AGENT agrees to waive any statutory amount which may be allowable or imposed for such termination as liquidated damages or other such statutory payments, if any.
    e) The termination of this Agreement, as herein provided, shall not affect AGENT's obligation to pay any amount accruing to M & M under the provisions of the Agreement while it was in effect.

b. ARBITRATION
Any dispute, controversy or claim arising out of or relating to this Agreement, which cannot amicably be settled, shall be finally settled by arbitration to be held in the English language in London in accordance with the Rules of the International Chamber of Commerce, except that in the event of any conflict between the provisions of those rules and the provisions of this clause, this clause shall govern. Regardless of where this Agreement shall have been executed, it shall be construed in accordance with the substantive law of the United States. The arbitration shall be before three English speaking arbitrators, one to be selected by each of the parties and the third to be appointed by the International Chamber of Commerce. Judgement upon any award rendered by all or a majority of the arbitrators may be entered in any court of any country having jurisdiction. The parties acknowledge that this Agreement and any award of the arbitrators rendered pursuant to it shall be governed by the United Nationals Convention on the Recognition and Enforcement of Foreign Arbitral Awards (1958).

7. WAIVER, ASSIGNMENT, NOTICE AND PREVIOUS AGREEMENTS
   a) This Agreement cannot be amended or modified except by the express written consent of both parties.
   b) This Agreement may be assigned by M & M to any of its affiliates without the consent of AGENT, but in all other cases shall not be transferable or assignable by either party without the prior written consent of the other.
   c) All notices of communications given hereunder by one party to the other shall be addressed to such party by registered airmail or by cable as follows:

   M & M: McMurphy and McNulty
            Borderwalk
            Mississippi

   AGENT: Timbuktu Enterprises
            P.O. Box 2160
            Lagos, Nigeria

   or to such other address as such party may from time to time designate in writing as its or their address for the purpose hereof.
   d) This Agreement superseded any previous agreements or understanding between the parties and all such agreements or understandings are hereby cancelled.

   IN WITNESS WHEREOF, the parties hereto have caused this Agreement to be executed by their duly authorized officers or representatives as of the day and year first above written.

WITNESS: McMurphy & McNulty

_____   By _____

WITNESS: TIMBUKTU ENTERPRISES

_____   By _____

GETTING PAID

When selling here in the domestic economy, the usual method of payment is an open account; the goods are ordered, delivered, and paid for in that order. Usually, goods are billed and paid for on a month-to-month basis. The system is built on the assumption of the credit worthiness of the customer and the relative ease with which the customer's ability to pay can be determined. Sometimes, there can be problems with delays or even default in payment. But there should be warning signals, and the supplier can usually apply adequate pressure to get payment.

In exporting to a foreign customer, it is far more complicated; the risks are greater, and when trouble arises it is much more difficult to do something about it. This is really one area where an ounce of prevention is worth more than all the cures in the world, and the prevention usually boils down to structuring the payment in such a way that payment problems will be avoided. There are basically four methods of payment: (1) cash in advance; (2) letters of credit; (3) bills of exchange, and (4) open accounts.

Cash in Advance: By paying in advance the foreign customer is putting complete trust in you that you will ship the goods according to the specifications and within the agreed-upon time frame.

You have the use of the customer's money and he or she is left with all the risk exposure. While it is by far the most attractive form of payment for you, it is unlikely you will be paid this way, and in fact, very little exporting is paid for in advance. The customer or importer is going to go for the best deal he or she can get, and a very important part of the best deal is the method of payment. You are competing for the customer's purchase, and in most cases you will not even be in the ball park if you require cash in advance. However, there are circumstances where you are not willing to sell under any other conditions, and these conditions are probably the same for your competitors as well. For example, if you have to modify a product or build to certain specifications or you have to incur a large up-front expense, you will have to insist on at least a partial payment, in advance. If the customer is a high credit risk, you may insist on payment in advance because not making the sale at all is better than going through a long hassle trying to collect. Moreover, if there are severe restrictions on foreign exchange leaving the country and if they are getting tighter, you may want to have your money prior to shipment. Cash in advance may be part of a total sales package where, for example, you negotiate a lower price in exchange for advance payment or you provide extra back up services to the customer.

Open Account: This is the opposite of cash in advance. Now you are taking all the exposure and all the risks. It is used with long-standing customers who have consistently paid in the past and who are known to have adequate resources at their disposal. It is also quite common, of course, between a parent and a subsidiary or a branch. In general, it is a risky business that requires continual monitoring on a case-to-case basis. Some firms have gone on open account on the basis that an open-account sale is better than no sale at all. But it depends on the size of the sale and the degree of exposure. One trading firm in New York shipped tens of millions of dollars of equipment and supplies on open account to a client in Saudi Arabia, including milk-processing equipment that cost millions of dollars. In this case there was no problem of payment, but the danger is that there always will be a first time. This is particularly true of large importing countries that may develop foreign-exchange problems or have serious political unrest. The credit reputation of your customer may still be first class, and he or she may sincerely want to pay, but the central bank or the government may not release the foreign exchange to do so. Also, companies that were excellent payers may overreach and you, among others, are left unpaid. With the recent drop in the price and the demand for OPEC oil there are many cases of bankruptcy in the Middle East and many horror stories by companies who have not been able to get paid. In general, an open account is less risky in a hard-currency country, in Europe or elsewhere, and you are likely to get somewhere through legal channels if problems arise. An open account is particularly risky where there are balance-of-payments problems and exchange controls.

Letters of Credit: Next to cash in advance a letter of credit gives you the best assurance of payment and is the most common method of payment in international trade. Basically, what it does is eliminate the risk of cash in advance for the buyer and of an open account for the seller. The buyer sets up a letter of credit for the amount of the sale at his or her local bank in favor of the seller. This is a promise by the bank to pay for the goods when the bank or its correspondent bank in the seller's country receives certain shipping documents proving the shipment has been made according to the agreed terms. Most letters of credit are irrevocable, which means that once the credit has been accepted by the seller, it cannot be changed in any way without the consent of the seller.

STEPS IN SETTING UP A LETTER OF CREDIT

1. You agree on the terms of sale, including the costs of the letter-of-credit transactions, which are usually assumed by the buyer.

Trading

2. The buyer's bank prepares the letter of credit, including the exact terms and documents necessary for payment.
3. The bank sends the letter of credit for confirmation to its correspondent bank in the United States.
4. The U.S. bank sends you the letter of confirmation and the letter of credit.
5. The exporter gets all the documents completed as he or she ships the goods.
6. The exporter presents the documents to the bank and gets paid.
7. The buyer receives whatever documents he or she needs to claim the goods at the port.

EXHIBIT 7.2

SAMPLE

CONFIRMED IRREVOCABLE LETTER OF CREDIT

NATIONAL BANK OF NEW YORK
444 Fifth Street
New York, N.Y.

DATE	ADVISED BY
June 2, 1986	Cable Telex

ADVISING BANK	APPLICANT
Foreigner's Bank Paris, France	Perfumers Inc. 630 Madison Avenue New York, N.Y.
AMOUNT	BENEFICIARY
$50,000.00	Perfume Manufacturers Ltd.

We hereby issue this letter of credit in your favor for the amount of $50,000.00 (fifty thousand dollars) by order of Perfumers Inc. 630 Madison Avenue, New York, which is available against your draft at sight drawn on us, when accompanied by the following documents which must cover full invoice value of the merchandise described below:

1. Signed commercial invoice
2. War/Marine Insurance Certificate in duplicate
3. Full set of clean ocean bills of lading, dated on board, freight prepaid issued to the order of The National Bank of New York, notify Perfumers Inc.

COVERING

    Perfume No. 60
    60 Bottles as per pro forma invoice dated May 10, 1986

SHIPMENT FROM	TO
Le Havre	New York
	SHIPMENT DATE
No partial shipments	On or before July 25, 1986

AUTHORIZED SIGNATURE

Bill of Exchange: Bills of exchange describe exactly what occurs under this method of payment: You exchange the documents, which enables the buyer to obtain the shipment when he or she pays you for the goods. Again, the transaction is usually done through your bank and the buyer's bank. Your bank draws a draft on the buyer and presents it with the shipping documents to the buyer's bank for payment. The buyer accepts the draft and authorizes his or her bank to pay, at which stage the buyer receives the documents necessary to get the goods from the shipper. Bills of exchange can be on sight, arrival, or time. An on-sight draft means payment is required when the documents are presented even if the shipment has not yet arrived. An arrival draft specifies that payment be made when the goods arrive, while a time draft indicates an agreed future date when payment will be made.

    The difference between a letter of credit and a bill of exchange is that in the former the credit of a bank or banks is involved, but in the latter you assume the risk until you are paid. When the letter of credit is confirmed by the bank, it means the bank is obligated to pay if you complete your side of the bargain. In the bill of exchange your customer may run into financial trouble after you have made the shipment and may refuse to accept the bill of exchange. The customer cannot get his or her hands on the goods, but you cannot get paid and, of course, you lose if you have to ship the goods back or abandon them or sell them at a discount to another buyer.

HOW TO BEAT THE PAPER CHASE

You have identified your market, you have the product, you have an agreement with your agent or distributor, you have ensured the best method of payment possible; now all you have to do is get the goods there. But therein lies the most irritating part of the whole process in the form of export documentation, barriers to trade, and the difficulties associated with bribery and corruption in many markets.

Export Documentation: At first glance, the amount of paperwork required for a single shipment is enough to turn anybody off. At its worst you may need 50 documents and 100's of copies. This is a significant cost in time and money because of the number of different parties or agencies involved in your shipment. These include yourself, your customer or representative, the freight forwarder, your bank, your customer's bank, the foreign government, and then, to cap it all, the customs at both ends. At second glance, it is not quite so bad. After you get some experience in export documentation it will become a routine matter, and the freight forwarders and the banks that handle international transactions are specialists in their own areas and can be of great assistance. Nevertheless, there are a lot of documents you have to prepare, and ultimately you are responsible for their accuracy. If documentation is not complete or correct, your shipment may be delayed or held in the port overseas or even confiscated. But nothing dramatic like this need occur as long as one responsible manager is supervising the export procedures. For firms probing or entering an export market for the first time, the local Department of Commerce office, or your bank or other exporters will be able to assist you in getting started. Of course, you could use an export management company or some other intermediary, but firms planning a long-term commitment to selling overseas will want to master the art and learn from experience.

Here is a list of the most important documents that are needed.

The Pro Forma Invoice and Purchase Order: These documents give the details of the terms of sale between you and your customer. The pro forma invoice outlines your terms for the sale including quantities and price of the goods and shipping and insurance rates. The purchase order from the customer confirms or modifies the terms of the pro forma invoice as regards quantity, cost, shipping date, export route, insurance, and payment method.

Bill of Lading: This is a very important document because it establishes who is the legal owner of the goods at the point of destination and is a key instrument for arranging payment. The bill of lading is issued by the international carrier and is a contract to ship the goods as well as a receipt for them.

Insurance Policy or Certificate: Because of the danger of damage, loss, or pilferage almost all shipments have to be insured. This is usually a requirement of the terms of sale, and most exporters have an open insurance policy against which they insure specific shipments by issuing a certificate of insurance.

The Commercial Invoice: This is issued to the customer. It gives details of the goods sold and contains the information agreed to in the pro forma invoice and purchase order. It is required in many countries for clearing purposes and is a key document in getting paid.

Export Declarations: This is required by the U.S. government and is principally a device for measuring exports and controlling them to avoid shipment of goods for which special licenses are required. This declaration is presented at the port of exit and includes a full description of the goods, their value, their destination, the exporter and the importer, and the name of the carrier.

Consular Invoices, Certificates of Origin, and Customer Invoice: The consular invoice is required by certain countries and contains essentially the same information as the commercial invoice, but it has to be certified by a consul of the receiving country. Usually there is a standard form that has to be returned in several copies with copies of other documents such as the bill of lading and the commercial invoice. The customs invoice may be required for custom clearance, and the certificate of origin, which certifies the country of origin of the goods, may also be required by the receiving country.

These are the main documents you need. A lot of them contain the same type of information, and many of them have to be duplicated for the different parties involved. For example, the bank will require the commercial invoice, the bill of lading, and the insurance certificate as well as other documents while the freight forwarder will also require the commercial invoice and the letter of credit as well as other documents including a packing list and your letter of instructions. One thing is certain: With the number of documents and copies required, an essential investment for the export department is a good copying machine.

But there is a little hope on the horizon. Moves are being made to cut down and simplify the documentation required especially between the main exporting countries. As the volume of world trade increases, the movement is likely to gain strength particularly as all of this is quite costly and in some cases can add up to 10 percent of the value of the goods, a 10 percent that is being paid by either the seller or the buyer or both.

Other Barriers to Trade: But you are not finished yet because so far we have only talked about getting the shipment into the port on the far side. Although it may be the responsibility of the customer or the agent or distributor to clear it through, you are making an investment for the long term, and you have to decide how serious other problems are likely to be and what impact they are likely to have on your projected sales volume. In particular, you need to watch out for barriers that may be imposed if serious balance of payments problems develop. While the most obvious danger you might face is a direct increase in tariffs, imports can be cut down by other nontariff means, not the least of which is increasing the quantity and complexity of the paperwork. The following are some of the most common means of doing this.

Import Licenses: The importer has to get this from some government department, and it can be used to limit some or all imports by delaying the issuance of a license or by allowing very short periods to apply for them.

Exchange Permits: Here the importer has to apply to a government agency or the central bank for the foreign exchange to pay for imports. In this way the government can determine priorities for import, delay purchases, or even prevent them altogether. They may also have differential exchange rates with one favorable one for essential goods and a less favorable one designed to cut down the import of luxury goods. Such a policy could, of course, have great impact on the price and demand for your product in the country.

Quotas: The government may also decide to limit the quantity of goods to be imported over a specific period of time. This may result from balance-of-payments problems or efforts to conserve scarce foreign exchange, or it may come from pressure from local businesses or employees who are threatened by cheaper imports. The United States had a so-called voluntary quota for the import of Japanese cars mainly to protect the domestic automobile industry. One possible favorable consequence of a quota is that although you may be limited in the quantity of goods you ship, you may be able to get a higher price if demand exceeds the limited supply or domestic prices are higher.

These are only some of the more obvious restrictions. A similar effect can be achieved by less obvious means. Paperwork can be slowed down, unrealistic standards can be set for packaging, labeling, or for health and sanitation purposes. There can be a customs slow down or certain items can be restricted to a few overcrowded ports. France, for example, limited the import of Japanese VCR's to one isolated understaffed port of entry, while the Netherlands requires the country of origin to be marked on imported eggs.

The Foreign Corrupt Practices Act

An export from you is an import for someone else, and if you think the paperwork is burdensome at this end, it is still easier because every country wants its citizens to export. Not so at the receiving end, and as we have seen, there are many ways to slow down imports or stop them altogether. But apart from these special ways, the normal port and customs regulations of many countries are made up of layers and layers of regulations laid on top of one another over hundreds of years. At the receiving end of an import shipment in the Middle East, I had to get more than 40 signatures including that of the provincial governor. It is a fact of life that in many cases these regulations and signatures are a source of income for the often low-paid bureaucrats that administer them. In other words, ports and customs houses are associated with bribery and corruption. No matter how you handle it, this is a cost to you, directly or indirectly, because although you are not going to be handling it yourself, it will make the price of your product higher, or your commissions higher. This aspect of doing business overseas has scared a lot of people because of the publicity surrounding the Foreign

Corrupt Practices Act. This piece of legislation resulted from large-scale bribery of high-level government officials to get large, multimillion dollar government contracts. High-level executives lost their jobs for giving the bribes, and the then prime minister of Japan lost his for taking them. Both the legislation and the severe penalties passed in 1977 were geared to "political" payoffs of a large nature. U.S. executives were regarded as being liable whether or not they had any reason to know that an agent in their employ was paying bribes. The United States is the only major Western economy that has this type of strict legislation, and some executives claim that as a result they are not competitive in bidding for contracts while the Germans, the British, and the Japanese are laughing all the way to the bank. In Germany you can even take some payments as business expenses and deduct them for tax purposes! How does all of this affect you and that customs bureaucrat that is sitting on your unsigned shipping documents until he or she gets a few dollars? Two fundamental questions for you are (1) If you have to make small payments to "lubricate" or "grease" or expedite the process of clearing your goods, is that a bribe? (2) If your agent is doing it under his or her agreement with you to clear your goods but out of his commission and without your necessarily authorizing it, are you liable? Although the legislation is ambiguous in many ways, it is pretty clear that payments made to lower-level government officials for the purpose of obtaining permits or getting them to do the job they should be doing anyway is not covered by the act and is a widespread practice in many countries anyway. From this it can be presumed that if your agent is doing the same thing, that is, making small-scale payments to small-scale officials, it is excluded as well. However, the act is very strict in large-scale contracts and particularly in dealing with higher government officials. So, apart from the morality or business-ethics point of view, unless you want to pay a large fine and possibly spend some time as a guest of the nation in a federal penitentiary, do not make any payment that is illegal. If your agent pays a bribe covered by the legislation you are liable. You are also caught in a very noncompetitive situation if the competition is free to do so. Realizing the ambiguity and uncertainty of the legislation, there is a move in Congress to modify it so that you are liable only if you have authorized a bribe rather than just "have reason to know." Another proposed change is that payments made to facilitate a sale, if lawful in the target country, are not bribes. It will take some time for the issue to be resolved. But not all the results are negative because in cases of large bids or contracts the client knows that a U.S. firm or executive cannot pay them off and therefore he or she doesn't expect it. Because this is not an expense you have to incur, your price may be lower and more competitive, and if your product or service is the best available you may get the contract without all the hassle associated with payoffs.

CONCLUSION

At this stage it must be pretty obvious that making an international shipment is a rather complicated business compared to sending a truckload to Baton Rouge, Louisiana. And so it is, although drawing out the details as we have done in this chapter gives the impression of a degree of complexity that does not always represent reality. In many ways what was presented was a worst-case scenario. Hundreds of U.S. firms, big and small, export up to $300 billion each year. Most of the trade is to countries with banks, customs services, and transport networks as efficient as in the United States, and the agents and distributors are well-established firms. But there are growing opportunities for exports in the lesser developed markets precisely because they don't have the capacity to produce themselves. And here there are difficulties, but difficulties that are far from being insurmountable. With a home staff having an eye for detail, your bank, a good freight forwarder, and a good agent or distributor there is no reason why your exports should not flow smoothly to their destination and why you shouldn't get paid—most of the time!

8
LICENSING: REWARDING OPPORTUNITIES WITH LOW RISK

Licensing used to be regarded as a second-rate method of entry into a foreign market. It was considered to be neither here nor there, in the way exporting is here and a fully owned subsidiary is there. But that is changing, even for the large companies, as they examine more closely the net risk-adjusted advantages in different markets. It is of even greater interest to smaller or medium-sized firms that lack the capital, management, or experience to go in and make an investment in a foreign market. In short, licensing may be the most attractive entry method because of the nature of the market or because of the resources or strategy of the firm, and this will be determined by the market analysis and the self-audit of the firm's own resources. Moreover, it can be quite rewarding financially, especially if a total package is put together, a package that includes technical assistance, engineering fees, a management contract, quality control, profit from sales of bulk materials or specialized machinery, and of course, royalties on sales.

But, although licensing is a relatively easy form of entry, it is controversial mainly because, overall, the transfer of technology is from the richer economies to the poorer nations that don't have the resources to develop or buy their own technology, or whose markets are so small they won't justify doing it. It used to be that the control and management of capital was the most controversial aspect of international operations, but recently the control and cost of technology has come to the fore, especially as the foreign-exchange shortages of many countries have highlighted all foreign payments and particularly licensing fees that are often for intangible or invisible assets. So, although licensing is a low-risk entry strategy, it has to be evaluated carefully to avoid the danger of licensing when one should not and not licensing when one should. Most of the large companies pick and choose between different strategies in different situations. Some companies do nothing except licensing. Fruit of the Loom manufactures nothing itself, but its trademark is on many products, manufactured in many different locations and sold throughout the world. For other companies the choice may be one of necessity even in larger markets. It is necessary, therefore, to take a look at the circumstances that make licensing the only or preferred entry method.

LICENSING: IS IT THE BEST FOR YOU?

Most companies decide to go the licensing road because of the characteristics of the market itself. Some firms may look at the market and because of the difficulties of the other more conventional forms of entry may decide to pass it up altogether. But if the world is your marketplace, that is not sufficient reason because licensing may be both possible and rewarding. The characteristics of the market that will indicate to you that licensing is the road to go include the following:

1. The market has low-volume potential, cannot be served by exports, but could generate extra revenues from royalties and fees.
2. It is impossible to export either because of trade restrictions or the inability of importers to get the foreign exchange to cover the cost of finished imports. Of course, this may also mean difficulty in getting foreign exchange for royalties or other fees, but these sums are likely to be considerably less than the cost of imported goods.
3. Competition in the market has made your products too expensive. This may be because of your high domestic production costs, the location of your facilities far away from a port, or the transportation costs involved in getting the product to a distant market.
4. The risk may be too high for an equity investment, or it may be too high relative to the resources at your disposal. You would not want to have had most of your eggs in the Iranian basket

Licensing

when the Ayatollah came to power. If you had a licensing agreement, you probably would have lost it and perhaps some infringement of your property rights, but it would be nothing compared to losing a wholly owned manufacturing plant in that country.

LICENSING: IS IT THE BEST FOR YOU?

	YES	NO
1. Is it the only feasible entry method?		
2. Is it difficult or impossible to export?		
3. Are your exports too expensive?		
4. Is the location too risky for a direct investment?		
5. Do you need an immediate cash flow?		
6. Do you want to make a low initial investment?		
7. Do you want to protect your technology?		
8. Does your product need extensive modification?		
9. Do your resources limit your choice to licensing?		
10. Is a good licensee available?		

Other factors related to your own company may determine that licensing is the best way for you to go even if other forms of entry are suitable as far as the market itself is concerned. Some of these factors may be

1. You need an immediate cash flow and a foreign manufacturer can begin production much faster than you could if you made a direct investment.
2. You don't have the resources now to manufacture for the market or invest in it, but you want to recover some of your R & D costs or to generate a stream of incremental income.
3. You want to protect your technology or patent from being copied in certain countries, so you officially license somebody to

use it. Although your patent or trademark is registered, it may have protection for only one year in foreign countries, and after that somebody else may be able to exploit the asset. So, the only recourse you might have is to license somebody to produce in order to protect your rights. You can buy a Cartier watch in a Cartier store in Mexico. It will have the same appearance, a similar dial and bracelet, but Cartier of Paris and New York have got nothing to do with it. And there is nothing much that Cartier, New York, can do about it in the Mexican courts.

4. You may have a good product and attractive markets, but the modifications required in the product are too many or too expensive for you to incorporate. But, it may not be so for a licensee who has a line of similar products.

5. Finally, although the market is attractive and the risk is manageable, you cannot afford to go in directly because of lack of capital, management skills, or experience. If there is a large difference in the operating environment between what you are used to and what exists and even if you have the capital, you might decide you don't have the experience and you could use the licensing arrangement as a stepping stone to a larger involvement at a later date.

WHAT'S IN IT FOR THE LICENSEE?

Like an agent or distributor agreement, the licensor/licensee contract has to be rewarding to both sides. The licensor chooses this method of entry because it suits him or her. But the licensor has to make sure that the licensee needs him for the long term. Some of the reasons the licensee is willing to pay for the technology are:

1. He or she is an entrepreneur who sees the potential for the product or product line in the market and is eager to cash in on it.

2. He or she has been your agent or distributor and wants to graduate into manufacturing, a goal that in certain circumstances could coincide with yours.

3. He or she is already producing other items, has excess capacity, and wishes to use it.

Licensing

4. He or she needs to update and keep up to date in technology in order to compete. In areas of production where technology is changing rapidly, it is extremely costly to get the most advanced know-how, and if there is free trade, outdated technology is a recipe for going out of business, as even the steel industry in the United States has found out.
5. Licensing may be the least costly way to get into production for the licensee just as it may be the least costly entry method for the licensor.

Although all of these are valid reasons for a foreign firm to want your technology, you still need to look beyond them to other qualifications that are also required. Look out for the following:

1. Can the firm get a production license? This may be difficult, even if the firm is already in production. Special permission may be required. It could be a great waste of time to begin negotiations, come to an agreement and then find your partner is not authorized to produce the product.
2. Does the licensee have the production facilities or access to facilities to produce the goods?
3. If your partner is a manufacturer, has he or she the skills or resources to market the product? If the manufacturer is already producing other goods, he or she probably has a distributor network. On the other hand, if your distributor or somebody with no manufacturing experience is going into manufacturing, does he or she have the required skills? You don't want a manufacturer who cannot sell your goods or a distributor who cannot manufacture them. So, technical competence as well as marketing and management skills are important.

Searching for and checking out potential licensees involves the same kinds of procedures and the same contacts as those used for finding an agent or distributor. Foreign branch managers of banks, other manufacturers, and of course, both the domestic and foreign representatives of the Department of Commerce are good sources of information. But, because of the importance of the choice to the success of this method of market entry it is essential to judge for yourself that he or she qualifies, that the chemistry is right, and that he or she has the facilities and financial resources necessary to make the venture a success.

SOME PITFALLS TO AVOID

Usually there is little or no capital investment made by the licensor. So the possibility of losing equity or being expropriated does not arise. But that does not mean an absence of all risk. It is just that the risks are of a different kind. Perhaps the greatest danger is the loss of your valuable asset, namely, a patent or brand or trademark. Of course, you will try to avoid this in the written contract, but in many countries that does not give full protection, especially if the licensee has the full knowledge and ability to produce the product. This is why licensors with an easily duplicated technology hold back specific components of the product that only they can supply. But even then, the product can be imitated and a brand name or trademark used, as for instance, when bottles of black liquid are sold as "Koca Kola." Products ranging from Hennessy brandy to Cardin jeans to helicopter parts have been manufactured under false trademarks.

Another danger is the loss of control of marketing, quality, and product image. Again, these factors can all be covered in the agreement, but it may be difficult to do anything about them in practice if you find yourself with the wrong licensee. As we will see later, they can be alleviated by technical assistance, management support, and quality control programs you provide. As in most such arrangements, a lot will depend on the working relationship of the parties involved. If things go badly, your brand name may be splashed on inferior products, and you may be getting little revenues because sales are low and there is poor market performance by the licensee.

PITFALLS TO AVOID

	YES	NO
1. Is there a danger of losing your secret, technology, or patent?		
2. Will your product image and/or quality be diminished?		
3. Could your licensee become your competitor?		
4. Are your payments secure?		

Beware of creating a competitor. What happens if your licensee in Brazil begins to export to Venezuela where you have a lucrative direct export market? Or if, after the license runs out, he or she continues to manufacture and faces you head on in foreign markets or worse still in your own domestic market? In the license agreement you can try to prevent all of this by restricting the licensee's sales to a specific territory and by requiring the manufacturer to stop producing after the contract ends. But it is easier said than done. Unlike a direct investor who can stop capital flow or cause a reduction in employment, you have very little leverage especially when the agreement runs out. In many countries an appeal to the courts will drag on and on and is unlikely to gain you anything in the long run except legal fees. Depending on the nature of the manufacturing process, you may be able to maintain a satisfactory level of control by supplying components or ingredients not easily obtained elsewhere. If you don't have such leverage, an alternate means of control is to be able to come up with improvements in the technology or know-how that you are licensing so that the licensee needs you.

Another risk is associated with payment. If you are supplying components or technical or management assistance of any kind, the problems and methods of payment are the same as we discussed when dealing with payments for exports. A letter of credit is the usual means of payment. The biggest problem arises with royalties on sales, the usual means of compensation of the licensor. Two problems can arise here. First, revenues may be low if the marketing effort is poor; second, you may have difficulty getting the royalties converted and out of the country. One of the disadvantages of licensing is that royalties are not large in the first place, usually 3 to 7 percent of sales, but if sales are low or foreign exchange is restricted, you may have given up a valuable asset and gotten very little in return. These problems can be overcome by, for example, requiring a minimum royalty payment independent of sales volume or by accepting payment in the form of part ownership of the licensee's business, in which case you are moving into a joint venture.

PUTTING SOME ICING ON THE CAKE

Although royalties from sales may be low compared with profits from exports or returns from direct foreign investment, there is the potential for increased income flows from the licensee for other services. A lot will depend on the nature of the business. Some large companies enter a licensing agreement not for the royalties on sales but for the revenues earned from supplying essential inputs into the manufacturing process. For the smaller or medium-sized firm and for firms selling technology or pure know-how, opportunities for incremental income can come from a variety of services supplied with the technology package. For example, the licensee may need you to design and assist in the construction of the manufacturing plant. He or she may need you in starting it up, operating it, and training local counterpart personnel. You may be able to procure or sell your own equipment to be used in producing the goods. The licensee may also require management and marketing assistance to effectively penetrate the market. Obviously, the licensee will be willing to pay for some or all of these services if it is profitable for him or her. In cases where your major source of income comes from supplying components of the product, you may have to supply some of these services free of charge. This is especially true of services related to quality control where product image is of importance to this and other markets. The licensee is likely to regard that as your concern and not something for which he or she should have to pay.

In providing these ancillary services to the licensee, the licensor may include them under the general licensing contract, but in general, it is much better to have them separate. These services are very expensive,

---

HOW YOU CAN ADD OTHER SOURCES OF INCOME TO ROYALTY PAYMENTS

	YES	NO
1. Can you be the sole source for an essential input in the manufacturing process?		
2. Are your services needed in the design and construction of the plant?		
3. Does the licensee need your equipment?		
4. Does the licensee need technical assistance to operate the plant?		
5. Can you provide management and marketing skills?		

costing the client at least $100,000 per year for a middle-level U.S. specialist when all costs such as family transportation, housing, fringe benefits, home leave, and fees are included. As soon as the licensee reaches the minimum level of competence in an area, he or she is likely to want to take over the function and terminate the technical assistance or management agreement. If there are two separate agreements, the important and long-term licensing one will not be affected and will not have to be renegotiated, a process that can be long and drawn out in the first place. Anyway, any technical assistance contract is likely to be of shorter duration than a desirable licensing agreement. But this does not mean that it is not worthwhile. On the contrary, fees and services associated with the start-up of the project and its continuing functioning could make this method of entry much more attractive than if the royalties on sales alone were considered.

Franchising

In many ways franchising is equivalent to licensing with some of the technical assistance, quality control, or supply factors included. In this case it is not just a license to use a technology, a trademark, or a trade name; there are also requirements on how the technology or trademark is used. The most common franchises in the United States are in fast-food restaurants, hotels and motels, car rentals, and services like Century 21 in real estate. Internationally, the most famous are in fast-food and car rental. Operations and procedures are supposed to be standardized so that if you buy a piece of the Colonel's chicken in Tokyo, the Yemen Arab Republic, or Tulsa it is supposed to have the same unique taste because of the international standards for ingredients and preparation.

Generally, a franchising arrangement involves a much greater support system than licensing. For the franchisor, product image is a valuable asset, and this has to be maintained in each market. This may require a continual supply of inputs and machinery as well as the advertising and promotional materials around which the international image or trade name is built. To reach the desired standards of service, technical assistance is usually supplied in areas like quality control, operating procedures, and, of course, marketing. Franchising also goes beyond licensing by often providing financial support, and it often moves from being a franchising operation to a joint venture with the local partner. As with exporting and licensing, franchising can be a first step into a market because it involves limited risk, but as we said earlier, there is usually a high correlation between the degree of risk and the level of control and profits. The move into joint ownership with the local partner may occur if financial support is converted into equity and if the franchisor sees the joint venture as a much more profitable way to go.

Finding a suitable franchising partner may be more difficult than to find one in licensing because what is being transferred is a whole system of doing business, rather than a license to produce or manufacture a product, something that the local partner is likely to have competence in in the first place. That is why most well-known franchise operations are in areas like fast food, car rentals, and hotel and motel management. They don't require much capital, and the skills are fairly easily transferable because many of them are mechanical duplications of a single process. If you move into the more technical service areas like real estate, accounting, or advertising, it is much more difficult to enter by franchising because much more sophisticated skills are required and regulations and accepted procedures differ so much from country to country. Nevertheless, franchising is not monolithic throughout the world. The marketing expertise of the major franchisors is far too sophisticated to allow a procedure that works in one country to interfere with sales in another. Changes are made in local markets to comply with that country's regulations, for example in the use of certain ingredients.

The risks associated with franchising are essentially the same as those found in licensing, the biggest being loss of control and the creation of a competitor. This may be one of the main reasons for the move nationally and internationally toward equity participation in the franchise. This gives greater control and makes your potential competitor your new partner. The entry method, therefore, has to be continually evaluated. Licensing or franchising may be most suitable for you as a first step in the market, but you may see later that to remain in it in a worthwhile way or to get bigger returns, you need to move into partial or sole ownership. Usually, the most attractive franchising areas are in consumer-type products where the capital outlay is not large. If you have that type of product or service, franchising with a view to a joint venture may be the way to go. If, however, your product requires an expensive plant or machinery with specialized technical competence, it makes more sense to license or go immediately into a joint venture or a wholly owned operation.

THE LICENSING AGREEMENT—THE MOST IMPORTANT COMPONENTS

In negotiating a licensing agreement, there are five particularly important guidelines for the licensee.

1. Clearly define what is being licensed. The technology package may have only one element, namely, a secret process or know-how. Or it may be quite complex involving not only know-how, but specialized equipment, secret ingredients, and a trademark. The total package may also include assistance in quality control, management, and marketing. A careful, detailed description of exactly what is covered by the agreement will close loopholes and prevent misunderstandings in the future. The more complex the package, the greater the control the licensor has. If all you are licensing is a trademark or know-how that can be easily adapted, the licensee may develop the capability of getting on quite well without you or even of becoming a major competitor.
2. Specify exactly what territories are covered by the agreement. Obviously, the licensor does not want the licensee competing with him or her in another country where the licensor is supplying the market directly or through another channel. So you need to limit the licensee's freedom to sell wherever he or she wants to sell. A problem you may face here, especially at a time of balance-of-payments difficulties, is that the host-country government may stop you or your licensee from signing an agreement that limits exports. And because licensing does not usually involve a transfer of capital by the licensor, but rather a drain of royalties out of the country, the local government tends to strictly regulate licensing agreements. As discussed earlier in the chapter on political risk, it is difficult for a company to operate in a country if that operation is having a negative impact on the balance of payments. So, if you are trying to limit the licensee to the local market and to restrict exports, you need to be able to show clearly the foreign exchange saved by local production, for example, by cutting down imports or by improving production downstream that increases exports.
3. Ensure high quality production. Your brand name or your reputation for quality or for the safety of the product may be a large

part of your asset. To safeguard it you may have to be sure of high-quality production. This is particularly important in an exclusive agreement, where the licensee alone can use the technology within the market because now you have no other recourse, and a poor or second-rate product could lead to loss of trademark rights. Depending on the product, you may visit the plant for inspection prior to signing an agreement, you may insist on the presence of your own technical experts, or you may specify the use of certain types of machinery or raw materials. In products where there is a safety factor involved like health products, electric tools, or foodstuff you will have to insist on high-quality standards and regular inspections to ensure they are maintained.

4. Make sure your valuable licensed asset remains secret or under your control. Obviously, if it were in the public domain it would be of little value, so in a licensing agreement you will need to protect the confidentiality of what you are transferring, not only for the duration of the agreement, but for a number of years afterwards. In practice, the confidentiality clause will be limited to information or knowledge that could not be discovered by any other means. Obviously, information the licensee already knows or that a third party reveals cannot be bound to secrecy.

5. Insist on a minimum performance clause in the contract. Essentially, this is to protect you from a nonperforming partner who has your asset tied up in an agreement but doesn't use it. If you are depending on royalties on sales, you will have no income. This point is elaborated under payment in a later section of this chapter.

OUTLINE OF THE LICENSING AGREEMENT

The following outline is presented to prepare the licensor for all the areas that need to be covered before signing an agreement. It is the equivalent of a checklist, each component of which will require a decision. Of course, the agreement itself will require legal help, a knowledge of local laws, and considerable attention to detail, but the major decisions are business decisions that you yourself will have to make.

The Outline

A. Formal Provisions: The first clause identifies the parties, their locations, what the licensor has to offer under license, and the date of the agreement.
B. Definition of Terms: This is an extremely important section because the clarity and preciseness established here will govern all that follows, and perhaps of more importance, it will prevent misunderstandings in the future. Definitions cover such areas as the licensed patent, what technology is involved, on what basis royalties are paid, and what law governs the agreement.
C. License Grant: This covers who is the licensor, who is the licencee, what is being licensed, whether if exclusive or not, sublicensing, and other conditions of use.
D. Royalties and Other Payments: This covers questions such as method of payment, currency of payment, royalty percentage, sales base, premarketing payments, minimum payments, and payment for any of the technical assistance, management, marketing, or other assistance provided.
E. Grant Backs: This refers to the right of access to new developments of the technology discovered by the licensee.
F. Patent Enforcement and Maintenance: This refers to the need to protect the secrecy of what you are transferring not only for the duration of the agreement but for a number of years afterwards.
G. Assignability: This clause clarifies the extent or limits of assignability to successors of the party involved or to a third party.
H. Effective Date Duration and Termination: This clause describes the length of the contract, terms of renewal, and conditions of termination by either the licensor or licensee.
I. The Reports Clause: This clause outlines the accounting required by the licensor to ensure accurate payment by the licensee and the right of the licensor to audit the reports.
J. Governing Law and Arbitration: This may be quite a complicated area because the laws of two different nations may conflict in areas such as antitrust. Arbitration outlines the specific disputes that are to be arbitrated, who the arbitrators will be, and how decisions will be reached.

K. Confidentiality: This covers the need by the licensor to protect his or her know-how or trade secret.
L. *Force Majeure* Clause: This lists the uncontrollable circumstances under which the licensor or licensee will be exempted from responsibility for nonconformance. These include such extraordinary events as earthquakes, revolutions, or accidents and might even include items like strikes, equipment breakdowns, or interference by the government.
M. Notices: These specify where notices are to be sent, how they are to be sent and on what date they become effective.

PAYMENT

In straightforward licensing agreements royalty revenues as a percentage of sales is the usual method of payment. Depending on the value of the licensed technology, trademark, or patent the percentage on sales usually runs in the range of 3 percent to 7 percent. The second clause of the agreement is very important because it clearly defines the base on which the percentage will be established. Are discounts allowed, or commissions to agents or distributors? Who pays taxes or expenses associated with faulty products or warranties? Usually all of these are deducted from gross sales and royalties are paid on net receipts from sales.

A very important factor is the question of minimum payments. This is to motivate the licensee to promote and market the product so that a minimum sales target is reached. The minimum royalty payment clause in the agreement would read something like this: "If total royalties payable under this agreement are less than $100,000 for a full calendar year after the commencement of this contract, the licensee will in addition to the royalties payable on net sales make an additional payment of an amount equal to the difference between $100,000 and the amount of royalty payable for the year in question." If the agreement is exclusive some such clause is a necessity if it is allowed by the law of the country. Otherwise, you may have your valuable asset tied up with a licensee who has little interest in fully exploiting it, and it may be an asset that could be earning a significant return if used by another licensee or if you entered the market through another method.

In developing countries it is important to specify the currency of payment and alternative payment methods in the event there are currency controls or the government limits future payments. Such an alternative might be an equity share in the licensee firm, a step that would move you in the direction of a joint venture.

CONTRACTING WITHOUT A LICENSE

Apart from licensing there are several other contracting arrangements that may be of interest to you in expanding overseas.

Management, Engineering, and Other Technical Assistance Contracts

Each year hundreds of millions of dollars are transferred from the industrialized world to the less developed countries in the form of loans from multinational banks and bilateral loans and grants from one government to another. The major multilateral banks are The World Bank, the Asian Development Bank, the Inter-American Development Bank, and the African Development Bank.

When the recipient country is unable to supply the goods or services itself, it is bound to advertise and award contracts under international competitive bidding. As can be seen from Exhibit 8.1, which is a page taken from the World Bank Operational Summary for Brazil, there are many projects in many different sectors of the economy. Such projects usually include a technical assistance component requiring foreign specialists in areas as diverse as construction design, telecommunications, or agronomy. In an earlier section we suggested that each company should take a second look at the range of goods or services it may have to offer because it might be in a competitive position to nail down one of these contracts. A few years ago a Cleveland construction firm was able to get such a contract under international bidding by forming a joint venture with a Chinese company that provided cheap labor and other factors while the Cleveland firm supplied the more expensive technical services such as engineering and management.

In country to country aid it is usually required that the goods or services be supplied from the donor country. The United States gives the largest amount of money each year, and the contractual components have to be supplied by U.S. firms. Opportunities under USAID are advertised in *The Commerce Business Daily*. However, one of the problems a firm faces here is the chicken-and-egg situation because often a requirement of the award of the contract is previous foreign experience. However, if you offer a specialized service or have a good in-house capability in a certain area, this may not be an excluding factor because in service contracts also you can enter joint ventures with an American or local firm.

A very big attraction of this type of business is that it is pretty safe from the payment point of view, as it is ultimately the financing source that is paying and then in hard currency.

EXHIBIT 8.1

BRAZIL

Min R	(COMPANHIA VALE DO RIO DOCE—CVRO). Up to 300.0 (Bank). Cararas Iron Ore Mining—Mine, rail and port facilities for export of up to 35 million tons per year of high grade iron ore. Appraisal mission in the field (Private co-financing expected to be needed).
Rwy R	(REDE FERROVIARIA FEDERAL, SA—RFFSA). Up to 200.0 (Bank). RFFSA III (Railways)—Expansion and rehabilitation program. Project preparation underway.
Fin R	(CENTRAIS ELECTRICAS BRASILEIRAS SA) (ELETROBRAS). 180.0 (Bank). Power Distribution—Credit line for power distribution sub-projects—sector loan. Project being prepared.
Rds R	Territory of Rondonia and Federative Republic of Brazil. Up to 240.0 (Bank). Northwest Region Development Program—Highway construction component. Total project cost estimated at $687 million of which $240 million in foreign exchange. Board presentation scheduled for December 1.
Rur R	Instituto Nacional de Colonizacao e Reforma Agraria (INCRA). 80.0 (Bank). Northwest Region Development Program III—New land settlement. Preappraisal mission scheduled for January.
Rur R	Federative Republic of Brazil. Up to 26.0 (Bank). Northwest Region Development Program II—Rural development in state of Mato Grosso. Total project cost estimated at $76.4 million of which $12.2 million in foreign exchange. Negotiations scheduled for December.
Rur R	50.0 (Bank). Maranhao Rural Development—Development project in two adjacent areas (Baixada Maranhense and part of Alto Turi region) to improve agriculture and social infrastructure, land tenure situation and access to land by landless farmers. Total project cost estimated at $145 million of which $29 million in foreign exchange. Post-appraisal mission scheduled for January.
Hea R	State of Sao Paulo. Up to 50.0 (Bank). Health—Development of health services in State of Sao Paulo. Appraisal mission scheduled for January.
Rds R	150.0 (Bank). Secondary and Feeder Roads III—Construction and improvement. Appraisal mission scheduled for December.
Urb R	110.0 (Bank). Integrated Urban Development in Recife Metropolitan Region. Appraisal mission in the field.
Agr R	30.0 (Bank). Amazonas Agricultural Development—Project aimed at improving production of foodcrops in selected areas of flood lands and introducing rational cultivation of highlands. About 5,000 ha of smallholder oil palm may be developed. The project would assist from 8,000 to 10,000 small farmers. Appraisal mission in the field.
Rur R	Territory of Rondonia and Federative Republic of Brazil. 67.0 (Bank). Northwest Region Development Program—Agriculture development and environmental protection. Consolidation and rural development in Territory of Rondonia, establishment of measures to protect forest reserves and ecological stations; ecological research. Total project cost estimated at $200 million of which $42 million in foreign exchange. Board presentation scheduled for December 1.
Hea R	Territory of Rondonia and Federative Republic of Brazil 13.0 (Bank). Northwest Region Development Program I—Health component. Total project cost estimated at $37.7 million of which $6 million in foreign exchange. Board presentation scheduled for December 1.
Wat R	(BANCO NACIONAL DE HABITACAO) (BNH) 200.0 (Bank). Water supply and sewerage in the low-income area of State of Sao Paulo. Appraisal mission postponed pending notification by Government of availability of counterpart funds.
Rur R	Secretaria de Planejamento da Presidencia de Republica 50.0 (Bank). Bahia Rural Development II—Integrated rural development in northeast Bahia to assist small farmers through provision of improved support services, land redistribution and infrastructure development. Preparation mission scheduled for January.
For R	Up to 70.0 (Bank). Forestry Development, including reforestation for production of charcoal in Minas Gerais. Preparation mission scheduled for December.
Edu R	Ministry of Education and Culture. Up to 50.0 (Bank). Education V—Strengthening of Brazil's secondary agricultural school system through provision of training, equipment, furniture, curriculum development and other technical assistance. Identification mission in the field.
Fin N	(BANCO NACIONAL DO DESENVOLVIMENTO ECONOMICO (BNDE)). 250.0 (Bank). Development Banking II—Implementation of integrated assistance programs for small and medium enterprises. Preparation mission scheduled for December.

Turnkey Contracts

These became quite popular in the Middle East over the past 10 years as governments and private investors rushed to bring factories, processing plants, hospitals and schools into operation. The "turnkey" element means that the contractor brings the project to the stage where it is immediately ready to operate. Usually the contract involves large sums of money, a high degree of complexity and considerable risk. Probably the biggest risk of all is the requirement for a performance bond by the contracting agency of the government. Middle Eastern and Eastern European governments require standby letters of credit guaranteed by a bank and callable at the discretion of the government. Believe it or not, what this means is that the contracting government can call a guarantee at any time even if there is no breach of contract and the contractor stands to lose a significant amount of funds. In practice, this does not happen too often although it is a considerable risk in countries where individuals can make such decisions on the basis of politics, favoritism or other emotional reactions. But, usually, the large contractor has a local agent or operator to assist him or her in avoiding such unpleasantness. In the countries where there are more established procedures, a guarantee will be called only for a default in performance, and then there are all kinds of arbitration procedures.

But, of course, this will drag on and on, and if your bond is not already called, at the very least you will be left without payment for work completed or in dispute. There are other means of protection like, for instance, sharing the risk in a joint-venture partnership or by taking out insurance, which is costly, because what you are doing is insuring yourself against the insurance you gave the government. Turnkey projects can be summed up as follows: highly attractive profits with correspondingly large risks.

Contract Manufacturing

Under this arrangement you pay the producer to manufacture the product for you to sell here, there, or elsewhere. It is close to licensing in the sense that know-how, equipment, and technical assistance are often provided, but there are no royalties, and you are responsible for marketing. Usually the technology or manufacturing procedures are mature and well known so there are no secrets involved. It was a growing form of foreign entry into many of the Eastern European countries until the development of payment problems and the cooling of East–West relations in the early eighties. But it is likely to revive because it has several attractions. It benefits the host country by providing employment, technology, and at least some foreign exchange. It benefits you because you get the product and access to the market without the hassle of local ownership, you may be able to supply several markets from a cheap production source, and you retain control over your real source of income: sales. The reason it was attractive in Eastern Europe included all of these reasons plus the fact that direct foreign investment was impossible in most countries, and opportunities for imports were limited.

OTHER OPPORTUNITIES IN A FOREIGN MARKET

1. Management or Technical Assistance Contracts
2. Turnkey Projects
3. Contract Manufacturing
4. Countertrade

Countertrade

The more things change, the more other things stay the same. Barter is back, and increasing, in the form of countertrade. Before it was simple barter involving the farmer exchanging eggs for a pound of tea. Now it involves multinational companies, governments, and a $100 billion worth of business per year. And it is likely to increase as more and more countries feel the squeeze for foreign exchange and try to barter their local production or raw materials for essential imports. It's a question of developing new methods of financing trade or giving up the market altogether. General Electric won the bid for a $150-million electric-generator project in Romania by agreeing to sell $150 million worth of that country's products. Several oil-producing countries have exchanged oil for other commodities. A country that does not have foreign exchange but has a large tender business could decide to award contracts only to countertraders, and they can make it attractive, for example by selling oil at a discount price or by compensating by allowing the bidder to ask and get a higher price. For larger companies that can use some of these countertrade goods, like steel, in-house or have marketing outlets in many countries, countertrade is a possibility and in some cases a necessity. Large companies like banks are thinking of setting up trading companies to handle the business. Sears has already set up its world trading unit to handle countertrade, among other things, for a commission.

Right now there are severe restrictions on imports in most Latin American, African, and some Asian countries because of the world-debt crisis and the drain on their limited amount of foreign exchange earnings to pay off interest and principal on the debt. Even the formerly lucrative OPEC markets are drying up. Countertrade may be the only way into such markets, and for companies that have bad debts or large uncollectable accounts receivable, countertrade may be the only way out. It is a complicated business if you handle it yourself, but the markets are large, involving the large tender business of Eastern Europe and the large markets that have limited foreign exchange. As in export you can use an intermediary like a trading company rather than doing it yourself. This cuts your costs and cuts your profit margins but at least it will not be you that ends up with an unmarketable tanker of Algerian wine.

CONCLUSION

International licensing is becoming increasingly important in large companies' strategies. Royalty receipts have risen from $1 billion in 1970 to $5 billion in 1980 and they cover almost every sector of production, from making rare drugs to shirts to building materials. For the smaller firm there is the attraction of incremental income with low risk and very little investment in extra facilities or management. It is not for every company and there are disadvantages, but for a firm that wants to enter a foreign market and cannot compete in exports or overcome tariffs or does not have the resources for direct investment this may be the only and best method of entry.

9

HOW THE JAPANESE DO IT: JOINT VENTURES

Setting up a good joint venture is like having a model child. It brings credit to its parents, contributes to their well-being and is effectively under their direction and control. A bad joint venture is like a delinquent teenager; its problems often arise from the fact that there are two parents, giving different commands, leading to a loss of control and maybe even a divorce! Indeed, it may not be a bad definition of a joint venture to describe it as the offspring of a marriage of convenience of two independent parents that might have preferred to serve the market in some more desirable way that was not possible. In more technical language, a joint venture can be described as the participation of two companies in the ownership, management, and control of a third enterprise designed to benefit both. In general, most companies prefer to fully control the investment if they are going into a country through any kind of direct investment, and indeed this is the path that most American and European companies have chosen. The Japanese have taken a different road using the joint venture much more extensively, keeping a low profile, and yet, in effect, controlling the enterprise. In the Philippines, for example, the Japanese have surpassed the United States in the amount of capital invested, yet anti-Japanese demonstrations there are almost unknown while anti-U.S.-capital demonstrations have occurred frequently. This may have something to do with the U.S. military presence in the Philippines, but on the other hand, it has been only 40 years since the Americans liberated the islands from a brutal Japanese occupation. The secret for the Japanese lies elsewhere. Their presence is less visible, and a lot of it has a local front. This is true not only of the Philippines but of other parts of the rapidly expanding markets of the Pacific Rim. But low visibility does not mean low levels of control. The Japanese have successfully entered the markets and maintained control by a series of stratagems that we will take a closer look at later on.

JOINT VENTURES: DIFFERENT COUNTRIES, DIFFERENT PARTNERS

Usually the choice facing a company entering a foreign market is to form a joint venture with a local firm. This may be done out of preference or necessity. It is done out of preference if the foreign company believes that, all things being considered, this is the best way of entering and being successful in this market. It is done out of necessity if it is the only way. For example, some countries will not allow a 100 percent ownership of a subsidiary. India is such a case, and many other countries limit foreign ownership in certain fields. The choice then is to forego the market altogether or to enter a joint venture. Other countries, as for instance Indonesia, announced policies whereby 51 percent of the capital had to be in Indonesian hands within a certain period of time. But, if partnership with a local company is the most common form of joint venture, it is important to realize some other alternatives that you may prefer or that may serve your purpose.

JOINT VENTURES: YOUR CHOICES

A. A joint venture can be formed with another U.S. company operating in a third country. This may be the best entry method for smaller companies with limited capital or skills, complementary assets, and the need to lower risk. When the risk and capital requirements are very large, as, for instance, in the development of minerals on the seabed, even very large companies like Lockheed or Kennecott may go this road. An extension of this type of arrangement is when two U.S. companies join with a local foreign company to form a local three-way venture.

B. A joint venture can be established between a U.S. company and another company from an industrialized country to operate in a less developed country. For example, this could involve a U.S. company and a French company in a former French colony. Again, for two small companies with complementary assets or technologies that could not go it alone, this could be the only way to get into a market.

C. There are joint ventures with state enterprises. This is when a private firm joins with a state-owned or semi-state body to form an independent enterprise. This has occurred in several of the more capitalistic-type countries like Brazil and Indonesia, and it is the only way of establishing production facilities in large markets like China or in the economies of Eastern Europe. American Motors recently formed a joint venture in China to produce their Jeep. Occidental Petroleum has done the same thing in coal production, and, of course, a lot of the oil exploration and development projects are of the same kind. But such ventures need not be confined to large projects as long as smaller companies have the longer-term vision and the resources to pursue such a venture. Indeed, in many cases smaller companies may be preferred because they are considered less of a threat and are likely to exercise less control.

D. A new and increasingly important form of entry in foreign markets is a joint venture between a U.S. firm and a Third World multinational to enter another developing country. U.S. firms have been increasingly noncompetitive overseas in industries like construction, service contracts, and basic manufacturing. The Koreans came to dominate many areas of construction in the Middle East; Indian companies have management contracts for hotels, and in certain countries in Latin America, Brazilian multinationals are exploring for and developing natural resources. They have the advantage of lower labor and management costs; lower input costs into the manufacturing process; a more appropriate technology; and greater familiarity with the social, political, and business climate. But they are often very short of capital. They lack new technologies to enable them to remain competitive, and they lack specialized skills. These are the complementary assets you could provide, especially management and marketing skills and home-office support that are often scarce resources for Third World multinationals, as they seek to expand.

So, in looking at a joint venture, it is important to look at all the options because one of the less common ways may be your best method of entry. Everyone hears of Toyota and General Motors joining up in California to produce cars for the American market or of Matsushita joining with General Electric to produce and market its video disk. But in certain niches of certain markets, your best choice may be one of the others, such as, for instance, a joint venture with a Filipino accounting firm to be competitive enough to get a World Bank contract in Indonesia.

ALTERNATIVE FORMS OF JOINT VENTURE

1. A U.S. company and a local firm
2. Two U.S. companies in a foreign country
3. Two U.S. firms and a local firm
4. A U.S. firm and a foreign firm in a third country
5. A joint venture with a state-owned company
6. A joint venture with a Third World multinational in another country

---

THE PROS AND CONS OF JOINT VENTURES

Although a joint-venture-entry method is often a matter of necessity rather than preference, it has a lot of distinctive advantages. For a small- or medium-sized company entering the market for the first time these advantages may dominate the decision and make this method of entry the best, at least for some markets. Even large companies have chosen joint ventures over direct foreign investment in countries like Japan, where they could have gone in alone but have opted to take advantage of a partner's knowledge of the local environment, production facilities that are already in operation, research already completed, or skills necessary for operating in a strange environment. But, this brings us to what the pros and cons are. Obviously, not all will apply to all companies entering all joint ventures, but it is a list to check off as you weigh the choice, particularly between a joint venture and a direct investment.

The Pros

A. Probably the single greatest advantage is that in most cases it requires far less capital and other assets, such as management skills, concentrated in one country. This may be particularly important for the smaller firm with fewer resources or for the firm that might prefer to diversify or spread the risk and commitment over several markets. Even for larger companies, the budgeting of resources may be important as projects get larger and as technologies get too expensive for one firm to develop.

B. Joint venture partners provide resources or skills that cannot be purchased even if you had the money to do so. These resources could be patented or specialized technologies but in most cases are much more mundane. I am referring to a knowledge of the local business and political environment and how to operate in it. It could also include knowledge of culture and language and personal access to officials of the government as well as important contacts in the financial, banking, or marketing communities.

C. A joint venture limits risk by sharing it and by providing a lot of political cover if the partner is a local firm. In many Third World markets, this is an important factor. The trend is towards local participation. You will have a much better bargaining position prior to entry, and you are unlikely to be forced to divest at a later stage.

D. In certain markets a joint venture provides a means of access where import controls or ownership restrictions make other forms of entry difficult or impossible. For example, Venezuela publishes a list of industries in which foreign companies cannot own more than 20 percent. India allows only 40 percent participation in many industries, and countries like Nigeria have similar limits. With large populations and, previously, with large oil revenues, these were markets that many companies were interested in but could not expect to invest in, except through a local partner.

E. Joint ventures may give access to marketing channels, distribution facilities or a dealer network that it might otherwise take years to build up. It may also qualify the venture for tax concessions or enable it to gain access to local capital markets.

In looking at these significant advantages you may wonder why any firm would take on all the risk and responsibility by going it alone into full foreign investment. The answer can be given in one word: *control*, which is the major "Con" that embraces most of the minor ones.

The Cons

A. The greatest disadvantage of a joint venture is loss of control. To have control is a basic human instinct, and it is a very strong instinct for companies planning and implementing a global strategy of production, distribution, and marketing. The goals and priorities of a local partner may diverge significantly from that of the foreign company. For smaller and mid-size companies, this conflict will be lessened because they are unlikely to be thinking in such large-scale terms anyway. Some issues of control are more important than others. Obviously and inevitably, the one that is likely to lead to the greatest conflict is money. For example, if you are supplying components, supplies, technology, or skills how much can you charge? Do you take out the profits or plow them back in to expand the joint venture? Very often the local partner will want to keep as much as possible of the profits in the country. What about exports to a market you are already serving directly?

B. Management is obviously very closely related to control. This refers to where decisions are made, who manages the enterprise, and who is ultimately responsible. In shared management, the positions filled by the respective parents are critical. It is obviously far more important to control the financial or production functions than it is to control personnel or public relations. Conflict over these issues can lead to lost opportunities, low production, low morale, and eventually to divorce of the parents, leading to the joint venture becoming a single-parent child; that is, if it survives at all.

C. Another problem with a joint venture is that even if you have a minority share or your investment is small, you may end up devoting an excessive amount of management time and effort to keeping the operation functioning while at the same time getting a smaller percentage of the return.

> THE PRO'S AND THE CON'S OF A JOINT VENTURE
>
> | Pro's | Con's |
> |---|---|
> | 1. Requires fewer resources | 1. Results in loss of control |
> | 2. Provides complementary resources | 2. Creates management conflict |
> | 3. Limits risk | 3. Demands too much time and other resources |
> | 4. Makes entry possible where other means are not feasible | |
> | 5. Gives access to marketing channels | |

Overall, the success of the joint venture for you will be determined by the return you get on your capital and the rewards you get for the amount of effort you have to put into it. So, although at first glance the pros seem to be very strong and to far outnumber the cons, the question of control in particular, will have a very large impact on the decision, precisely because it has an impact directly on transfer prices and profit distributions.

MAKING THE JOINT VENTURE DECISION: TEN QUESTIONS TO ANSWER

In Chapter 6 we outlined a way to decide on the best entry method. If you are now focusing in on a joint venture, it is because you have decided this is the best form of entry for you to this market at this time. In making the decision and, in particular, in calculating expected returns, you need detailed information on many factors. This information can be summarized in the following ten questions:

1. What are the costs to me?
2. What are the benefits to me?
3. What percentage of ownership do I require?
4. Who are my potential partners and what have they to offer?
5. Does ownership distribution reflect what my partner has to offer?
6. How do I value a partner's assets, such as knowledge of the local environment or political and financial contacts?
7. Will the contribution of each partner change over time?

Joint Ventures

8. Is this reflected in the ownership structure?
9. How much control do I need?
10. What restrictions does the local government impose?

We will now take a closer look at each one of the questions to elaborate on what you need to look for in each.

1. Your immediate costs can be broken down under financing required, technology supplied, supplies required, and very important, the management and marketing time that will be taken up by the joint venture, especially in the start-up period. But, there are other costs, for example, the loss of exports now being sent to the market or the loss of the most economic use of resources caused by a loss of control.
2. The benefits will primarily be from increased sales in the new market and possibly from increased sales in nearby regional markets with preferential trading arrangements. There will be associated benefits to the parent, for example, dividends, interest payments, and payments for any other assistance like management, marketing, or technical assistance.
3. Once you have calculated the costs and the benefits, you can determine your expected returns. But, perhaps of more importance, you can decide what percentage ownership of the joint venture you require to justify your contribution. In many countries what you can own will be limited by law, but under the upper limit there may be a wide range and your share of that should reflect your contribution to the joint venture.
4. Screening distributors, agents, and licensees to get the right one for you is serious business, but most of the time a mistake may be undone. With a joint venture the stakes are much higher and questions of control are much more important. A mistake here is going to be costly. You need to go through a systematic screening process to determine the right fit for your goals. In practice, the number of candidate firms will not be that great because you are likely to be looking for a very specific set of requirements, like, for instance, experience in producing or marketing a similar product line. And you will have at your disposal all of the information the foreign representatives of the departments of Commerce and State can provide. If you were already active in this market, you probably are familiar

with the operations of the best candidates.

In the case of government restrictions on local private ownership you don't have much choice; you join with the state agency responsible for that area of production or operation. Reynolds has recently gone into a joint venture with the Chinese for the largest cigarette factory in the world. It had no choice in its partner; it was preselected in the form of the agency responsible for this sector in China. Choosing the right partner presumes you have some kind of profile of what you want, and you know the assets you require to complement your own in the joint venture. For example, you may require existing production facilities because you want a quick start-up. You may require a certain level of financing or a marketing network in place. The more detailed your requirements are the easier it will be to narrow down your choice. Apart from your profile, the partner may have special assets. For instance, the firm may have a multilingual sales force in a country with many dialects. Or it may have developed high-level political and financial contacts that will ease the operations of the venture.

5. Distribution of ownership is a crucial element in a successful joint venture because it has a large impact on the distribution of payments and on control. The basic rule is that each partner should be getting out of the joint venture rewards proportionate to what they are putting in. One problem is that contributions may vary over time, and the distribution of ownership remains rigid. For example, some of the contributions of the local partner, such as knowledge of the market or of the work force, are important at the beginning but become less significant as the joint venture itself gains experience. The danger is that the contributions of the partners go out of balance without a change in benefits, and the result is dissatisfaction or even joint-venture divorce.

6-8. Putting a value on some of the assets of the local partner is a difficult job. How, for instance, do you quantify something like a knowledge of the local market? Although such a valuation will be a rather crude measurement, it should be done. More important, all contributions of both partners should be quantified over time so that benefits accruing to each partner can also be adjusted over time. It is not just the local partner's contribution that may decrease in importance. You may have very important contributions to make up front, for example, technology, money, or machinery, but they may cease as the

Joint Ventures

joint venture develops its own skills or ability to finance itself out of its own profits. If significant changes in the contribution of each partner are likely to occur after the start-up of the joint venture, then the benefits should be adjusted accordingly. If it is not possible to adjust them by the distribution of ownership, it may be possible to rectify an imbalance by payments for management time or technical assistance or increased dividends.

9. How much control you need, what level of control you require, and in what areas is a question that is obviously related to the earlier questions on what contributions each partner makes and how ownership is distributed as well as how independent your product makes you. In a later section we will be examining closely the means a foreign partner can use to exercise control with or without majority ownership. Here the focus is on the critical areas you need to control and how you intend to structure the joint venture to ensure that control. Important areas of control can be outlined as follows:

   A. Which partner is responsible for which management positions? Obviously, this is a controversial area due to the sensitivity and power of certain positions, for example, the financial manager.

   B. Who selects and appoints the management?

   C. How are the earnings and profits of the joint venture going to be used? The local partner may want to expand and diversify the joint venture. You may want profits to be distributed to the parents.

   D. How are prices determined for machinery, supplies, or other inputs supplied by a partner?

   E. Who makes key decisions on new products, expansion, financial structure, hiring, and the amount of advertising?

   The amount of control you need will obviously have an impact on the earlier question: "What kind of partner do I want?" If you are interested in high levels of control in most areas here outlined, you may decide to disperse ownership through several partners, or you may choose dummy-type firms, with little bargaining power, or silent partners. On the other hand, if you want a real operating joint venture and you want to make good use of local skills, you will choose a partner that may lessen your control but who will be involved actively in strategic business decisions and will make a significant contribution to a successful venture. You may even decide to

pick a public-sector partner, and again there are several kinds. Many countries like Brazil have enterprising profit-conscious public or semi-public companies that would be active joint venture partners. Many in other countries are more politicized and stagnant, with overweighted managements, too many employees, and high overheads.
10. The local government may restrict your options in a joint venture. The most significant limits may be on ownership and requirements to place indigenous managers in key positions. The ownership limits may be general, limiting the degree of ownership any company may have in any industry. Or they may be specific to certain industries, like telecommunications.

Many countries want local managers in key positions if not at start-up, then within a definite period. There are several valid local reasons for this but, for you, it could have a big impact on control. Apart from explicit legal requirements, you also need to analyze what the direction of policy is likely to be and how it will affect your operations. Usually after the initial transfer of capital, technology, and skills, the ongoing contribution the foreign firm is making, relative to its return, will appear to be getting less and less. In these circumstances the pressure may be put on to increase the investment of profits in the country or to reduce the outflow of earnings in other more direct ways. One way that the uncertainty in this situation can be reduced is by an entry agreement where both the firm and the government agree to specific arrangements over a definite period. Such an agreement will not always be possible. But you don't want to take the risk of losing your investment or of being forced to divest it. In the analysis of political risk you have made the best judgment possible on the likely direction of policy. If it is toward further restriction of ownership, you will want to stick with exporting or licensing. Of course, it may also go in the opposite direction, in which case you might now be entering as a joint venture partner with the intention of becoming a 100 percent owner at a later date.

EXERCISING CONTROL AS A MINORITY PARTNER

As mentioned earlier, one of the most important questions in a joint venture is the question of control. Many international companies used to rule out joint ventures because of the loss of management control. Of course, this need not be a major problem if you have a majority share, but it may be a problem where this is ruled out by the government or where you choose not to take a majority share. But minority ownership does not necessarily mean minority control, particularly if the joint venture is dependent on a critical flow of inputs from the minority partner. This can easily be concluded from the method of operation of Japanese multinationals in Asia where they have very effectively controlled joint ventures despite having minority ownership.

The Japanese have expanded their investment in Asia very rapidly in the last 15 years and have seemed to have done so while maintaining a fairly low profile in countries where they were only recently an occupying military force. Many of the countries like Indonesia, Thailand, and the Philippines have restrictive ownership laws, at least in certain areas, and in-built mechanisms for gradually increasing local ownership and management control. However, this does not seem to worry Japanese managers very much because the government's policy and their ability or resources to implement it are very far apart.

But it is not just the Japanese who adopt strategies to control the joint venture, while remaining a minority partner. Here are some of the well-known methods used in any country where a company can get away with it:

A. Keep control of key inputs or functions that are essential to the success of the joint venture. These could include:
    Financing for the venture
    A key part or ingredient for the product
    Equipment essential for production
    Expertise essential for production
    Access to international markets
    Management or marketing expertise
    Channels for marketing the product, national or international

    If the foreign joint-venture partner is supplying one or several of these, it has a lot of power and control, despite a minority share of ownership. Of course, neither can you cut your own nose to spite your face. If you already have made significant commitments of money and time in developing and setting up a joint venture, you don't want to fail. This also can be a strong bargaining chip for your partner, especially if you are supplying only one key component.

B. Another common practice is to use nominal or dummy shareholders to create the required local majority ownership. In an agribusiness joint venture in Indonesia the major contribution of the local partners, led by a prominent general, was the land. But the land had previously lain fallow and unused and in its undeveloped state was worth little. By assigning a high value to the land and by financing a lot of the other inputs, majority local ownership was ensured. In another case a loan was given to the local partner to purchase his share in the joint venture, with the understanding that the loan would be repaid from the earnings of the joint venture. If the sole purpose is to meet the requirements of the law, this does it. However, if you want a local partner that can really contribute to the venture, you will go for a real operating joint venture. Of course, it may be difficult to find such a partner because of a general shortage of capital or a lack of interest of local firms in a project that you consider attractive.

C. Choose as partners nonmanufacturing investors, like banks, insurance companies, or retail owners who have no interest in the day-to-day running of the enterprise.

D. In order to ensure that local shareholders hold a majority of equity, structure the venture so that it has a very low level of equity capital and a high level of debt, which the foreign partners control either by granting the loans themselves or using their own credit rating to raise them. Again, the leverage this gives the foreign investor may be a two-edged sword. Obviously, if the joint venture has to pay back the loans or ensure a continual stream of future financing, it is dependent on the source. But what if there is conflict and a divorce where there is very low capital contribution by the local partner? Then it may be the foreign partner who is left to pay the bills.

E. Another related technique is to arrange a deal with a friendly local firm that is a majority owner, but that is willing to give you effective control over operations. Of course, this leaves open the possibility that the friendly firm may turn out to be not so friendly when it comes to determining how profits are to be distributed, how much should be plowed back into the joint venture, or whether someone's first cousin should be hired.

F. A friendly deal can be formalized in an agreement independent of the ownership arrangement, where the parties clearly divide responsibility between the two sides regardless of the division of ownership. Most of the critical functions of the new enterprise would be the responsibility of the foreign partner, while the local firm looks after functions like public relations, labor relations, and payroll. Very often, of course, the local firm does not have the capabilities to carry out important functions like foreign procurement or foreign marketing, and it will welcome such an arrangement. On the other hand, the foreign partner may make more money out of these functions, done by the parent company, than from the joint venture itself. One element of such an agreement that is important and may be controversial concerns exports. One of the reasons you may decide to go into a joint venture in the first place is to gain access to cheap factors of production like raw materials or labor. But you may still be supplying an adjacent market from your home base or another plant. You do not want your child, the joint venture, competing against yourself at lower prices. Meanwhile, the joint venture itself, as a firm trying to maximize its profits, will want to export, and the government will certainly want it to do so. This is a difficult and controversial area of control that could be straightened out in an agreement, if the government allows it.

G. Besides ownership, another requirement of many countries all over the world is that the management be nationalized within a certain period of time. This, in practice, means increasing control. Many firms have gotten around that one by having a nominal manager in a key position, but the real power lies with a "consultant" who on an organization chart has no line of responsibility at all. For instance, even with local firms in the Middle East the person with the title of president or general manager may have little real power while someone who never turns up at the office makes all the key decisions. This may be particularly true if the real power in the firm is a politician or a member of the ruling elite. In a similar way, a key figure can control a joint venture by the sheer level of competence he or she brings to the task, or by agreement between the partners. And this is true despite the fact that he or she is a foreigner.

In many cases, of course, it may be difficult to find qualified local managers to put in key positions, although usually the firm can bring them up from the ranks if there is a sufficient commitment to training. There are also cases where the local firm may not want the responsibility, or they feel the joint venture will lose if the foreign firm gives up control. Many local firms go into a joint venture in the first place because they could not compete with imports into their markets. What they are primarily interested in is a successful enterprise, and they don't care who is managing it.

We have just seen some of the ways to control a joint venture, even if you are a minority owner. But I think it should be clear that in an international economy, where you are carefully selecting a method of entry and a joint-venture partner, you are not interested in control for control's sake. What you want is to achieve your marketing goals, not to gain power, and the best way to penetrate the market is to purposely choose a joint-venture partner with real contributions to make. It is not without reasons that joint ventures have been described in terms of a marriage, suggesting a good working arrangement rather than one side having more power than the other. In practice, one side may not be able to exercise the power effectively, and that is where these methods of exercising control are necessary.

CONCLUSION

Throughout this book there has been a strong emphasis on the attractions and opportunities in the less developed economies. Many U.S. companies discovered these a long time ago and have located their production facilities there to manufacture products for the home market at a lower cost. But it's not just the costs of production that are attractive; the markets themselves are growing, and these countries have very large populations.

But, there is a risk, and the environment is unfamiliar. In particular, there is a strong economic nationalism that often is incorporated in laws restricting ownership of local assets by foreign companies. This is particularly true in the area of natural resources. For the small firm in particular, a joint venture has two powerful attractions. It spreads risk, and it gives you access to local management or marketing skills and to partners who have a familiarity with the environment. It is often difficult to put a price on such assets, but very often they make the difference between success and failure in a foreign market. But, as in most things, there is a trade-off, and the trade-off is a loss of some degree of control. Depending on what you want from your joint-venture partner, there is another set of trade-offs. If you want an active, operational, contributing partner who may have significant contributions to make to the venture, you will have less control and probably more areas of conflict. If you

Joint Ventures

have a silent type of partner, you have less local contribution and more control. Different environments will often determine which is the best way to go. In the long run the joint venture will survive and succeed as long as the benefits outweigh the costs for both partners, and that is why a high degree of flexibility is required on both sides so that the benefit/cost ratio between the partners remains in balance.

10

DIRECT FOREIGN INVESTMENT: BIGGER RISKS, BIGGER REWARDS

Compared to other entry methods the decision to invest in a wholly owned subsidiary in a foreign country is a giant step.

Many theories have attempted to explain such a step, why it is necessary, and why a foreign company can succeed against local or regional competitors. For most companies the answers are fairly straightforward. The market is attractive or growing, other means of entry like exporting may be cut off, or the competition is eating into a market share. In short such a big investment is justified because the rewards will be greater in the long run. Some companies want to combine the factors of production that they have a lead in with cheaper foreign labor, raw materials, or energy. High transportation costs or high tariffs or high home production costs may leave them little choice. For example, in 1985, just a few days after the U.S. government announced the lifting of "voluntary" quotas on car imports by the Japanese into the United States, Lee Iacocca and Chrysler cancelled plans to open two small-car plants in the United States and decided instead to go to some kind of foreign sourcing.

Large companies like Chrysler have the resources to pick one or the other option, but for smaller or medium-sized companies with limited capital, this is a big decision, and they cannot afford to be wrong. You

Direct Foreign Investment

don't have to have the expertise to make such critical judgments yourself. Such judgments are a team effort involving input from economists, financial analysts, tax lawyers, and legal experts. But, of course, the decision is not usually a team decision. The buck has to stop someplace and you need to know all elements and get the global picture in order to make the final decision. But, in order to know the global picture you need all the input you can get, and, inevitably, the most critical input concerns the bottom line for you and your company, or in other words, whether the investment will give you a better return on your money than anything else. This chapter concentrates on explaining how that is evaluated, so that you know the basis on which the decision has to be made. Before getting into that, we will take a look at the special risks and advantages you face, what makes it worthwhile and how both your home and host country may be willing to help you. Having looked at the returns on the investment, we will, at the end, look at the advantages of buying or acquiring a foreign firm instead of starting from scratch yourself.

EXTRA RISKS, GREATER RETURNS

The essential difference between a direct form of investment and other entry methods is that in the latter case you are transferring an entire facility, or the capital to build or acquire it, to another country. In contrast, in exporting or licensing you are transferring products, services, or a patent or technology. In licensing, exporting, or even in a lot of joint ventures there are strict limits to your control in the foreign market. In investing, since you own the facility, you have much greater control over production, quality, labor, and the way the enterprise is managed financially. Of course, there may be legal restrictions governing labor, prices, or taxes, but that is true of your home country as well. What is really of significance is that now, from within the market, you can fully utilize your particular resources for the best possible returns.

In investing in a foreign country the advantages come from: (a) location or (b) the firm itself. It is usually a combination of both of these that makes the risk and return of the investment worthwhile in the first place.

Location Advantages

The first item of importance here is the size or attractiveness of the market itself. When you look at Brazil or Indonesia, sheer size and demand can be the real attraction. But the market in the country itself may not be the main location advantage. Hundreds of U.S. companies have invested in Ireland for two very significant location advantages; the access it gives through a reasonable transport system to one of the best markets in the world, that is, the EEC and second, because of the incentives provided by the host government to attract foreign capital. But there are other advantages. Labor costs are the most significant and are probably the single greatest reason why U.S. companies have moved to low labor-cost areas like Mexico, South Korea, or the Philippines. In many countries wages for doing the same job, in producing the same item, are one fifth of the home cost and in other cases even less. The situation is aggravated by the value of the dollar which is still quite strong and, which makes it that much more difficult to compete, not only in exports, but with other companies exporting or re-exporting back into the United States. If there is a lot of labor involved in the manufacture of your product, this may be the single greatest location advantage. As capital has moved overseas and as the United States has continued to purchase its steel, cars, and electronic equipment from cheaper production sites in Asia and elsewhere, the service sector of the U.S. economy has taken up the slack, and the earnings from these services have partially offset the trade deficit in the balance of payments. But it is uncertain how long this will last, and it may be only a matter of time before engineers, accountants, and other professionals from good universities in India or Egypt or Manila are providing services at a fraction of the U.S. cost.

There are other location advantages. Taxes may be lower; raw materials, land, or electricity may be cheaper, but more important, since you are inside the market, you are not subject to the import limits or quotas that could cut off your market at any time. Mention was already made of the advantage of having access to a preferential trading area. But it does not have to be preferential to gain the advantage. The cost factors mentioned here will make your product so much cheaper, and what may really give you the advantage over your competitors is transportation costs. Several years ago a firm I knew was putting together a complex tender bid for a multimillion-dollar irrigation project in Saudi Arabia. It involved very large quantities of PVC pipe. At that time the firm could supply almost every item, including the pipe, at a cost competitive with European suppliers. But when the inland shipping costs and the ocean freight were added it did not have a chance compared with a company shipping out of Europe and through a Mediterranean port. The same is true in supplying a regional market. Transport costs alone can give the competition, or a local producer, a clear edge.

Finally, the investment entry method can give a much greater thrust to the marketing effort. You are there, your marketing people locally or centrally have the expertise and have control, you know what the market needs and in what quantities, and you are not as dependent on agents or distributors or middlemen who may be satisfied with a few slices of bread rather than going for the whole loaf. You will have your own sales force, your own service department, and much more direct contact with the final consumer.

The Firm's Advantages

Usually these are fully exploited in combination with the location advantages. You have some advantages that some customers consider specific to you, otherwise, you would not be in business at all. If these are unique, you probably will be able to sell, export, produce, and compete from any base. If your technology is exclusive, your product outstanding, your brand name or trademark known worldwide, you may not be as dependent on the location advantages because you can charge a premium price to cover your costs. But this is not usually the case, and the advantages you have will need the cheaper factors of production to survive in the market in the long run. These firm specific advantages are what are likely to make the investment a success. You have the technology or know-how, you have the specialized equipment or trade secret or patented ingredients, you have the management skills, and perhaps, more important, you have the marketing skills to sell the product. Fundamental to all of these are the financial resources to choose the investment-entry method. When you combine these with the location advantages, it can be a winning combination not only over exporters or users of other entry methods, but even over producers inside the local market. In a word, the direct foreign investment allows you to exploit to the full advantages you have, or to gain a competitive advantage you have lost, or would not have in another entry method.

But there is a price to pay. The risks are greater, although as we saw earlier in Chapter Four they are usually exaggerated. You are pouring a lot of capital into a jurisdiction outside your own. Murphy's law may apply, a bearded revolutionary may appear on the horizon, and what can go wrong may go wrong and at the worst possible time. But, as we saw, that's not the real risk. Of much greater importance are the operational risks like being able to reach and maintain the market share that makes

FIGURE 10.1

DOES YOUR PROPOSED LOCATION HAVE THESE ADVANTAGES?
                                                    Yes   Yes
---

(a) A large market
(b) Access to a regional market
(c) Access to a common market with low tariffs
(d) Low labor costs
(e) A trained work force
(f) Cheap raw materials, rent, electricity, or other factors of production
(g) Low taxes
(h) A package of government incentives

FIGURE 10.2

WHAT ARE YOUR ADVANTAGES?

(a) A distinctive brand name or trade mark
(b) A technology that gives you an advantage
(c) A trade secret
(d) Adequate financial resources
(e) Management and marketing skills
(f) Access to or distribution channels in another country

the investment worthwhile in the first place, managing the labor force, handling currency difficulties, being able to ensure the source of supply of your inputs, and most of that has to do with good management. There is no doubt that a manufacturing subsidiary is a method of entry involving a level of risk higher than any other entry method. It involves a very careful judgment on market, economic, political, and social factors for a longer period of time than any other entry method. The size of the potential loss is of a completely different dimension than exporting or licensing or even a joint venture. And when you're in, you're in. It is almost impossible to get the investment back out if a change in strategy is required. You cannot afford to make a mistake because the payback period is so long. But if the risks are greater, so are the rewards in greater rates of return, greater profitably, and an opportunity to exploit other markets. What is often forgotten is that even if the risks of investment are high, so may be the decision not to invest. You may end up being excluded from an export market or losing competitiveness and even being wiped out in the home market by cheaper imports. And it is not as if you jump straight in. In practice, you are likely to have built up experience and confidence in exporting or licensing, and then you invest.

THE PULL AND PUSH IN DIRECT FOREIGN INVESTMENT

In discussing foreign manufacturing, it is necessary to realistically analyze political risks as there are some inevitable conflicts between the goals of the nation and the foreign investor, but there are also very important areas of common benefit. The most fundamental is that they need your capital and you are willing to invest it. You have many choices, and with limited resources you will be selective on where you go. Often this will depend on where you get the best bargain. Countries offering incentives for investment are trying to pull you in their direction. This is nothing new. Here in the United States almost every state was trying to get General Motors to locate their new Saturn production plant in their area. A foreign country has basically the same goal; they need the capital, the employment, the taxes, and the exports generated. Countries like Italy, South Korea, Singapore, the Philippines and Jamaica, to mention a few, have packages of incentives. In Exhibit 10.1 a summary is presented of the incentive package presented by the Irish government through its Industrial Development Authority. Most packages contain most of these elements although they may be targeted to certain areas of production or certain depressed geographical areas. But they are significant and can make a big difference in deciding the financial feasibility and return from the investment.

The incentive package that could make the investment entry method very attractive may include some or all of the following:

The Pull Factors

A. A maximum tax rate, tax holidays, or tax deferrals
B. Liberal depreciation allowances

C. Guarantees that foreign exchange will be provided for the repatriation of profits, dividends, and capital
D. Nonrepayable cash grants toward the cost of fixed assets
E. Training grants for employees
F. Ready-to-occupy factories in industrial parks
G. Rent reduction
H. Loan guarantees and long- and short-term loans at special low interest rates
I. Duty-free entry for equipment and/or raw materials used in production
J. Protection in the host-country market by import duties or other controls on competitive products

These incentives are confined to investment-entry methods, for obvious reasons. But the fact that they are offered at all says a lot about what the political climate is likely to be in that country although a country may offer an attractive set of incentives, and if other political fundamentals are not stable, there is likely to be little investment despite the incentives. For example, Jamaica offers a very attractive package, but it has not drawn the expected investment because of perceived political risks.

These are the pull factors. The United States also gives you a push to encourage you to invest at least in certain areas by giving a set of incentives of its own. How long many of these will remain is unknown, especially if direct investment overseas is seen as the export of jobs. Countries like Sweden do the opposite. They have restrictions on the movement of capital if it leads to the loss of jobs at home. The United States has broader foreign-policy goals, and the assumption still remains that investment overseas leads to extra jobs at home from exports and inputs and that, anyway, it is the only way U.S. companies can remain competitive in certain world markets. It is becoming a bit more controversial, as U.S. companies use the cheaper overseas source to supply the home market. But for the moment two important policies remain, namely, the ability to freely move capital into production overseas and the absence of punitive taxes on overseas earnings. There are other incentives that may assist you greatly in making an overseas investment. These include:

Direct Foreign Investment

EXHIBIT 10.1

IRELAND

A favourable tax environment

A most important element in Ireland's financial incentives for new industry is a generous package of tax relief:

— a maximum corporation tax of 10% for all manufacturing companies until the year 2000.

— industrialists in Ireland benefit from generous capital allowances for tax purposes, including free depreciation. In all parts of the country, a company can depreciate 100% of the total cost of fixed plant and machinery and write it off against tax — and in the first year if preferred.

— industrial buildings also qualify for free depreciation i.e. 100% of the cost, less any grants received, may be written off against tax in the first year the building is used.

— losses can be carried forward indefinitely for tax purposes.

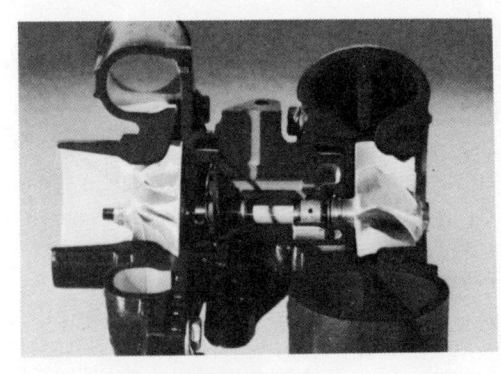

Garrett Corporation is a subsidiary of the US Signal Corporation and manufactures turbocharger components at Waterford. The company, which established in Ireland in 1978, will employ 100 workers at full production.

Generous incentive package

Capital Grants
The wide range of non-repayable cash grants is the second main incentive offered by the IDA to new engineering industries setting up in Ireland. The IDA gives cash grants towards the cost of fixed assets, including land, site development, buildings, machinery and equipment.

Grant levels range up to 50% of fixed investment depending on location, type of project, etc. For large capital intensive projects the grants are calculated on a per capita basis and also related to location. The Authority also subsidises the cost of research and development programmes, and feasibility studies on new products.

Training Grants
The IDA provides training grants of 100% of the cost of agreed training programmes for workers in new industries. The grants also cover the cost of sending personnel abroad for training; the salaries, travel and subsistence expenses of training personnel; management training expenses; the cost of hiring training consultants etc. AnCO operates training courses designed to meet the needs of specific industries.

Low Cost Financing:
Machinery leasing and other loan capital is negotiable at low interest rates from the Irish banking system arising from favourable tax and incentive systems.

The Result: On a manufacturing investment in Ireland, the payback period is significantly reduced and the return on investment is very much higher than for an equivalent investment elsewhere.

Industrial Estates, sites and advance factories:
The IDA owns many serviced industrial sites which are available for approved projects. It builds advance factories on its own industrial estates or on single sites so that accommodation for new industry is in many cases immediately available. This factory space may be rented or bought; rentals are usually subsidised. IDA's Building Operations Division can arrange for the design and construction of purpose-built factories on an agency basis.

Support and After Care
In addition to the incentives already outlined, IDA operates advisory services on raising finance, manpower, site selection and legal formalities — and it continues to help and advise firms when they are established.

The IDA has a network of regional offices throughout the country. No matter where you locate in Ireland local IDA representatives are on the spot to help.

The Push Factors

A. Free movement of capital
B. Absence of punitive taxes
C. Support in making the investment decision by OPIC, the Private Sector Bureau of USAID, and by investment missions or technical support
D. Foreign Risk Insurance provided by OPIC, which is a government agency
E. The research and wealth of information provided by the Department of Commerce and commercial attachés overseas
F. Incentives offered by the Export/Import Bank to purchase U.S.-made equipment for overseas operations
G. Last, there is the political clout the U.S. government carries in the event foreign investors are threatened by foreign governments' controls. These include vetoes on loans from multilateral banks, the cutoff of U.S. foreign aid, and restriction on imports to the U.S. market.

HOW TO DECIDE ON THE BOTTOM LINE: THE RETURN ON INVESTMENT

If some of the earlier forms of investment were like dipping your toe in the water, direct manufacturing is really jumping in at the deep end. So, it requires a full-scale financial analysis and an analysis of all the factors that affect the profitability of the enterprise. But the financial analysis is not done in a vacuum. You already have much of your homework done. Let's summarize what you already know or what you need to know in order to have the full framework for the financial analysis.

What You Know Already

A. You know the political risks. You have analyzed the political climate and decided that it is acceptable and will remain acceptable for the planning period in which you are interested.
B. You are aware of the financial risks. From your examination of trends in the balance of payments, tariffs, exchange rates, and

inflation you feel this is an environment you can succeed in. In fact, one of these may be the main reason for going into direct investment because it is the best or only long-term way of ensuring a presence in this market if there are growing balance-of-payments problems or tighter control on foreign exchange or imports.

C. You may already have some experience in the market through exporting or licensing, so you are making a decision in a familiar context. This should not be underestimated because in many countries a knowledge of the operating environment, of key people, business customs of major customers, port problems, and so forth, puts a high degree of realism into a financial analysis that otherwise is in danger of taking place in a void.

D. You know the market, its size, growth rate, and the marketing infrastructure. You have estimated export possibilities to third countries and you know the competition you face. In analyzing the costs and benefits of the different entry strategies, you have calculated the costs of exports that will be lost from the home base by this entry method.

E. You know the incentives available from the host and home governments to assist you, the so-called push-and-pull factors. In particular, you know the factors that will lower your start-up costs, like availability of a plant site or production facilities and the types of tax benefits you are likely to get.

There are other contextual factors you will know like, for instance, the availability and cost of skilled and unskilled labor, a subject that will be covered in a later chapter.

BACKGROUND INFORMATION YOU HAVE ALREADY

1. Political Risks
2. Financial Risks
3. Knowledge of the Operating Environment
4. Knowledge of Market Size, Growth Rate, and Marketing Infrastructure
5. Home- and Host-Country Incentives to Invest

CAPITAL BUDGETING

Capital budgeting is the framework within which you have to make the investment decision once you have gathered all of the information previously listed. Basically, the question capital budgeting forces you to ask, and answer, is whether you would be better to forget about the whole deal, put the money in the bank, and sleep better. The reason you won't do that, of course, is that you expect that the investment will give you a far higher rate of return. A more technical definition of capital budgeting is that it compares the advantages from the alternative uses of funds with the cost of alternative ways of getting the funds.

To carry the financial analysis through a logical way follow these three steps:

Step One: You calculate revenues and costs over the life of the project for the project itself.

Step Two: You estimate the contributions of the project to the mother company, namely, your home base.

Step Three: From the point of view of the firm as a whole determine how the incremental net cash flow compares with alternative investment possibilities and calculate the estimated return on investment.

Step One: Calculating revenues and costs over a five-or-ten-year planning period involves an element of crystal-ball gazing because of all the assumptions you have to make about inflation rates, labor costs, exchange rates, and levels of sales. But you have to take it one step at a time based on the best information you have. The market analysis covers local sales as well as export receipts. This may be considerably complicated by the different ways different transactions are treated for foreign-exchange purposes. Mexico, for instance, has an official rate and a free-market rate, and different transactions come under each. The rate may also be negotiable, but one way or the other it has to be factored in for export sales, equipment imports, or production supplies. Costs of the project include investment in land, plant, and equipment to get started. Then there are the ongoing production costs, which depend on the cost of labor, raw materials, energy, and other inputs into the manufacturing process. All of these could, of course, be significantly affected by host-government incentives like tax-free import of required equipment or ingredients, low interest loans, or training programs for workers. Finally,

TABLE 10.1 NET PRESENT VALUE OVER 20 YEARS OF ONE DOLLAR AT DIFFERENT DISCOUNT RATES

Year	5%	6%	7%	8%	9%	10%	12%	14%	15%	16%	18%	20%
1	.952	.943	.935	.926	.917	.909	.893	.877	.870	.862	.847	.833
2	.907	.890	.873	.857	.842	.826	.797	.769	.756	.743	.718	.694
3	.864	.840	.816	.794	.772	.751	.712	.675	.658	.641	.609	.579
4	.823	.792	.763	.735	.708	.683	.636	.592	.572	.552	.516	.482
5	.784	.747	.713	.681	.650	.621	.567	.519	.497	.476	.437	.402
6	.746	.705	.666	.630	.596	.564	.507	.456	.432	.410	.370	.335
7	.711	.665	.623	.583	.547	.513	.452	.400	.376	.354	.314	.279
8	.677	.627	.582	.540	.502	.467	.404	.351	.327	.305	.266	.233
9	.645	.592	.544	.500	.460	.424	.361	.308	.284	.263	.226	.194
10	.614	.558	.508	.463	.422	.386	.322	.270	.247	.227	.191	.162
11	.585	.527	.475	.429	.388	.350	.287	.237	.215	.195	.162	.135
12	.557	.497	.444	.397	.356	.319	.257	.208	.187	.168	.137	.112
13	.530	.469	.415	.368	.326	.290	.229	.182	.163	.145	.116	.093
14	.505	.442	.388	.340	.299	.263	.205	.160	.141	.125	.099	.078
15	.481	.417	.362	.315	.275	.239	.183	.140	.123	.108	.084	.065
16	.458	.394	.339	.292	.252	.218	.163	.123	.107	.093	.071	.054
17	.436	.371	.317	.270	.231	.198	.146	.108	.093	.080	.060	.045
18	.416	.350	.296	.250	.212	.180	.130	.095	.081	.089	.051	.038
19	.396	.331	.276	.232	.194	.164	.116	.083	.070	.030	.043	.031
20	.377	.312	.258	.215	.178	.149	.104	.073	.061	.051	.037	.026

you assign a terminal value to the project, which reflects its estimated market value at the end of the planning period.

Having collected the data on revenues and costs of the project itself, they now need to be brought together in a financial analysis. The most common form of analysis is done by determining the present value of the sum or stream of benefits expected over a certain planning period in the future. The logic behind this is straightforward. Since you are making the decision and the investment now, based on future returns, it is better to reduce future revenues to their present value at some financial rate. Table 10.1 is a straightforward discount table that shows the present value of $1 received at any of a number of years in the future and discounted at a variety of interest rates. This is essentially the same procedure as we used in Chapter Five to compare the advantages of two entry methods. The difference is that in this case you are looking at one investment with a view to ranking it with alternative uses of scarce capital. A simplified cash-flow analysis of a project for 10 years is presented in Table 10.2. A big decision, of course, is what discount rate you use and what, if any, premium should be included above the required rate of return for your domestic investment. Here, 16 percent is used assuming a 14 percent domestic requirement rate and a 2 percent risk premium. The negative cash flow in year one represents the initial investment in site, plant, and equipment. Receipts from sales are projected over a ten-year period. So are costs, taxes, and all the other factors that are required in a manufacturing facility. This gives you the net after tax inflows for the 10 years. Using Table 10.1, you discount each year at 16 percent to get the net present value of after-tax inflows. Now you can figure out the cumulative inflows, and you see they become positive on year seven, showing that the project's required rate of return is exceeded.

Step Two: What you are really interested in is the flow of funds back to you, and that's a different question than the flow to the project itself. Here at home, if you had two units no such problem would arise because you could assume cash flows to one unit would be available to another or to headquarters. In a foreign investment what you have to take into account are ceilings on repatriated profits, special taxes, or required reinvestment policies by the host country. Probably most uncertain of all is the translation of the flows that are possible into home-country currencies over the planning period.

You also have to figure in any extra revenues the home base may be getting from exports to the subsidiary of inputs or fees for management services, just as you would have to figure in as a cost the loss of exports you formerly had to this market.

Step Three: Now you are ready to compare the results with alter-

Direct Foreign Investment

native uses of your resources. There are several ways of ranking investments, and they will be covered only briefly here. A detailed treatment is part of any financial management textbook.

TABLE 10.2 CASH-FLOW ANALYSIS (MILLIONS OF FRANCS)

	Net Cash Flow	Discounted @ 16% per $1	Present Value of Net Cash Flows	Cumulative Discounted Value of Net Cash Flow
Year 0	(400)	1.000	400	(400)
Year 1	45	0.862	38.79	(361.21)
Year 2	65	0.743	48.3	(312.91)
Year 3	80	0.641	51.28	(261.63)
Year 4	95	0.552	52.44	(209.19)
Year 5	150	0.476	71.4	(137.79)
Year 6	200	0.410	82.0	(55.79)
Year 7	250	0.354	88.5	32.71
Year 8	275	0.305	83.88	116.56
Year 9	300	0.263	78.9	195.49
Year 10	350	0.227	79.45	274.94
Terminal Value	650	0.227	147.55	422.49

METHODS OF RANKING INVESTMENTS

A. Payback Period: This method ranks investments on a scale according to the time it takes for each investment to give back earnings equal to the cost of the investment. Obviously, the sooner your investment is paid back, the sooner your risk is reduced and the capital is available for other investments. Using a simple example, assume you make a $10,000 investment in two different projects. One pays back $2,000 per year for five years. You then have your money back, or in other words the payback period is five years. But if the other pays back $3,000 for the first two years and then $2,000 for the next two years you get your money back in four years, making this the more attractive investment by this criterion.

But it is a limited technique because it does not take into account the income stream beyond the payback period, and it fails to account for the time value of money. In areas of high political risk, however, the payback period will be looked at closely along with other measurements. In such an environment it tells you that if worse comes to worse, and as long as it does not happen before such and such a year, you will at least have your investment out, even if longer-term goals are not yet reached.

B. Net Present Value: We have used this method already to determine what the present value of the projected income is. This method is used very widely to decide on the best investment based on how much each discounted income stream exceeds the cost of the investment. Let's take an example. Assume two investments, Project A and Project B, involving an investment of $750,000 each and different payback periods as in Table 10.3.

TABLE 10.3 RANKING INVESTMENT BY PAYBACK PERIOD AND NET PRESENT VALUE

$	Project A	Project B	A @ 16%	B @ 16%
Yr 1	150,000	187,500	129,300	161,625
Yr 2	150,000	187,500	111,450	139,313
Yr 3	150,000	187,500	96,150	120,188
Yr 4	150,000	187,500	82,800	103,638
Yr 5	150,000	150,000	71,400	71,400
Yr 6	150,000	150,000	61,500	61,500
Yr 7	150,000	150,000	53,100	53,100
Yr 8	150,000	150,000	45,750	45,750
Yr 9	150,000	-----	39,450	-----
Yr 10	150,000	-----	34,050	-----
Total	1,500,000	1,350,000.00	724,950	756,512
		Less Investment	750,000	750,000
		Net Present Value	($25,050)	$6,512.00

Looking at this table, project B wins on two counts, although total income is less. First, it has a quicker payback period, namely 8 years, compared with 10, and second, when the income stream is discounted at 16 percent for both, project B exceeds A by $31,562. What is more surprising is that at a 16 percent discount rate, Project A makes no economic sense because from an original investment of $750,000 the present value of total income is only $724,950 or less than the investment, while B is only marginally more rewarding at $756,572. Of

Direct Foreign Investment

course, 16 percent is a high discount rate, but if the expected rate in the home country is 14 percent and the foreign location is in any way shaky, a 2 percent premium is not that much. It is like an investor looking at AT&T and expecting to make an 11 percent total return on his or her stock investment. To invest in a new, upstart telephone company, he or she would have to at least expect a few percentage points above AT&T.

C. Internal Rate of Return: This is essentially the same procedure as calculating the net present value except that in the latter case an expected return is identified and the income stream discounted at that rate. Here you know the cost of the investment and the income stream you will have, and you are looking for the rate of return where that income will equal the net value of the investment. There is no formula to find the internal rate of return, but you can get very close by following these four steps:

Step One: Make an approximate calculation of the rate of return.

Step Two: Using that rate, calculate the project's net present value.

Step Three: If the present net value is more than the investment, try a lower rate; if it is lower try a higher rate.

Step Four: Narrow the range until you get a rate where the net present value and the net investment are equal.

Using a simple example of an investment of $50,000 for five years you project a cash flow as outlined in Table 10.4.

TABLE 10.4 CASH FLOW DISCOUNTED AT DIFFERENT RATES

Year	Net Cash Flow	@ 10% = $	@ 15% = $	@ 12% = $
1	$ 5,000	× .909 = 4545	@ .870 = 4350	@ .893 = 4465
2	$10,000	× .826 = 8260	@ .756 = 7500	@ .797 = 7970
3	$15,000	× .751 = 11,265	@ .658 = 9870	@ .712 = 10,680
4	$20,000	× .685 = 13,360	@ .572 = 11,440	@ .636 = 12,720
5	$25,000	× .621 = 15,525	@ .497 = 12,425	@ .567 = 14,175
		53,255.00	45,645.00	50,010
		−50,000.00	−50,000.00	
		3,255.00	− 4,355.00	

You first discount at 10 percent, and you see your rate is too low because the discounted income stream is greater than the investment. But, at 15 percent you are too high because the income stream is too low by $4,355. Taking a midpoint of 12 percent, the difference between the investment and net present value is only $10, so for all practical purposes your internal rate of return is 12 percent. If your expected rate of return were more than 12 percent, then this project would not make sense. If 12 percent is above your acceptable rate and you are considering alternatives, you will pick the project with the highest internal rate of return, all other things being equal.

D. Profitability Index: This criterion is again quite close to the idea of net present value and can be expressed in a cost/benefit ratio as follows: The Profitability Index = Benefits/Costs where the benefits are the present value of future net cash flows over the life of the project and the costs are the net investment. Using the figures from the previous example, if your cost of capital plus a risk factor were 15 percent, then your P.I. would be $45645/50,000 = .91. If your cost of capital were 10 percent, your P.I. = 53255/50,000 = 1.06, and at 12 percent it would be just at 1. This means that at 12 percent the project will earn your required rate of return but nothing more. At 15 percent you have a premium over your expected return whereas at 10 percent you would be losing.

All of the foregoing techniques can be used to evaluate the viability of the project itself as well as the return to the headquarter's investor. If you are investing, it is this latter question that is most important. And, of course, there are many elements to take into account like the increased export sales or any other kinds of fees or royalties paid by the subsidiary. There may also be a considerable number of intangible benefits to the company as a whole like, for instance, better knowledge of foreign markets, new management skills, or demand for new or adapted products the company had not previously considered.

Where Do You Raise the Money?

One of the biggest decisions the investor faces and one that will greatly influence the financial results is how the project is financed and how it is structured. If you can raise money in the local currency you can reduce both financial and political risks. This would, in turn, reduce the

Direct Foreign Investment

premiums and so the investment would become viable and more attractive because it has a lower expected rate of return.

It is not always so straightforward. Some countries have precise regulations on the use of local capital by foreign companies, and in general, what the government wants is a transfer of capital into the country, or if local capital is going to be used, that it is raised by selling equity to local investors, rather than by borrowing from local sources.

There are several important factors to take into account in making the decision, assuming your options are not limited by the government and you have a number of choices open to you.

   A. Exchange Rate Changes: From an investment point of view there is a lot of money to be made or lost by the original decision on which currency to use to make the investment. In the early eighties the British pound was strong, based, among other things, on the rapidly increasing prices for oil in the seventies and the expectation that they would continue to rise. If an investor's income was going to be in pounds or a currency tied to the pound, he or she could borrow in another currency and pay off the debt with a lower exchange rate. On the other hand, if you invested one million dollars in Mexico when the peso was 40:1, you would need 40 million pesos to get your investment paid back. In a matter of a few years you would have needed close to 500 million. If you raise the capital locally, the devaluation does not have this radical effect because you will be paying off that debt from within the currency area.
   B. Interest Rates: Normally you would expect a company to borrow money from the cheapest source, but many U.S. companies borrow, when they can, at a higher rate in the local currency mainly because of the exchange rates risks here outlined. What makes the difference is the forecast about how the difference in interest rates and exchange rates will interact with one another. It may be better to take on the higher interest rates in order to lower the exchange-rate exposure.
   C. Political Risk: If local institutions lend you money or local investors have an ownership interest, political risk is likely to be lower because powerful local interests want to protect your income stream for their own sake. One of the ways local financing and the financial analysis closely interact is that any risk premium is reduced or eliminated altogether. So, a project that did not make sense because of a political-risk premium when

financed from the foreign country could make economic sense if financed locally.
D. Host-Country Regulations: The government may not allow you to borrow locally. There may be an ambivalence about this position in the sense that the government wants local participation but does not want foreign firms soaking up scarce local capital in competition with local firms. The government's regulations on foreign exchange may also affect the decision because, again, in a situation of scarce foreign exchange, a company is much more likely to get dollars to pay off debt and to pay interest on debt than to pay dividends on equity.
E. Taxes: The way the debt/equity structure and the local/foreign sourcing of funds is affected by taxes in the host and home countries will have an impact on net cash flows and therefore on your investment decision.

In summary, the information you need is complicated and may give off different signals. There may not be a clear-cut answer, but enough information is needed to make an informed judgment. In most cases core financing for fixed assets overseas will come from the parent company because it is only when it shows its own willingness to take a risk that it is going to be credible as a borrower at home or overseas.

If you borrow locally you lower certain risks, but you might raise others if capital is scarce. If you bring in capital as you almost inevitably will, you face risks from currency fluctuations, varying inflation rates, and possible exchange controls. Whatever road you go, you can see the direct impact it will have on the question raised in the earlier section, that is, whether or not this is a good investment.

CONCLUSION

Most business people assume they know their home environment and the risks associated with business there. And yet, events like the oil-price increases of the seventies or the massive increase in manufactured goods imported into the United States still came as shocks. Overseas, the unforeseen and the risks are compounded. To enter a market the firm needs to have a vast amount of accurate information available to it and, of more importance, the analytical skills to handle it. This data includes areas as diverse as the regulatory and legal framework, tax law,

Direct Foreign Investment

economic trends, political risks, exchange rate expectations, labor conditions, cost of inputs, and market potential. One or all of these factors are changeable, and the analysis of the investment proposal would have to take into account many of the "if-then" scenarios. A direct foreign investment is a long-term commitment of assets. It's easy to go in, but difficult, if not impossible, to get your assets out if things go wrong. The basic rule is that you invest up to the point where the discounted stream of future earnings is higher than, or at least equal to, the cost of the investment. Deciding that is the crux of the matter.

11

THE SECRET OF SUCCESS IN AN OVERSEAS MARKET: THE MANAGER AND THE WORKFORCE

What are the three most important factors in the success of an overseas venture? The manager, the manager and the work force, the men and women on site who make the project work. Talking about an overseas manager appears, at first hand, to imply a direct-investment or joint-venture form of market entry. But an overseas manager may be involved in several other ways. Service contracts or technical-assistance contracts, with or without licensing, require a manager or somebody to perform the management functions. An overseas manager may have responsibility for a region; he or she may be based in Athens, for example, and be responsible for developing and supplying markets by export in the Middle East, supervising a licensing arrangement in Algeria, a joint venture in Yugoslavia, and a manufacturing plant in Greece. Performing several roles in this fashion is exceptional, but the point is that in dealing with the overseas manager, much more is involved than a direct form of investment. Moreover, many of the topics discussed have relevance for the home-based manager responsible for foreign markets. He or she will have to deal with several markets; he or she will be continuously in and out of the country dealing with agents, distributors, suppliers, carriers and local officials. All of this requires a set of management skills, some of which are quite distinctive and cannot be learned from a book or a college course. Let us take an example. Kaiser Aluminum have a modern aluminum plant just outside Accra in Ghana. They also have several plants in the Northwest of the United States. In Ghana as well as the United States, most managerial and technical functions in the plant are performed by Americans but in surroundings and in roles that are very different. The manager in Ghana has a much broader role and needs an added set of skills to perform them. A successful manager in Washington State does not, *ipso facto*, make a successful manager in Ghana. For example, a manager in both countries has to deal with government leaders and regulatory authorities, but consider the difference in issues. The government in Ghana has been very unstable ever since Kaiser built the plant, but in recent years there have been several coups, some involving sharp swings to the left. Kaiser is one of the biggest local taxpayers, one of the biggest earners of foreign exchange, and one of the largest employers in the country. The manager of such an enterprise is a powerful person in the local political scene, and his or her plant is a very visible symbol of power and wealth and consequently, a very likely target of political rhetoric, petty interference, and imposed delays. In a sense, a socialist-leaning government cannot live with Kaiser and cannot live without them. The manager, dealing with political leaders in this environment, is responsible for the very survival of the enterprise and his or her political, diplomatic, and cultural skills are probably far more important than the set of managerial skills his or her counterpart in the United States needs on a day-to-day basis. Of course, the manager will have considerable back-up in a situation like this. For instance, there will be regular contact and support from the head office, a local counterpart manager with good access to the levers of power, and the manager will have experience working in an environment that prepared him or her for this challenge.

Not all situations are as extreme as Ghana's, but I will put most emphasis on situations that are remote from the United States because the difficulties and challenges are most demanding and often apply, but to a lesser degree, in foreign markets closer to home.

WHERE DO YOU FIND OVERSEAS MANAGERS?

If you are looking for overseas managers, you have three options open to you: You can limit your selection to personnel from the home country, you can use local nationals, or you can try and find the most suitable candidates anyplace, and then appoint them to any post at home or overseas.

Home Country Managers

In practice, most international firms feel they need to have at least a few top-level managers from their home country in each operation overseas. This makes more sense in some of the less-developed countries where talent is scarce, but as companies develop into real international firms, rather than national firms with foreign operations, the policy is changing toward foreign management of foreign operations. It is also becoming a more attractive policy as economic nationalism grows, and because it is so much cheaper. In practice, and especially at the beginning of a foreign operation, it may make more sense to have key positions filled by home-country nationals. Look at the way the Japanese structure the management of their investments in the United States, which is the MBA capital of the world. Key posts are filled by Japanese nationals, and there is a general feeling that this is necessary to maintain rapport with the parent firm as well as for transferring Japanese levels of efficiency and ways of doing things into the American workplace. In this case, the Japanese consider it an advantage to export the Japanese management style into their U.S. plants while the conventional wisdom used to be that this was one reason for not using U.S. managers overseas.

To determine whether a home-country national is the most appropriate, it is helpful to answer the questions in Figure 11.1. The more answers checked "Yes" the more reason for hiring a U.S. manager for the job.

Several of these questions, although answered in the affirmative, may involve poor long-term strategy. For example, to use a foreign assignment as a training ground for home-based managers is to assume that the home-office position is more difficult than the foreign position, a questionable assumption that may affect the success of the subsidiary if it is a key post. Equally questionable is the policy of sending surplus management personnel overseas. This could be all right if the best were sent, but of course, if the best don't want to be sent the not-so-good will have little choice. Unfortunately, many companies have had such a policy in the past where the misfits were shunted off to the international division either at home or abroad. The international division was often so small and lacking in clout that it had no choice. Domestic sales were

The Manager and the Workforce

FIGURE 11.1

Checklist to Determine When a Home Country Manager Is the Most Appropriate for a Foreign Operation

	Yes	No
1. Are you starting up a new project?		
2. Are local managers scarce?		
3. Does the foreign operation, e.g., a technical-assistance contract, have a definite life span?		
4. Will the firm have greater prestige and more power by having a U.S. manager?		
5. Does the firm have surplus, under-utilized managers in domestic operations?		
6. Is it difficult to get suitable foreign managers because of race, religious, or language differences?		
7. Is the foreign operation isolated from the local environment or more focused on relations with the home base or other foreign activities than on host-country markets?		
8. Does the firm have an exceptional home-country manager available for the job?		

often 90 percent of the company's business, and the result was a vicious cycle for the international division because poor management led to less effectiveness and less clout. But, here again, times have changed as the domestic divisions have come under pressure from foreign sales and the international division becomes a window on the world marketplace.

Finally, although there may be a scarcity of local talent or a foreign manager may have more prestige, that situation can change very rapidly with, for example, a change in the political climate. Then you may need local managers, and the way to have them, if they are scarce, is to hire them and train them at headquarters or on the job.

THE ADVANTAGES AND DISADVANTAGES OF HIRING LOCAL MANAGERS

If local managers with the required skills are available, the advantages of hiring them appear overwhelming. Here are some of the most obvious.

1. They know the language.
2. They know the culture.
3. You cut costs because local salaries are so much lower, and you don't have to provide transport, housing, and the like, for a whole foreign family.
4. Your firm takes on a local image or lowers its foreign image.
5. A local manager hired at a premium salary over local levels is likely to provide long-term service and continuity of management to the foreign operation.
6. They have access to local leaders in industry, banking, and politics that it may take foreigners years to establish.

But there are several difficulties the firm may face with local managers. They have no "feel" from the inside for the firm, and there may be considerable difficulties in communication between local and headquarter's management. Even between the United States and Europe, which have so much in common, there are problems arising from different business, educational, and cultural backgrounds. For example, in some countries a business manager has considerably less prestige than other professions such as medicine, the military, the legal profession, teaching, and farming. In others it may be so prestigious to work for a foreign firm that the manager may not want to dirty his or her hands and do the nitty-gritty work that a foreign manager may be required to do.

Finally, the local manager may be subject to more government pressure and may be able to withstand it less than a foreign manager. As a manager of a foreign company, he or she has a loyalty to it, but the government may appeal to his or her nationalism and put pressure on the manager to make decisions that are not the best for the company. For example, a local manager's uncle may have his request for the development of a large tract of land on the outskirts of the city delayed for "environmental" reasons, while the real reason is to bring pressure on his nephew, the local manager.

The Manager and the Workforce

Hiring the Best Manager Irrespective of Nationality or the Location of the Post

In an ideal world this would appear to be an ideal policy and would be the most consistent with the idea of a true international company, that is, one that tries to make the best use of financial, technical, and personnel resources on a worldwide basis. Although international firms are at the forefront of the movement of goods and resources across national boundaries, however, when it comes to managers, there may be much stronger nationalistic forces at work. For example, some companies operating in countries in the Common Market in Europe prefer to bring in an American manager rather than raise nationalistic jealousies by appointing a manager from Germany, France, or England. The multinational policy is also expensive because you are paying for the cream of the international crop and there is considerable expense in training, moving families, and providing housing. Of course, even if you have such managers, you run into controls the national government may impose or to the problem that managers of certain ethnic or religious backgrounds may not be accepted in some countries.

HOW DO YOU SELECT THEM?

We have already dealt with one of the fundamental criteria involved in the selection of overseas managers, namely, their nationality. There are other criteria of equal importance that need to be taken into account in the selection process.

1. Company Experience: This is a highly desirable quality in a manager but should not be a necessary condition of assignment. The idea is that a manager with company experience knows the way the company works and knows its policies and its products as well as other managers, and so communications and relations with the head office will be so much better. However, a lot of this can be achieved by training, familiarization programs, and regular meetings.
2. Technical Competence: This is required not only to do the job effectively but also to gain the respect of the local government and business, banking, and labor leaders. Sometimes companies send less qualified managers overseas on the assumption that, overall, lesser skills are required. In general, the

assumption should be exactly the opposite because of the many roles the manager will play and the fact that he or she may be called on to perform a broader set of tasks in his or her professional capacity than if he or she were home based.

3. Language and Culture: Finding somebody who knows the language and also has the required technical skills will be the exception rather than the rule. And, it is unrealistic for most managers to learn the language especially if they are on limited-time assignments. If the language is critical for doing the job, the best thing to do is to hire a local national. What is much more important than a knowledge of the language is a "feel" for the environment and the culture. A manager with a perfect knowledge of the language may make a mess of the job if he or she is insensitive to the culture. Most managers who have been really successful overseas did not know the language but knew how to operate in a very different environment. As well as that, a knowledge of English is now widespread at the levels of business and government at which the manager will operate. The biggest handicap of not having the language is in dealing with a local work force.

4. Motivation: Is the manager going overseas for valid motives or is he or she at a dead end in the home front or is he or she running away from something?

5. Age: Managers interested in going overseas are likely to be younger rather than older, and in a different and often stressful environment the younger person may be better able to do the job. However, in certain societies age is a sign of wisdom and is respected, and it may be difficult for a younger person to command the attention necessary to do the job.

6. Ethnic Background: Obviously this is a delicate area surrounded by equal-opportunity restrictions. What is real, though, is the question whether an Italian-American is more effective in Italy, a black American in Kenya, or an American-born Japanese in Japan? Although such assignments would seem to have benefits, there is also the possibility that such a manager may provoke hostility either because of position, salary level, or the status of the job.

7. Status: This quality is close to being indefinable, but it is very important. Perhaps the best way to describe it is the ability of the manager to project a presence and to command respect

without demanding it in the environment in which he or she works. In more traditional societies, status is often ascribed to a person by his or her family background or his or her religion or by some other quality not acquired by the person. Obviously, this is a relevant factor in selecting local managers as long as the manager also has the technical competence necessary to do the job.
8. Family: When hiring a manager, you are really hiring a family, and the manager's performance is likely to be influenced by the way the family adapts to the local environment. In the domestic environment it is almost unknown that a wife be interviewed before offering a job to a husband. For an international assignment, especially in developing countries, this should be a requirement so that both partners have an accurate knowledge of the working and living conditions.

There are some formal tests that can assist you in the selection process, and some of them may highlight deeply felt cultural prejudices. But in the end the selection process boils down to a judgment of whether the manager has the required personality and skills; whether the family knows exactly what they are getting themselves into, for example, housing, schools, cultural and social limitations, and medical facilities; and whether the manager and his or her family can deal with the extra pressure and stress that may be associated with working in a foreign country.

HOW YOU CAN PREPARE THEM: OUTLINE OF A TRAINING COURSE

Formal training for overseas managers has been the exception rather than the rule for most companies, although it is very costly if a manager has to be repatriated because he or she is the wrong choice, or if he or she cannot adapt to the environment. On the other hand, large corporations have an "on the job" training procedure where managers are sent overseas at lower levels of responsibility and then promoted and rotated into other areas so that the company ends up with a cadre of experienced international managers. A smaller firm cannot afford the inevitable mistakes that this approach presumes and will not be big enough to absorb one unsuitable manager in a key position overseas. However, a formal training course is expensive, often the assignment may be for a

FIGURE 11.2

Summary of the Selection Process

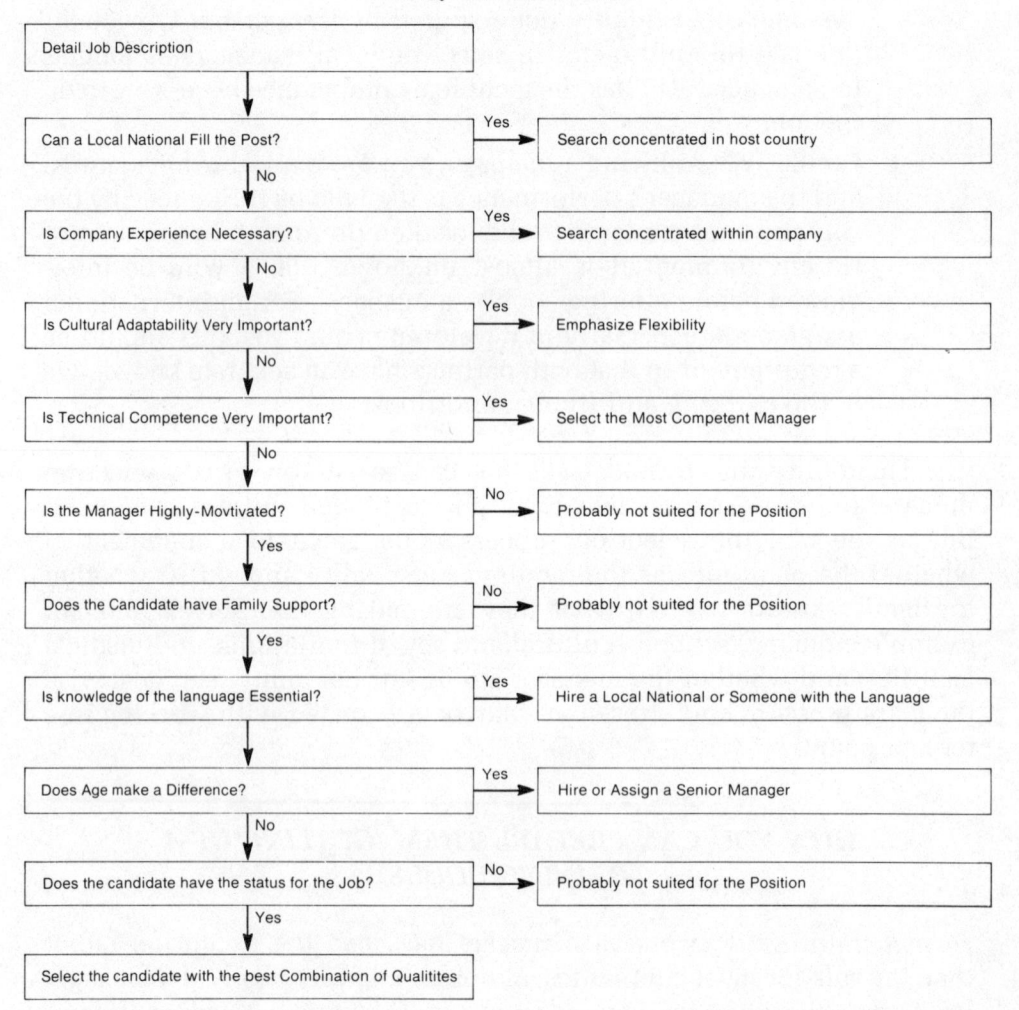

```
Detail Job Description
         │
         ▼
Can a Local National Fill the Post?  ──Yes──▶  Search concentrated in host country
         │ No
         ▼
Is Company Experience Necessary?  ──Yes──▶  Search concentrated within company
         │ No
         ▼
Is Cultural Adaptability Very Important?  ──Yes──▶  Emphasize Flexibility
         │ No
         ▼
Is Technical Competence Very Important?  ──Yes──▶  Select the Most Competent Manager
         │ No
         ▼
Is the Manager Highly-Movtivated?  ──No──▶  Probably not suited for the Position
         │ Yes
         ▼
Does the Candidate have Family Support?  ──No──▶  Probably not suited for the Position
         │ Yes
         ▼
Is knowledge of the language Essential?  ──Yes──▶  Hire a Local National or Someone with the Language
         │
         ▼
Does Age make a Difference?  ──Yes──▶  Hire or Assign a Senior Manager
         │ No
         ▼
Does the candidate have the status for the Job?  ──No──▶  Probably not suited for the Position
         │ Yes
         ▼
Select the candidate with the best Combination of Qualitites
```

short time, or the manager is needed immediately, all leading to a direct placement with little or no preparation.

The Japanese take the job of training a bit more seriously. The Ministry of International Trade and Industry set up an Institute for International Training and Studies near Fuji, and major corporations send their prospective overseas managers there for a full year of full-time formal training. This includes intensive training in English and another foreign language, area studies, and international management studies. Although you are unlikely to use anything as formal as this, there are a number of organizations in the United States like the American Management Association (AMA), or the World Trade Institute, that provide shorter courses geared to the manager's getting ready for an overseas assignment.

AN OUTLINE: Whether formal or informal, long or short, the course should be geared toward developing the skills necessary to operate overseas effectively. One of the best ways of determining these skills would be to ask Americans who have worked overseas what they are and then build or choose a training program that develops these skills. From the experience of most companies it is obvious that cultural sensitivity human relations skills, and ability to adapt are extremely important to success. It can be argued that you are born with or without these skills, that you either have them or you don't, and that a training course will not be needed if you have them and will be no good if you don't. The one statement that I would disagree with is that you don't need a training course. Obviously, you cannot learn a culture or how to adapt while sitting in a classroom, but you can learn a lot about the country and its people that will ease your entry into the job.

Whatever the length of a training course, be it one day, a week, or longer, the important elements can be covered around these five basic themes:

1. Culture, Religion, and Social Structure: This would cover such areas as methods of communication, greetings, colors, folklore, music, attitudes to work, time, wealth, and the future. It would describe class and ethnic divisions, family structure, and sources of status, as well as the content and influence of religion.
2. Politics and Economics of the Country: This would cover such areas as political structures, interest groups, corruption, freedom of expression, the role of the military, and in the economic area, the content of the GNP, balance-of-payments situation,

foreign-exchange controls, and income distribution. For example, to many Americans the concept of a one-party democracy is a contradiction in terms, but in certain countries where it operates, it need not be so at all. Similarly, since the manager will be dealing with the government, it could be of great significance to realize that what looks like an absolute dictatorship from the outside is, in fact, one-man rule that survives by reconciling the interests of many groups in a way not unlike a democracy.

3. Business Customs and Methods of Operating: This would cover areas such as labor conditions, methods of negotiation and resolving conflict, managerial styles, perception of foreign managers, perception of the company, and attitudes toward foreign investment.

4. Educational, Health, and Recreational Facilities: Since the assignment is really a family assignment, a thorough knowledge of these factors is very important.

5. How To Deal with Culture Shock: This would prepare the manager and the family for a series of symptoms that hit most people transferred into a culture that is very different from their own. Often, the assignment begins with a period of excitement and euphoria and descends into a period of culture shock. The degree to which this is overcome by the manager and his or her family will often determine the success of the manager in the post. To be prepared is half the battle, and to recognize the symptoms is the first step in overcoming the shock. It is a matter of amazement, still, to see highly educated and competent managers placed overseas, and hit by culture shock, who have no idea how common it is or how to overcome it. Local people's behavior seems to be stupid; institutions of government, frustrating; the culture, irrational; the workers, lazy; one's home country, identical to paradise; all leading to a tendency to withdraw from social relations with local nationals and into the expatriate ghetto, which reinforces all the prejudices that are already rapidly developing. This is the point where all the abstract qualities of flexibility, adaptability, and sensitivity to the culture are tested in practice, and the managers who succeed are probably those that have the greatest "feel" and understanding of the content outlined in the first three sections of this outline.

COMPENSATION: HOW MUCH WILL THE MANAGER COST YOU?

You send a manager overseas to make your business do better, operate more efficiently, and make a better product. But there is also a valid negative reason for careful selection and good preparation: A failure or the wrong choice can be very costly. Repatriation of a manager and his or her family is the worst-case scenario, but it can also be very costly if the manager stays on, performing at a level way below par. And, that is before you come to actual salary and benefit costs. In the case of an overseas manager, these escalate rapidly. For illustration's sake let's say you have a manager you plan to send to a fairly tough assignment, for example, Saudi Arabia or Indonesia, and his or her present base salary is $60,000. Here is how the escalation works:

TABLE 11.1   SALARY ESCALATION

Base salary	$60,000
10% Increase on promotion to the new post	66,000
Fringe benefits at 22% of base salary	14,520
Subtotal	80,520
15% overseas allowance	9,900
Post-differential adjusted to World Bank or U.S. government rates = 20% of base	13,200
Provision for housing at $2,000 per month	24,000
Travel costs annually, family of four (home leave)	16,000
Education allowance (2 × $6,000)	12,000
Subtotal of Special Overseas Allowances	$75,000
Total cost to the firm	$155,620

What you find, in other words, is that the cost of having a manager overseas is almost double the domestic cost, and, of course, if you start with a higher and more realistic base salary, the final total cost will be that much higher. There are also other extras that may be offered to make the job attractive to a home-based manager, like special insurance, moving and storage expenses, costs of selling or buying a home, and covering of tax differentials. It is easy to see why it is becoming so much more attractive to hire local or third-country nationals, except when rare specialized skills are needed or the operation is in a start-up phase.

MANAGING A FOREIGN WORKFORCE: WHAT YOU NEED TO KNOW

One of the most important functions of a foreign manager is to get the best out of the workforce. Before even getting to the country, here are some of the important facts you need to know:

A. Wage Rates: Salary levels have become a critically important factor in remaining competitive precisely because labor costs make up such a large part of production costs. This does not mean, however, that a low-wage area necessarily determines the location of a plant because there are other important factors like, for instance, transportation costs, import duties, or the economic or political situation. But when labor costs per day for assembly work in some Asian locations are lower than American costs per hour, it is easy to see why large parts of the textile and electronics industries have moved there.

B. Fringe Benefits: Fringe benefits can vary greatly from country to country, so it's important to see what the final labor cost is in a country when wages and fringe benefits are added together. For example, this can vary significantly in Europe where fringe benefits can cost the company as much as the base salary, while in other countries it is about 45 percent.

C. Are Benefits Required by Law? In the United States most benefits are negotiated, while in many other countries they are mandated by the government. Legislation may cover profit sharing, paid holidays, year-end bonuses, maternity leave, medical benefits, severance pay, disability, retirement insurance, and payments to the family if the employee dies.

D. Levels and Availability of Skills in the Areas You Need Them: If you wanted to hire accountants in the Philippines as part of a service contract, you would have a good selection of well-trained graduates. However, if you were looking for people to maintain sophisticated equipment, it might be more difficult. Of course, what many companies require in an overseas location is cheap, unskilled labor. But even then, within an existing pool of labor workers, it may be important to segment them into different categories, for example, the level of basic literacy or other skills you may require.

E. Training Required: The analysis of the levels of skills and wages

The Manager and the Workforce

leads directly to this question because you may have low wages and high training costs, or you need to know the availability of skills in order to determine the training costs.

F. Work Attitudes: This refers to attitudes toward manual labor, punctuality, assembly-line production, and supervision. We deal with how these attitudes vary in the chapter on culture, but this is an area where stereotyping can affect the judgment of a manager. There is a surprising similarity in workers' goals, everywhere, with the opportunity for individual achievement being a widely accepted value.

G. Social or Racial or Family Factors: Social status is a complex phenomenon in many countries, involving family trees, wealth, sex, number of children, race, religion, regional origin, and education. The manager needs to know how these will affect his or her operations, particularly in such areas as appointing supervisors, assigning jobs, and developing good working relations in the workplace.

KNOW THE LABOR LAWS

In some countries with strict labor laws it has come as a shock to many companies to realize how much their hands are tied or how much it costs to terminate a worker once he or she is hired. A number of countries, for example, require firms to give severance pay to any employee who has obtained permanent status, and permanent status may be reached in 60 to 90 days. Some U.S. firms jump to the conclusion that there is an unregulated labor market in most countries that have low wages or high unemployment or both. The opposite may be the case. Nearly every country has laws concerning working conditions, wages, and fringe benefits.

In South America, in particular, the severance pay may be very costly. For example, a subsidiary of a U.S. firm won a service contract that lasted three years at a fixed price. Everyone was delighted when the contract was extended for two more years. The firm was under the assumption that when the contract ended, the workers could just be let go. In fact, at the end, the severance pay was so costly that it almost ate up the profits of the five-year contract. In Mexico any worker discharged after a brief trial period must be paid three months' wages, and each year beyond the trial period the worker accumulates 20 more days.

IMPORTANT LABOR LAWS

1. Basic wage levels
2. Wage controls
3. Profit sharing
4. Paid holidays
5. Vacation time
6. Severance pay
7. Retirement insurance
8. Obligations to the worker's family
9. Health benefits
10. Laws governing unions
11. Laws applying to strikes
12. Restrictions on visas for foreign workers

Another law that may have serious implications for a firm concerns workers' visas. It has eased up now, but a few years ago it was difficult to get workers to do certain kinds of work in several European countries. Then you may need a foreign work force. Or you may need non-managerial expatriate technical specialists while you are starting up or while operating, and it may be difficult to get them into the country and to keep them there.

MOTIVATION, COMPENSATION, AND PERFORMANCE

What motivates people to perform well or poorly is a complex question that is far from being fully understood even in this, the most analyzed work force in the world. In a foreign environment it may be much more difficult, as different cultural values play a fundamental role in motivation.

Obviously, the most fundamental motivation for anyone is the need to eat, drink, and to have clothes and shelter. But once those needs are met motivations may vary considerably. For example, satisfaction of higher-level human needs in the job is not a common expectation of a worker in the western world. Rather, work is often regarded as a state or place of endurance necessary in order to get the money to do the fulfilling things of life elsewhere. So there is a sharp distinction between the work and nonwork life, and the effort to motivate workers may be concentrated on their physical or monetary needs. In contrast, the Japanese have tried to fulfill other higher needs, by building work-

The Manager and the Workforce

group identity, promoting loyalty and pride in the corporation, getting workers involved in decision making, and developing pride in their job.

In some countries, promising a worker security in his or her job or a clean job may be more important than offering him or her higher pay. A person may get higher status in the group or extended family from the type of job he or she holds, and this may be more important than promotion within the firm itself.

Another important element in motivation may be the management style. In this country this tends to be formalized and impersonal and associated only with the work environment. In other countries the expectations and motivations of the work force may be highly personalized in the manager, and performance may be closely tied to his or her attitude rather than to a monetary reward.

What all of this boils down to is that the manager needs to appreciate what motivates the workers in this particular foreign location, and that means he or she really needs a good understanding of the important values and priorities in the culture.

Compensation

In determining wage levels and the whole compensation package, six factors need to be taken into account:

1. Local law and government policy
2. The pay level necessary to recruit and hold on to competent workers
3. The balance between being vulnerable to the charge that workers are underpaid and exploited or overpaid and therefore creating an elite group of workers
4. Union contracts
5. The types of incentives and bonuses that increase productivity levels beyond what is normal in traditional local enterprises
6. The need to create a loyal work force for political reasons

Within these broad guidelines, the four major components of the compensation package will be the following:

1. Basic Wage
2. Fringe Benefits Required by Law or Union Contract: In some

countries these may be as much and even greater than the base salary

3. Voluntary Fringe Benefits: These are offered over and above what is required by law and may have several purposes like, for instance, building company loyalty, holding on to a trained work force, and creating a local interest group tied to the firm. This can be a useful tactic when the foreign firm wants to achieve these purposes without paying salaries that are way above local standards. Such benefits may include special training courses, low interest loans, a company clinic, transport allowance, and educational subsidies. One U.S. company in West Africa, in a delicate political environment, provided the following extra benefits to their workers: three hot lunches per week, two cold meals, family food packs, free medical care for the family, housing subsidies, and a recreational center. This has created a loyal work force, but there is always the danger in providing these services of highlighting the local government's inability to provide them, not only to the workers' families, but to all the people.

4. Performance Incentives: These may include piece rates, bonuses for exceeding established quotas, rewards for cost reduction or higher quality, and profit sharing. Profit sharing is legally required in some countries and is so much a part of tradition in others that it should be regarded as part of the basic wage. As a real performance incentive, profit sharing needs to be selective and to be continually reviewed. Otherwise, it quickly becomes the expected reward for all workers. Foreign firms should carefully examine local practices prior to initiating an incentive plan so that it does not antagonize the work force by being too restricted or antagonize other local firms by being too generous.

Performance Evaluation

This is also complicated in different social and cultural environments. In many countries position and status are determined ascriptively and not by ability or performance. Age, birth, and lineage are important bases for power and influence. In rewarding performance or promoting workers, the manager may run into ascriptive barriers that when breached can lead to conflict in the work force. It may also be difficult to discharge or even discipline incompetent workers not simply because of legal constraints, but because of links to supervisors, nepotism, or the position of the workers in the local community. This heightens the urgency of appropriate motivation as well as a good selection, training, and compensation package.

WORKING WITH FOREIGN LABOR UNIONS

Unions are a fact of life in most countries where multinational companies do business. One of the dangers for international managers is that they project their own domestic experience onto unions where the history and pattern of labor relations may be different. To understand the diversity of unions and union attitudes in less developed countries, it is necessary to look at the way historical and political events have shaped the way unions react today.

The origin of unions as we know them began in Europe with the breakaway from the tightly controlled organizations of crafts in the feudal system. The traditional crafts and their organizations began to break down with the emergence of an urban, modern economy in the Industrial Revolution in England and Germany. The union movement was strongly influenced by the analysis and research of Karl Marx and Frederick Engels, which highlighted the appalling condition of the working class. The Communist Manifesto was a revolutionary call for workers of the world to unite to overthrow the capitalist owners and to confiscate the means of production. This never materialized in the industrialized societies of Western Europe which Marx saw as the prime targets for proletarian revolution. Instead, both worker and political forces were able, through agitation and legislation, to change working conditions and to limit the almost absolute power of capital that existed in the early stages of the industrial revolution. The result was legislation in most countries in Europe on things like wages, holidays, length of the working day, safety regulations, and child labor.

But if history did not follow the path worked out by Marx, it was greatly influenced by his ideas with the result that European labor unions are closely associated with socialist ideology and several political parties have their base of support in labor unions. This is in sharp contrast to the United States where unions are generally nonideological, apolitical, and primarily interested in salaries and working conditions. Also, in Europe there is a history of collective action and struggle and of suspicion springing from the history of general strikes and violence. The manager in Europe will meet in the union leaders a group of men and women who really believe capitalism is an oppressive force and needs to be fought and restricted, if not overthrown. Such a position in an American union would be the exception rather than the rule even if manager–union confrontation is at times equally intense.

In less developed countries the tradition is much closer to the European example than to the American. This results from the ties that were established between the unions of the colonial powers and the unions in the colonies. The matter is complicated by a distinctive factor in the history of Third World unions, namely, their active involvement in the national struggle for independence against the colonial powers. The leaders of the political or military revolt and the leaders of unions were closely united in the pre-independence struggle. The result has been that most of these unions are highly politicized and some have very close contacts with ruling parties that they helped place in power in the first place. Moreover, the multinational company, whether from the former colonial nation or not, is very easily identified with the foreign power and the former freedom struggle. The result is that it may be difficult for the firm to confine its discussions and negotiations purely to economic issues. The management's best interest lies in dealing with unions that are strong locally, that are nonpolitical, representative of the work force, and concerned for the workers' welfare, as their number one priority.

CONCLUSION

There are many opportunities in the international market and many require a foreign manager to exploit the opportunity effectively. These opportunities vary from the regional market that needs an aggressive marketing manager, to the production plant or subsidiary that needs a production or financial manager, to the technical assistance team under a World Bank contract that needs a chief of party. Other members of an overseas team may have weaknesses, workers may not be fully trained or there may be government intervention that makes efficient operation impossible. But, if the manager is up to the job, he or she will be able to get the best out of a bad situation. But, on the other hand, no matter how good the other factors in the operation are, a bad manager usually means a less-than-efficient operation. This is particularly true in the markets of the developing countries where the manager has to play many roles and the most important skill of all may be negotiating with the government and getting documents signed. The irony is that a manager may have the best technical skills available and still be a very inefficient manager overseas. That does not mean that technical skills are not important. It has to be presumed the manager has the required technical skills to do the job. But what is of even greater importance is the ability of the manager to play an expanded role and to adapt and adjust in a new and strange environment. That's why a clear and detailed description of the job is important as well as a clear set of selection criteria. A training or orientation course will, in the long run, only provide some fundamental information that will be used to good effect by the manager who has the latent ability to do the job and will be of little help to the one that cannot.

12

BREAKING THE CULTURAL BARRIER

A major U.S. package-goods exporter forgot that many residents of the Middle East read from right to left. In an ad featuring a laundry detergent, dirty clothes were shown in a pile on the left-hand side, the soap powder in the middle, and the spotlessly clean clothes on the right. For a woman looking at the ad in the Middle East the soap dirtied the clothes. General Motors made a car called the Nova in the United States that sold very well over many years. It was a failure when they tried to sell it under the same name in Spanish-speaking countries where "Nova" means "it does not go."

Double-meaning words or sentences are a great source of humor for the British. They found it immensely amusing when a U.S. packager instructed the customer to open the package by "stripping off the top and pushing in at the bottom." Another ad said that a certain product was "as smooth as a baby's bottom," which in translation into Japanese comes out as being "as smooth as a baby's arse." And it's a good job that not too many women do business in the Middle East. A laundry list in a hotel, among many other errors, left out the "R" in "lady's shirt." Another hotel in Tokyo wanted to instruct its occupants that the maid would do the ironing for them. The instruction informing them of this read as follows: "The flattening of underwear with pressure is the job of the chambermaid. To get it done, turn her on."[1] And it is not just at the level of poor translation that problems arise. Saudi Arabia is a very large customer for British exports, so it was a breakthrough when the Saudi king decided to visit Britain. At the airport to meet him, the prim and proper male prime minister of the time took two steps backward when the king went to kiss him on both cheeks in a traditional Arab greeting. As the cameras covered all details of the event, a major diplomatic incident was barely avoided.

The one common mistake running through all of these incidents is the misuse of language or symbols that mean one thing in one culture and have a different meaning in another. In short, the cause of the problem of cross-cultural difficulties is communication, and by that is meant not just the spoken or written word, but all the elements of a culture that form a barrier to mutual understanding. As the preceding examples show, there is room for costly mistakes. But a more positive way to look at the problem is to examine how communication can be improved precisely because it affects so many areas of business.

Good communication is essential between your firm and its customers, with your agent or distributors, with your employees, and with the government and other important actors in the international business place. In order to understand the context of the problem and how to overcome some of the difficulties in practice, it is useful to look at the idea of cultural distance, communications across cultures, and components of culture that have an impact on marketing and management.

FROM HERE TO CHINA: A LONG CULTURAL DISTANCE

In the domestic business environment it has become standard practice to use cultural analysis in understanding the local market. The modern marketing manager is expected to understand the impact of cultural and behavioral patterns, such as the role of family members in decision making, different consumption habits, the spread of innovation, and the role of social classes. And, that is in a market that, in general, has the same language and culture and shares the same values, assumptions, ways of action, and social conditions. Of course, there are significant cultural minorities with distinctive tastes and values in the U.S. market, but they fit more logically into one of the non-U.S. groups later described than into the overall description of the U.S. market.

For illustration purposes cultural distance from the U.S. market can be described in three steps:

1. The first step outward in cultural distance is to the markets of Europe, Canada, Australia, and at some levels the industrialized nations of South America. These markets have unique qualities and differ in several respects from each other and the U.S. market. But they share a common tradition and way of thinking coming from their common heritage in the Judeo-Christian religion and in the Greek and Roman method of logic, language, and reasoning.

2. At a greater cultural distance are the Islamic countries of the Middle East, Africa, and Asia that became such attractive new areas of international business with the sharp rise in oil revenues. They share a lot of the elements of the Western tradition described above including the Judeo-Christian religion and elements of the Greek and Roman way of thinking. But there are also large differences associated with the belief in Islam and the values, assumptions, and social relations that go with it. There is a tradition of trade, commerce, and negotiation. There is also a distinctive independence, pride, and confidence springing from the belief in Allah and the security of knowing that they possess the most recent revelation of God through Mahommed and that all other religions, to one degree or another, are still in the dark.

3. At a greater cultural distance are the countries of Asia and particularly of the Pacific Rim where two-way trade and investment to and from the United States is becoming increasingly important. There is little in the foundations of these cultures with which Western business people have a direct familiarity. The languages are different, as are the ideas, assumptions, and values on which communication is based. The religious traditions of Animism, Buddhism, Taoism, and Hinduism are very distinctive, and even where there is a Western superstructure like, for instance, Christianity in the Philippines, the real motivating force continues to be ideas and values more fundamental to the culture. Obviously, it is a large oversimplification to lump cultures as rich and diverse as these into one category, but it is useful in outlining different degrees of difficulty in communicating into these cultures and in preparing oneself for the different problems that arise in different markets. For example, take the problem of "losing face." Nobody wants to lose

face, but in the rough and tumble of American business dealings it is regarded as part of normal procedure and a more senior executive has little problem overruling someone in order to clinch a deal or get the job done. In the Middle east "face" is important, but there is a directness and bluntness at many levels of communication. Indeed, many Western business people are surprised at the apparent ferocity with which Arabs may argue even when one party is far more senior and important than the other. But it always tapers off to an amicable conclusion and nobody loses face because the rejection of an idea or a position is not considered a rejection of the person. The Far East can be very different. Saving face is extremely important and requires a lot of time and effort. In the Philippines, to raise your voice in anger or reproach is a mortal sin the size of a bulldozer. Indirect communication and the use of intermediaries to convey unpleasant messages are common techniques, and the subtleties are very easily missed. For example, there are many different ways of refusing someone, and there are different ways of saying "No." Getting behind the subtleties of a culture to what is really meant or being conveyed is a difficult process and requires years of living in the culture as well as thorough knowledge of the language. From a practical point of view, for a home-based or field-based manager dealing with many cultures, the goal of getting inside one or several cultures is unrealistic. But it is essential that a person involved in international marketing or management have cultural sensitivity and understanding of some of the basics involved in trying to communicate across cultures.

BREAKING THE COMMUNICATION BARRIER

One way of looking at communication is to see it as involving three steps:

1. Putting your meaning into words
2. Sending the message
3. Deciphering of the meaning by the target audience

This process is illustrated graphically in Exhibit 12.1. The problem lies in the fact that the words or symbols that carry your message or bear

EXHIBIT 12.1

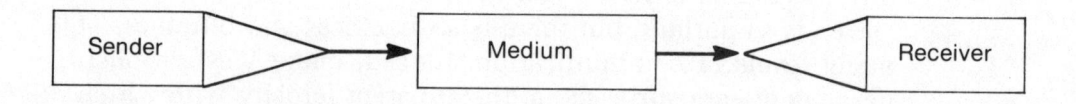

```
[Sender] ▶ [Medium] ▶ ◀ [Receiver]
```

the meaning you want may mean a totally different thing for the person receiving the message. In other words, the medium does not convey the meaning intended, or indeed it may convey a totally different meaning. For example, many ads in this country depict a situation of relaxation or satisfaction with a product by showing the happy consumer with his legs on a table or desk facing the camera. In the Middle East pointing the sole of the foot at another person is an insult. Here, there is a message that is intended, satisfaction with the product by a medium, that is the photo, and the message conveyed is very different from the message intended. The photo is no longer a means of communication, but rather a communication barrier.

The greater the cultural distance the greater the barriers, and of all the barriers the greatest is language because in many ways language is a window into a culture. Many people see a new language as just a different set of signs that convey the same meaning. For example, the British will say they want their "lorry filled with petrol," while Americans say they want their "truck filled with gasoline." In this case it is just a case of different symbols conveying the same meaning. But language is a much more complex thing than just a set of cold signs. The words, the structure of sentences, the background meanings all convey different content in different languages. That is why learning the language is the best way of learning the culture because in learning the language, you are learning the culture. But, if you learn the language as just another set of symbols, as you would use a new mathematical formula, then your difficulty may be compounded because now you are using *his* words to convey *your* meaning, and because they are his words, he is picking up a very definite meaning that you may not intend.

The problem is further complicated by the degree of explicitness in verbal communication. In the United States and other Western countries

Breaking the Cultural Barrier

messages are explicit, direct, and to the point. There is little left unsaid and few nonverbal signs. In other cultures it is very different and the greater the cultural distance, the greater the difference. Now there is less of the meaning in the words and more in the facial expressions, the tone of voice, the place of communication, the words chosen. The message may be contained more in what is *not* being said than in what *is* being said. This is why it is so important to get beyond the language to the real meaning that is being conveyed. Not understanding the message being conveyed can be costly. A consulting firm in the Middle East put a lot of time and effort into preparing a complex technical and cost proposal for a Saudi client. Negotiations dragged on, and at the end the client requested a new, extensively revised and costly proposal. The firm was preparing to put more money into the effort when an American manager, working in another part of the business, informed them that this was really a way for the Saudi to let them know that he was no longer interested in their proposal.

If communication across cultures is so difficult, what steps can be taken to overcome the barriers? Here are ten steps that can be taken that will make communication easier.

TEN STEPS FOR EASIER COMMUNICATION

1. Before visiting the country or beginning to do business, study the important distinguishing features of the culture. You will not really be learning the culture, but rather *about* the culture and that is sufficient to avoid the bigger mistakes.
2. Don't take chances with jokes or "off-the-cuff" comments that may convey a very different meaning than you intend.
3. Use an interpreter to bridge the cultural gap. But be careful in selecting him or her because you are adding another link to the communication chain and the interpreter needs to understand both sides of the culture gap if he or she is not to distort your message.
4. Use your agent or distributor to communicate with local customers. He or she has a business orientation, knows you and your product, and even if your agent or distributor doesn't speak your language that well, he or she may be more useful than a professional interpreter.

5. Use local specialized personnel where possible. For example, relying on their communication skills, you can use a local advertising agency, a local writer to write important letters, or a local lawyer or manager, all in their areas of expertise.
6. Don't force the pace of communication. Your client knows your goal and what you want, but your client may need a lot of time to digest information, to gain a consensus, or to reach a decision.
7. Realize that you too are communicating nonverbally. When you sit impatiently for two hours waiting for the meeting to begin and then have it interrupted by what appears to you to be all kinds of irrelevancies, realize that your impatience may show no matter how you try to cover it up.
8. Know that as an explicit communicator in an indirect culture you may be at a disadvantage because you are not proficient at reading nonverbal signs, whereas the people on the other side are.
9. Do not turn down social invitations even if you don't speak a word of the language and your host or fellow guests don't speak a word of yours. This may be part of their process of building trust and learning more about you.
10. Learn from the experience of other expatriates who have work experience in that country. It is possible to pick up more good tips in one hour from a culturally sensitive expatriate than from days of reading about or trying to understand the culture.

THE CONSTITUENTS OF CULTURE AND HOW THEY AFFECT YOUR BUSINESS

You don't choose a culture, you inherit it, and the most spontaneous and natural thing is to believe that the way you act, think, behave, and organize is the best way and is the standard by which all other cultures should be judged. Indeed, the differences in other cultures are likely to be regarded by many as exotic, retarded, or at least, strange ways of behaving. Very often it is only when you really begin to see another culture from the inside that you can begin to appreciate why people act differently. And very often it is only then that you appreciate what makes your own culture distinctive, that you realize it is only one among many ways of looking at the world. Most of us take our culture for

Breaking the Cultural Barrier

granted and fail to realize how relative it is. One way of testing your knowledge of your own culture and of highlighting it is to answer the questionnaire in Exhibit 12.2.

The questions appear straightforward at first, but turn out to be a bit more difficult to answer in practice. What you have as a result is a profile of your own culture and your own way of doing things. Now you can examine the components common to all cultures. Even if every culture is different, there are elements of culture that are universal, and by looking at these you can get an idea of the way each has an impact on your business. The important parts of any culture can be broken down in several ways. For our purposes here we concentrate on technology, language, law, education, values/attitudes, religion, and social organization. This provides a useful framework for looking at all cultures and for examining how some components have an impact on your business. We have already seen the impact of politics, law, and language. We have dealt with the work force and with levels and types of education. Here we will examine the impact of technology or material culture, values and attitudes, religion, and social organization.

EXHIBIT 12.2

CULTURE QUESTIONNAIRE

1. List in order of priority the three top values of most Americans:
   A.
   B.
   C.
2. List in order of priority three American status symbols.
   A.
   B.
   C.
3. Give three examples of how messages are communicated non-verbally between Americans.
   A.
   B.
   C.
4. How are American social classes differentiated?
5. Describe an American tradition that another culture might regard as ridiculous.
6. Name two colors you would not use in packaging or advertising in the United States.
7. How do Americans measure time?
8. What is distinctive about the way Americans greet one another?

9. What role does religion play in life decisions?
10. Describe the qualities of an American role model.
11. How would outsiders describe an American stereotype?
12. What is an American's attitude toward work?
13. What is an American worker's attitude toward his boss?
14. Identify a ritual specific to America.
15. Describe a taboo specific to Americans.

TECHNOLOGY

Technology is really a bad name for a very simple thing, namely, the way things are produced in a particular market.

In a highly sophisticated market like Japan or West Germany, it is possible to develop input-output tables that are based on the needs and end products of a highly developed mechanized method of production. This can help determine the demand for your product. In a society with a lower level of technology, or means of production, no such conclusions can be reached.

But levels of production can have a more direct effect. Even in Europe the lack of freezer capacity in the home means there is a much smaller market for many frozen products. Similarly, the presence or absence of electricity or its costs or voltage can affect you if you are selling washing machines.

In less developed countries there is a big emphasis on what is called "appropriate technology." What this usually means is machinery that is durable, simple to operate, and easy to repair. Above all, in a situation of high unemployment, production should be labor intensive, that is, it should create jobs, not make them redundant. In short, what different levels of technology or production mean is that you may need a cheaper, adaptable product that fits the technology of your new market.

VALUES AND ATTITUDES

Looking at the values and attitudes of a culture is a complicated task, as you probably discovered in answering the preceding cultural questions. It is a bit like self-analysis made more difficult by the fact that all aspects of a culture are intertwined. What we will concentrate on here are attitudes and values that have the most direct impact on the marketing effort in a foreign culture.

Attitudes Toward Material Possessions

In the absence of a traditional hereditary class system and the status that goes with it, Americans often use their material possessions as indicators to others of how they wish to be perceived. The location or size of a person's house can indicate his or her status, as can the size of his or her office. One danger of this attitude is that what is perceived as giving status here can be regarded as showing lack of class elsewhere. In positioning a product in the market, or in advertising, it may be a mistake, for example, to highlight the status role of a product rather than its use or the extra benefits it can give. A U.S. consumer may be impressed with a product with a new faddish design; a European may be far more impressed with durability or convenience. A recent radio ad for cable TV has two kids comparing how smart their dads are by the fact that one has installed cable TV and the other hasn't. In other countries, this could be offensive as a sales pitch, particularly where there are different parent-child relationships where children have little say on purchasing decisions or where parents are never criticized in public, even by implication.

Very often competition or acquisition is viewed with suspicion as a danger to the social cohesiveness that has been built up over centuries in many countries because of a situation of scarcity. Obviously, a society of abundance, like the United States, is a marketing manager's dream, where possessing the newest and latest may be a status symbol and where there are frequent changes in taste and a shorter life cycle for products. Marketing these types of products in other countries demands careful market research and perhaps a very different positioning than in the home market. For stable consumer items, or industrial products, the problem is much less severe.

Attitudes Toward Time

In negotiations, planning, meeting deadlines, and getting paid there may be nothing quite as frustrating as different attitudes toward time. Very few cultures give the same importance to time as Westerners do.

The Filipinos are so sensitive to this difference and the upset that it can cause in business and other relationships that it is quite common in setting the time of a meeting with a foreigner to ask: "American or Filipino time?" The former means a 1 o'clock meeting will usually take place before 2 o'clock; the latter means it can take place any time later in the day! And it is easy to draw the wrong conclusions. In trying to nail down a contract in Latin America, an American businessman was left sitting for hours in the antechamber of a deputy minister's office. This he interpreted as a very bad omen indeed. To his surprise, after he was called in the minister proceeded to finalize and sign the contract. The delay was an effort to get all the smaller things out of the way to concentrate on this large question.

One of the advantages of this flexible attitude toward time is that fixed delivery dates for goods or start-up or completion dates for contracts are not nearly as rigidly adhered to as in the domestic market. But, on the other hand, counterpart services or goods that are to be supplied by the other party are often delayed. One of the biggest mistakes that can be made in many environments is to set deadlines for yourself or others. Be careful of mousetrapping yourself on the one hand by setting unrealistic target dates. On the other hand, imposing deadlines on others may actually lead to a slow-down or the dropping of a "glass window" over further communication or cooperation. It is important to realize that despite every best effort by a local partner or manager, he or she is unable to deliver on time, not because of any lack of good will on the partner's or manager's part, but because of the lack of supporting staff, procedures or institutions.

Attitudes Toward Change

In introducing a new product into the domestic market, most companies use adjectives like "new," "breakthrough," or "unique." That is because change is rapid and rapidly accepted. Other countries have a much greater allegiance to tradition and may stick with the old reliable and even out-of-date product rather than choose the new for newness's sake. In such a society, and even European nations have quite conservative markets in this sense, it may be much better to relate the new to the traditional than position it as a "breakthrough." The problem may be compounded if your product affects traditional ways of doing things or is a threat to existing skills or power structures. For example, many accountants in small businesses resist computerization, not because it's costly but because they fear the change or they see the threat of somebody doing in a few hours what he or she takes several days doing. It is reported that when King Faisal wanted to introduce television into Saudi Arabia, the religious leaders strongly objected until he explained that a television is like a drinking glass; it's neither good nor bad in itself unless you put whiskey in it. And, since television could be used for preaching and prayers as well as entertainment, the mullahs consented. So change can be resisted because people fear that it may change religious, social, or political traditions. Many companies have identified a market need for their product like, for instance, a new and better means of production, but discover the demand never meets expectations, often because of resistance to change.

Attitudes Toward Color, Music, and Folklore

Sometimes the color of the package or product can affect demand because colors can mean different things in different cultures. For example, black is a color for mourning in the United States and many European countries, while white is the color for mourning in Japan and other Asian countries. So, a marriage picture with the man in a black tuxedo and the woman in a white wedding dress could mean the man is happy and the wife-to-be is mourning or vice versa depending on where you live! But other colors may mean very different things to different people. To many Westerners pink and yellow are feminine colors while blue is masculine. In contrast, in Iran, blue is one of the least acceptable colors. To illustrate how subjective, emotional, and culture-bound colors are all you have to do is see the usage in the United States, where it is common to talk about "feeling blue," "being in a dark mood," "green with envy," or "red with anger." So colors affect products, packaging, and advertising. A safe and practical rule to follow is that the colors of the national flag are safe to use.

Music is also quite distinctive from country to country, as is folklore. It is quite easy to make a mistake using a folklore image or stereotype. Marlboro has run their cowboy ad successfully for years in the United States, where the cowboy is a romantic figure that conjures up all kinds of historic value-laden traditions. But in Paraguay the cowboy is no hero; he is literally a worker who lives on the range with his cattle for weeks and is paid little. The urban consumer may want a very different cigarette than the cowboy. On the other hand, if you are able to tie in your product to folklore in the host market, it may be of great assistance in marketing and advertising. For example, many of the newly rich urban Saudis long for their Bedouin roots and drive out into the desert at night for parties and get-togethers. A tie-in of the product to that tradition would have a powerful appeal.

RELIGION

Religious values are the source of many aspects of human behavior even in the industrialized countries. Many sociologists and social historians attribute the start and success of the Industrial Revolution to the beliefs springing from Luther and Calvin that hard work and thrift glorified God. This tradition carries on in many countries today and is sometimes used to explain why the Protestant countries in Northern Europe are more economically advanced than the Catholic countries of Southern Europe. A bigger contrast still exists between the Protestant ethic and Hinduism and Buddhism where, far from riches being a sign of the favor of God, they are viewed with suspicion, as is strong competitive behavior or acquisitiveness. The role of marketing and advertising is to stimulate wants and desires. A central tenet of Buddhism states that the way to be content and at peace is to suppress these feelings. Obviously, this is going to affect marketing and advertising.

Islam, in its stricter forms, forbids direct contact between men and women in the workplace. Every day time has to be set aside for prayer, and during Ramadan, the month of prayer and fasting, both production and consumption of goods and services may drop off. There is also a fundamental fatalism at the center of Islam where many Muslims believe that what will be is already predetermined. So, when you are planning a project or projecting sales or laying out a critical path for action to achieve a goal, the final word most often is "Inshallah," namely, "God willing" with the implication that if things do not materialize the way your rational, carefully worked out plan intended, it is not because of human weakness or error, but because it was not meant to be.

SOCIAL ORGANIZATION

This refers to the position of men and women in a society, the kind of family structure they belong to, and group organizations and behavior and relationships people have with one another. Such structures directly affect marketing. If the family structure is extended, rather than nuclear, then it may be more effective to address the family as a unit in the selling effort rather than just as individuals. Another important factor relates to who makes the purchasing decisions. In many countries it may be the man, in others, the woman. Social organization is also important in market segmentation. For example, the senior citizen segment is very important in the United States because senior citizens are primary purchasers for their own needs while in countries where the family is more extended or less nuclear the segment may not be as important. Similarly, in countries where fewer mothers work outside the home, or children have little or no say in purchasing decisions, directing the marketing effort at children will have little effect.

Perhaps the most important factor of social organization is class structure and class mobility. In many Western countries and particularly in the United States there is, generally speaking, relatively easy upward mobility based on merit. In other cultures, movement is far more rigid, and from a marketing point of view it is important because the distribution of purchasing power and class structure are closely related. In summary, you need to know what is the purchasing unit, who makes the purchasing decisions, and what class structure exists and how it affects the segmentation of the market.

In evaluating the impact of culture on your marketing effort, it may be helpful to synthesize as many of these components as possible in a matrix to highlight the likely consequence of each component for different parts of the marketing effort. An example of such a matrix is given in Exhibit 12.3. It can be adapted depending on your product, your market, or the elements of culture that affect your marketing effort. What it gives you is a systematic way of checking out the major implications, and it could be useful as a checklist with a local distributor or research firm to make sure that major implications of some components of the culture are not being overlooked. For example, under social organization, if there is an extended family structure it would affect research in the way the market is sampled and who is interviewed; it may affect design by, for example, making a larger product or container for a larger family size; it may affect advertising depending on who is making the family decision; it may affect positioning by downplaying labor-saving qualities where there is abundant free labor; and it may affect price by the fact that family resources, not just an individual income, are available to pay for the product.

EXHIBIT 12.3—A CULTURAL MARKETING MATRIX

MARKETING IMPLICATIONS					
Components of Culture	*Research*	*Design*	*Advertising*	*Positioning*	*Price*
Language					
Technology					
Values and Attitudes					
Religion					
Social Organization					
Color					

SOME BASIC DO'S AND DON'TS

We have discussed several important aspects of culture and drawn out some of the implications for the international marketer or manager. Obviously, it takes a long time to penetrate into and adjust to a different culture, but a lot of what has been said can be summarized in a few basic rules that will serve as guidelines when entering a new market or before getting an opportunity to get to know it first-hand.

Do's

1. If you are dealing with one major market or area, or are assigned to a country, learn the language.
2. For important letters, contracts, and other documents always back-translate. In other words, get a good translator, but after the job is done get someone else to translate it into English, and then check it.
3. As well as learning how things are done in a strange culture, also learn why. By getting behind the actions to the values and traditions that motivate them, you are likely to develop a much greater understanding and tolerance of different forms of activity.
4. Draw up a checklist of the important components of each culture you will be working in, and ask how each element is likely to affect different aspects of your marketing or production effort. The matrix given on page 235 will assist you.

Breaking the Cultural Barrier

5. Be backwards about coming forward. For better or for worse, many countries perceive American business people as aggressive and overbearing and accuse them of projecting a superiority image. Little notice is taken of this type of behavior inside the U.S. market, but even in some European countries and especially in the Far East, people downgrade their achievements or attribute them to others or to Allah or to luck. A direct blunt hard sell in such an environment is often the wrong approach.

Don'ts

1. Don't try to set the pace at which business must be done in another culture. For most American executives time is scarce and costly, and business transactions are quickly agreed to based on the judgment of advisors or experts. In most of the rest of the world there is a very different pace, and to be successful, you have to fit into it.
2. Beware of being suicidally direct in business matters. The people with whom you will be dealing are likely to be just as keen to do business and to make a profit, but there is a ritual and an understanding they need to build up prior to finalizing any deal. So the first meeting, or even the second, may be spent on what appears to be pleasantries and social chatter, but it is far from being wasted time and to short-cut it may be costly.
3. Unless you know the language well, don't use it casually. Many foreigners appreciate the attempt to learn the language, but others are turned off by the throwing around of a few words you have picked up. And sometimes it may cause damage, if only to your own pride, if you use a word or an idiom incorrectly.
   what appears to be pleasantries and social chatter, but it is far from being wasted time and to short-cut it may be costly.
3. Unless you know the language well, don't use it casually. Many foreigners appreciate the attempt to learn the language, but others are turned off by the throwing around of a few words you have picked up. And sometimes it may cause damage, if only to your own pride, if you use a word or an idiom incorrectly.
4. Don't assume that what works or is best in the U.S. market is easily transferable to other markets. It sometimes is, and marketers are trying to make it more so by the development of

world brands. But the assumption that it isn't transferable is safer, especially if the cultural distance is great. This applies more to consumer goods and is not changing very fast because often there are deeper reasons than simple taste for the difference, reasons such as religion, tradition, national pride, or independence.

5. Don't accept stereotyping of markets or consumers by "old hands" who may be "burned out" because of some of the methods they adopted in the market in the first place. Stereotyping attributes qualities to people on the basis of the assumptions made about the culture or the country as a whole. Behind it lies the belief in the superiority of one's own culture and ways of doing things so that everything is judged by that standard. You hear statements like "The Mexicans never pay you on time," or "A contract with a Turk is not worth the paper it is written on," or "British managers have no imagination," or "Getting anything done in Indonesia requires a bribe." Obviously, there is no smoke without a fire, but it's a bad start in a market to begin with such blanket assumptions.

DOING BUSINESS IN THE ARAB WORLD

Culture is such a nebulous concept that the danger is that you could theorize about it all day and at the end know little of what it means in practice. To avoid this we will now take a look at what it means in practice in doing business, first in the Middle East and then in the Philippines, two areas that are quite a distance culturally from the United States but are also countries with a large U.S. involvement.

In many parts of the Middle East, including Saudi Arabia and the Gulf States, many of the external appearances indicate a cosmopolitan environment. You arrive at a modern airport with efficient immigration and customs procedures, you drive in a General Motors taxi to a Hilton or a Sheraton hotel, and you have a choice of cold cereal for breakfast. But at your first meeting the familiarity ends, and you realize you are in the middle of a very different cultural world. You are greeted with elaborate handshakes or if you know the client well, with a kiss. The meeting may last an hour with no discussion at all of the business at hand. And the same may happen at the second meeting. And just when you think you are getting down to business, others may walk into the meeting to get their business done or the phone may ring or even two

Breaking the Cultural Barrier

phones and your client has one on each ear as he also talks to you. Then tea is served, and again as you get down to business the meeting has to break up, for now it is prayer time. All through this you must never show or appear impatient and you must be very gracious in accepting any invitations or gestures of hospitality. It is an honor to be invited to an Arab home. To refuse is a major gaffe. When there, remember that his wife or older female children do not exist for you and should not be mentioned in conversation. It is unacceptable to spoil a good meal with conversation on a serious topic like business. In contrast to the Filipinos, Arabs can be very loud and animated in discussion amongst themselves on any number of topics, but this is a delicate area that, for you as a guest, it is not wise to imitate. Physical contact and handshaking at the beginning and end of a meeting are common. Facial expressions are quite expressive and can carry quite a weight of nonverbal communication. Clicking of the tongue usually signifies a negative response. You may sit in the traditional Arab style on the floor on cushions. It is very rude not to remove your shoes on entering the house, and you must tuck your feet under you so that the soles of your feet are not pointing at anybody. Be very careful you do not eat with your left hand or pass anything to another with it and be careful of the hand gestures you make. After a meal loud gastronomical noises that we regard as rude are sometimes considered a compliment to the host's excellent meal.

Meanwhile, business may be languishing, and you cannot really speed it up. But it's not really languishing from their side because all of this socializing and conversation is part of the effort to get a measure of you, your firm, and what you have to offer. Things may be considerably speeded up if you are "well connected," but it is quite common to have to make several trips before you get your foot in the door. But, there is one positive element in this, especially with private clients: When they get to know you and trust has been built up, the relationship is intended to be long and fruitful for both sides.

DOING BUSINESS IN THE PHILIPPINES

The same kind of superficial, modern similarities exist when you reach Manila as they did in the Arab world with the added attraction that the Filipinos you will be dealing with will speak English and will have gone through an educational system modeled on the American system. But, again, quite soon the differences begin to emerge. The family is the center of life, and questions about children and children's children and cousins and cousins of cousins are most acceptable. Business or progress or money can never interfere with the family. A strong social control is what is called in Filipino "hiya" and is very inadequately translated by the English word "shame." One of the greatest accusations that can be made against a person is "Walang hiya" or "They have no shame," or otherwise they would not have behaved in a certain way. If you do something consciously or unconsciously that breaches the "hiya" rules of behavior, it may seriously affect your future relationships.

A high priority is friendship, camaraderie, and smooth interpersonal relations. Open conflict is totally unacceptable as is overt competition or aggressive bargaining. There is a complex system of indirect communication used to convey information, especially information of the unpleasant variety. One such indirect method is the use of intermediaries who may also be verbally indirect. It is quite difficult at first for a foreigner to understand what is really being communicated, but the Filipinos themselves are quite familiar with the signs and nuances of indirect and nonverbal communication.

It is unrealistic to expect to find the drive and initiative of the American culture in the Philippines. Overhanging everything is a strong fatalism and the feeling that things are the way they are and there is very little you can do to change them. So planning and motivation of people by economic incentives are not as successful as elsewhere. Two of the most commonly used words in the language are "Bahala na," which really mean "That is the way things are and there is little we can do about them."

Progress is made in the Philippines by persuasion, compromise, and discussion. Nobody must ever lose face, and even if you raise your voice in frustration, it causes a loss of face and a retreat behind a veil of superficial friendliness by the Filipino. Again, all of this has a positive side because there are probably very few places in the world for doing business that are as friendly, light-hearted, hospitable, and cooperative as the Philippines.

CONCLUSION

International markets would be so much simpler to manage if they were all the same culturally. They would, of course, also be very boring. Many experts see a move toward a common culture and the acceptance of common products and brands. But, the evidence would seem to point, if anywhere, in the opposite direction with the growth of religious fundamentalism in the West and the Middle East, and the move in many groups to retain their distinctive cultural identities like, for example, the French in Canada. So the cultural challenge to the international business person remains and, for the American, it is a particular challenge in the large markets of Asia where strong manufacturing countries like Japan and South Korea are much closer culturally to the local markets. But, unlike many other obstacles in a foreign market, culture sensitivity and flexibility is one you have control over, and while it may take a considerable learning effort, with the right approach it is not a factor that will prevent you from effectively operating in most markets.

REFERENCE

1. There are numerous examples of similar incidents that have been part of international marketing folklore for years. David A. Ricks gives examples of the mistakes in communication in *Big Business Blunders;Mistakes in Multinational Marketing*. Dow Jones-Irwin, Homewood, Illinois: 1983

13

PROTECTING YOUR PROFITS: PRICES, TAXES, AND EXCHANGE RISKS

When everything is said and done it all comes down to the bottom line, to the profit you make and how you protect it. Financial management has become increasingly difficult as exchange rates have fluctuated back and forth ever since the break between gold and the dollar in the seventies. It is not just that it affects your immediate cash flow, but as we saw earlier, it raises the question about where you raise your money, in what currency, how you protect your income stream, and how you minimize your taxes. It also directly affects prices. The dollar has gone from strength to strength in the eighties, and American exports have become so much more expensive overseas and imports have become so much cheaper. As a result, many companies are whiplashed both ways. As they try to export, their prices become increasingly less competitive in dollar terms, while in the home market they are hit by imports that are so much cheaper. For example, in the early eighties the French franc went from less than 2F = $1 to close to 10F = $1. A bottle of French wine that was $10 in 1981 would be competing head-on with a bottle of similar quality from California, also at $10. Three years later, if nothing else intervened, the French wine should be $2. while the California wine still cost $10. This has put intense pressure not only on the domestic prices for many items, but also on export prices and the price companies can charge for their goods produced overseas.

HOW TO SET YOUR PRICE

In the normal run of things the first pricing decision a firm faces in an international market is the price of exports because that is usually the first step into the market. Even within exports, there is a difference between occasional sales, where the motive is to get the highest price possible, and a long-term pricing strategy for a long-term export market. Some exporters examine the export price in relation to the domestic price and try to determine whether it should be greater, equal to, or less than the domestic price. But that is the wrong starting place. If you are making the decision for a long-term commitment to an export market, the basic rule is "Establish an export price that will give you the greatest return on investment." That price can be higher or lower than domestic prices and may vary from market to market.

With this as your starting point, you are looking at conditions in the export market and then moving backwards to the price. We have already examined several of the important factors of the foreign market, but from a pricing point of view the two fundamental facts are demand and the competitive situation. These will determine the price range, and then the firm has to decide whether it can sell at that price. It is of little use to set a price related to the domestic price and then find that because of demand or level of local incomes or competition, you cannot penetrate the market. It is also of little use to set a price you cannot live with at the production end. So, the two ends of the equation are

1. What will the foreign market allow me to charge granted existing levels of demand, incomes, and the competition?
2. What is the minimum price I can afford to charge granted my costs?

Both sides of this divide are imporant; you cannot sell below production cost, but at the same time, from market to market, you may have considerable discretion on price.

Cost

In deciding on your cost, you have two choices as a domestic producer, that is, variable cost pricing or full cost pricing. In variable cost pricing you see exports as an added extra, over and above the domestic market, and so you are only interested in the extra or marginal cost of producing goods for the overseas market. The extra sales make a contribution to net profit while all other costs like R & D and company overhead are charged against the price of domestic sales. This could lead to a company being charged with dumping or with the charge that it is selling abroad at a price cheaper than at home. For a firm with surplus or underutilized plant capacity, this pricing strategy is attractive especially as the price is likely to be lower and more competitive in the foreign market. In a full-cost-pricing strategy, on the other hand, all products bear an equal share of fixed and variable costs of production and therefore should start off at the same basic price. Distinctive features of each market can lead to a change in this basic price. For example, you may have special packaging for international sales or special advertising in domestic sales. For the firm looking at international markets for the long run, and especially as international sales expand proportionate to domestic sales, or new investment is needed in production facilities, there is little choice but to go to full cost pricing.

The Retail Price to the Consumer

A phenomenon unique to the international market is the escalator effect that begins to work immediately in determining the price once the product leaves the plant. Figure 13.1 shows the resulting retail price in the home and foreign markets.

TABLE 13.1   PRICE ESCALATION

	Home Market	Foreign Market
Cost from Manufacturer	$50.00	$50.00
Overseas Transport	-0-	8.50
Insurance	-0-	1.35
Import Tax at 14%	-0-	8.38
Importers Margin 12% on CIF	-0-	7.18
Cost to Distributor	50.00	75.41
Distributor Mark-up at 15%	57.50	86.72
Retailer Mark-up at 28%	73.60	111.00
Percentage Difference		50%

This gives an idea of how much the price can increase compared with the domestic price. In this case, using an importer, the price is almost 51 percent more than the domestic price, and in many cases sales may be made where incomes are much lower. And, that price may go even higher if inland shipping costs are involved or if there are extra costs associated with credit or service.

If the firm can sell at this or a greater price at the retail end of the chain, good and well, and this is where the judgment comes in on market demand and the competition. If the price is too high and if there is excess capacity, the company may revert to marginal cost pricing, thus lowering the base on which the export price begins to escalate. Another alternative is to eliminate some of the steps on the escalator. For example, you can lower your price significantly by eliminating the importer and the distributor and selling directly to the retailer. You might be able to reduce the size or remove certain features of the product to make it cheaper, or if it was easy to assemble, you might ship it broken down under a lower tariff classification. Last, of course, you may be driven to move your production overseas to a low-cost area that will benefit all of your markets, including your domestic market. In this case, you are once again betting on exchange rates as well as production costs. Consider what happened to Volkswagen in 1974 when their big American sales were declining due to a strong mark. They moved to the United States for lower wages, lower transport costs, and lower-priced components. In 10 years a lot has changed, including a sharp turnaround in the value of the dollar, which made the German-produced Volkswagen relatively cheap.

HOW TO REDUCE YOUR PRICE	Yes	No
Can you bypass the importer?		
Can you bypass the distributor?		
Can you get a lower tariff classification?		
Can you adapt the product to make it cheaper?		
Can you reduce the mark-up of the middlemen?		
Can you produce the product cheaper?		

THE ROLE OF GOVERNMENTS IN PRICING

You don't make your pricing decision in isolation. In many countries the government can intervene in various ways to set prices. In determining the price you expect to get for your product and in evaluating the market generally, this is an important element to look at because, after all, your price will largely determine your net revenues and the return on the investment. Countries with high inflation rates are particularly prone to government controls of prices and also, most likely, of the movement of foreign exchange. There are some countries in South America where inflation is now in the area of 200 percent per year. This may look like an opportunity to make a killing, but for the exporter costs go up also inside the market, and the exchange rate is likely to deteriorate at, or near to, the rate of inflation, so locking in prices for any period of time becomes extremely risky. It is even more so if the product is manufactured in the country.

If the government imposes price controls, a firm could find its margins being eroded. Controls occur in countries with high rates of inflation, but in other countries with much lower inflation rates price controls have been used, as in the United States under Nixon, in Belgium in 1981, and indeed, in many of the other Western European countries. The controls may be across the board or limited to certain, usually consumer-sensitive industries, like pharmaceuticals or utilities.

Common Ways of Controlling Prices

A. Set a maximum price for products. This is usually done as part of a package where wage increases are also curtailed and prices of basic commodities are held down by price controls. Argentina, for example, introduced such a plan in 1985 to reduce inflation.
B. The government can control mark-ups imposed by importers, wholesalers, and retailers so as to keep the price to the final consumer at a certain level.
C. An elaborate bureaucratic permissions procedure may be established for all or some price increases. It may take months for any increase to make its way through the system.
D. If the government is in production itself or has stockpiles of commodities, it can force prices down by cutting prices or flooding the market with goods, thereby changing the supply and lowering the price.
E. The government may penalize a foreign supplier or assist a local producer by tariffs or tax concessions.

F. Government marketing boards also control prices. The government buys up all the local product and sells it both domestically and internationally. The purpose is usually to keep the price paid to the producer at the lowest acceptable level, eliminate the middlemen who really make the profits, and bring in revenue for the government. The result, usually, is inefficiency and the development of new competition overseas if the government's marketing board keeps the price high.

In setting the price, therefore, you are placed within fairly rigid limits that include costs like transport, insurance, and tariffs, but a different mode of entry like a joint venture or a direct investment can help you get around these. These different modes of entry bring us to the question of intracompany or transfer pricing.

TRANSFER PRICING

There is hardly any other area of international business that has attracted such criticism and attention by both the United States and foreign governments than transfer pricing. Transfer pricing refers to the price charged by the firm or the subsidiaries themselves, for goods and services transferred within the company. Most of these transfers are taking place across national boundaries into and out of countries with different tax rates, duties, and foreign-exchange controls, so you can see the scope that exists to achieve the maximum profits for the corporation itself. For example, you could lower duty costs in a high-duty country by undercharging your subsidiary for the product, or you could transfer profits out of a high-tax-rate country by overcharging a subsidiary, or you can move funds from a country that has exchange controls to one that hasn't, by overcharging. From there the profits can be transferred back to the parent. Given the opportunities to shift funds and profits, transfer pricing is obviously something that is going to occur if the company is able to get away with it. Needless to say, it is not a subject that company managers are willing to give details on while being interviewed on the six o'clock news. In practice, in countries where most of the major companies do business, the tax and customs authorities are capable of spotting abnormally high or low pricing. Second, the tax base and custom duties of most of the major trading countries are very close to one another in range, and most of them don't have exchange controls. The idea of having tax-haven holding companies in the Bahamas or Liberia or Panama to syphon off profits from high-tax countries is just not realistic anymore, as the IRS and other tax agencies long ago plugged that particular loophole. Anyway, in big companies it presumes a high degree of control by central management because, after all, what manipulative transfer pricing does is make one country manager look bad and some other one look good just on the basis of corporate practices. For the smaller or medium-sized company, the problem is obviously not that complex, but, nevertheless, it will face pricing decisions for the supply of services or ingredients or parts for the production process, even if it has only one plant overseas. You need to know the choices you face.

1. If you want to build up your subsidiary to make it a strong profit center with a good credit rating or if there is severe competition, you could supply it at manufacturing cost or at some margin lower than to outside buyers. If the product is a finished component selling at a higher price domestically, you could face problems because, in effect, you are transferring the mark up overseas. On the other hand, the profits may all be coming back later on.
2. You can employ an arms-length policy. You simply sell to the subsidiary at the same price as to any other unrelated buyer. This obviously is the most acceptable to the domestic tax authorities of all countries involved.
3. You can charge cost plus transfer prices. This is a strategy that lies someplace in between the two extremes outlined in paragraphs 1 and 2, and it can usually be worked out in a way that satisfies both foreign and U.S. tax authorities, especially if it is a uniform formula for all items for all countries.

In general, the move is more and more toward an arms-length policy, but if that is not the best for you it is appropriate to look at feasible alternatives. In the long run what will determine how well you are doing is how much you sell and for what price to buyers outside the firm. In other words, we are back to where we started, in the foreign market, with a product, trying to determine the best price granted the level of demand and the competition.

YOU GOT YOUR PRICE; WHERE'S THE MONEY?

It is possible to insure against commercial risks and political risks, but the best insurance against foreign-exchange risk is your own ability to forecast it and manage it to your own advantage. Of course, you could decide that you were only going to do business in dollars, which means you are not going to do too much foreign selling. More realistically, what you are going to have to do is shift the risk or create insurance for yourself by hedging and other techniques. The awful thing about foreign-exchange exposure is that you might have made a great sale, made a very good investment, and then have all the advantages wiped out in a sharp foreign-exchange swing. For this reason, management of foreign-exchange risk has become one of the most important management functions. Before going into the details of how you can shift risk and protect yourself, it is worthwhile to take a look at the scope of the problem faced by the large companies and how one company attempts to deal with it. In 1984 IBM estimated that the continual rise in the value of the dollar against the currencies of the many countries IBM operates in reduced its earnings by $278 million. Of course, in the period prior to 1980 the opposite was the case, as each pound, mark, Swiss franc or yen was worth that much more in dollars. Kodak is another company that is particularly vulnerable because, in 1984, 35 percent of its $10.6 billion in revenues came from sales overseas.

Kodak bills its subsidiaries overseas in their currencies and its exports are billed mostly in foreign curencies, so it has considerable exposure to currency fluctuations. Kodak actively manages its own foreign-exchange exposure in 16 different currencies to protect its imports, receivables, royalties, dividends, and service fees. At any one time up to $300 million is being moved in and out of different currencies at all hours of the day or night because the international-currencies markets operate in different time zones all over the world.[1] Some companies that have been burned by the exchange swings and wrong projections of the last few years tend to hedge all or most of their foreign-exchange exposure so they know what their cash flow will be and can make planning, pricing, and budgeting decisions accordingly. But hedging everything, when everything involves hundreds of millions of dollars, can be quite expensive and then may turn out to have been unnecessary, or worse still, may have led to missed opportunities if the rates go your way. Kodak takes a more activist approach, hedging much of its exposure and trying to make a profit or at least cover the costs of overhedging and making some extra cash on the currency swings. Of course, this presumes 24-hour-a-day monitoring and realiable, up-to-date information both on currencies and on where the company's exposure is at any one time. Not doing anything at all can be quite costly.

In 1984 the experts' consensus was that the dollar was going to drop. If you, as an exporter, had expected to receive 75 million German marks at the end of the year and you followed the consensus you would have done nothing because you expected the mark to strengthen. On the first day of trading in 1984 in Frankfurt your marks to be transferred at the end of the year were worth $27.3 million. At the end of the year they were worth $23.76 million because the mark went down, not up, went from 2.7458 to 3.1570. In January you could have locked in, in the futures market, a rate of 2.6450 marks to the dollar that would have given you $28.34 million at year's end. But, of course, that is the wisdom of hindsight. The real question is how you could have made an informed judgment of what was going to happen and what steps you could then have taken. The first part of this question was addressed in Chapter 3. Now we look at how you can shift and manage foreign exchange risk.

MINIMIZE YOUR MAXIMUM REGRET

Minimizing your maximum regret in foreign-exchange exposure is a matter of judging the extent of exposure, the amount of risk you are willing to take, and the price you are willing to pay for protection that may or may not be needed. Some of the steps you can take are relatively straightforward and involve an adjustment to risk as conditions change. Other techniques shift risk and can be costly. Here are some of the well-known steps you can take:

   A. Increase your prices in local currency terms to keep up with the devaluation you expect. In this way, even if the local currency drops, you are getting more of it for the same amount of product, and it should translate into an equivalent amount of dollars. Of course, this may not be as simple as it sounds. Price controls may prevent you from raising prices, or you may price yourself out of the local market or be driven out by the competition.
   B. If you are in a joint venture or assembly or manufacturing you could cut down on components with foreign content and reduce inventories of imported items. Of course, it may not be possible to do this because you cannot find local supplies or a significant component, or an input can be produced economically only in a central location.
   C. Run up local debt by increasing payables in relation to receivables. This reduces foreign-exchange exposure because if and

when a devaluation occurs, the debt can be paid off with less foreign currency. Of course, you better be right in your forecast, and this is a longer-term strategy. In a matter of a few weeks in early 1985 the British pound ranged in value from $1.08 to $1.21. A debt of a million pounds could be paid off by $1.08 million dollars at the low rate, but it would have cost $130,000 more at the high rate, all in a matter of a few weeks.

STEPS TO PROTECT YOURSELF FROM FOREIGN-EXCHANGE EXPOSURE

1. Increase your prices to keep up with rate changes.
2. Cut down items that use up hard currencies.
3. Increase debt in the vulnerable currency.
4. Speed up or slow down payment.
5. Balance currency exposure.
6. Use Hedges and Options.
7. Swap currencies.

D. Speed up or slow down payment. In this strategy you speed up or slow down payment depending on what you expect to happen to the currency in question. For example, if you are exporting and you expect a devaluation, you could shorten the payment period so you get your money out faster, or if you were paying for an import and you expected the foreign currency to revalue upward, you could prepay or pay immediately on purchase because if you were to wait and that currency were to go up, you would have to pay more in dollars. The same applies to other transactions. If you had a subsidiary in Mexico and you correctly predicted the great devaluation of 1982, you could have had the subsidiary make early payments for goods, services, fees, dividends, and any other payments due late in the year. At the same time if you were transferring dollars to the subsidiary, you could have delayed, and later in the year the purchasing power in pesoes would have increased significantly. But it may not be that easy, especially in the countries with weak currencies, where you most need it. Leads and lags put obvious pressure on the currency and contribute to the devaluation forecasts' becoming self-fulfilling. The country in question is likely to impose time limits on leads and lags and force payment within a certain period of time.

E. You can apply the strategy of balancing currencies in two ways: You can balance out payables and receivables between the different subsidiaries of a company so that the amount of exposure is limited to the subsidiaries that are owed a net surplus. For example, one subsidiary may have more British pounds than it needs while another may have a bill in sterling. By shifting these funds internally, a company saves the cost of buying and selling currencies through a bank. Balancing also saves the cost of hedging, and it can be used to take advantage of currency shifts. It is also used to describe a situation where you accept exposure in two or more currencies expecting them to balance one another out, also saving you the cost of hedging. It would work, for example, if you had a payable and receivable of equal amount in two European currencies that tend to move with one another. A riskier strategy is where you balance payables or receivables in a strong and weak currency with the expectation that any movement would balance itself out between the two.

F. You can use hedging and options. Hedging involves a contract, usually with a commercial bank, made now to exchange a certain amount of one currency for a certain amount of another at an agreed future date. A currency option is different. Here you purchase the right to buy a currency at a certain rate in the future, but you don't have to exercise the option when the time comes if it is to your advantage not to do so. Take the example of a British importer of textiles who has to pay in dollars but has to sell at a fixed price in pounds to retailers. In 1984 the pound's high and low against the dollar were 28.5 percent apart. The importer could buy dollars forward at a fixed exchange rate so that he has, in effect, locked in the price he will be paying for the textiles. But if the pound had strengthened by 15 percent, he would not get the advantage because he is locked into a specific rate. If the importer is in a very competitive business with low margins, he could be severely undercut by a competitor who did not hedge, who can now buy the textiles cheaper and therefore sell them to the retailer cheaper.

As an alternative, the importer could have purchased a currency option that protects him if the pound goes down but which he does not have to use if the pound goes up that 15 percent. The problem is that options are expensive, often around

5 percent of the total amount covered, and they must be paid for at the time of purchase.

For an exporter, another possibility is what is called a money-market hedge. As an importer or exporter, instead of buying or selling currencies forward or using options, you can set up a money-market hedge that works like this: Suppose you make a million-dollar export to England payable in pounds in 90 days. On the day you sign the contract you could borrow one million pounds, change them into dollars, and now you have your dollar price, less the transaction costs. In 90 days when you get paid in pounds you repay the loan. What you have done is lock in the price, and you have the use of the money for 90 days. Your cost is the difference between the interest on the sterling loan over the 90 days that you have to pay and what the dollars earn for you over the same period, plus the transaction costs.

G. Swaps are designed to give a subsidiary, a branch, or a joint venture local currency without actually changing currencies. This can be done in several ways. For example, you could deposit a million dollars, in dollars, in an Indonesian bank in, say, Switzerland, and in exchange the bank loans your Indonesian subsidiary a million-dollars worth of local currency. The subsidiary's liability is in local currency, the bank's liability to you is in dollars. After the subsidiary has paid back the loan you can withdraw your dollars. In this way the exchange risk is eliminated, but you have to calculate the cost in terms of the interest paid by the subsidiary and what alternative rates of return you could have received on the million dollars.

All of the means of protecting your foreign exchange exposure implies some cost, a cost that it is to be hoped you are able to build into your price. More fundamentally, financial management involves a lot of judgment in determining how much risk to accept, how much to cover, in what currencies, and over what period of time.

FACING THE INEVITABLE: TAXES

If you think the U.S. tax system is convoluted, wait until you start operating in several different countries. There are different types of taxes, different levels, different patterns of tax administration, and different tax incentives and overlaps in tax systems. And they have an impact on almost every aspect of international business. They affect the way you decide to enter a market, where you decide to locate, how you finance the venture, how much debt you incur and in what currency, and how prices and profits are arranged within the enterprise as a whole. An international tax specialist who knows the tax laws of the countries you are planning to enter will advise you on most aspects. What you need is the overall perspective so you can make the best judgment on entry method and on protecting your stream of profits.

Exports

Earlier, I mentioned the tax incentives offered to companies by both host and home countries to encourage them to invest overseas. There is also a tax incentive for exports. Many countries that have an indirect tax system give a rebate of most taxes once the item is exported. The United States has a direct tax system, and rebates of direct taxes are not allowed under the GATT rules. This has become quite a controversial issue in Japanese trade because in cars, for example, lower taxes and the tax rebate alone could give the Japanese manufacturer up to a $900 advantage per car in the American market. The United States adopted a different approach. Until 1985 a U.S. business could set up what was called a DISC, or a Domestic International Sales Corporation, that allowed an ongoing tax deferral on income derived from exporting. A DISC was really a dummy corporation used to defer taxes on up to 42.5 percent of profits earned from exporting. A DISC could be set up in any state with a nominal capital of $2,500. At least 95 percent of the DISC's gross receipts and assets had to be export related. The shareholder, namely the parent company, had to pay taxes on dividends paid by the DISC from profits that were previously deferred. But the DISC could hold on to the profits and use them as loans to the parent for production or research and development. A liberal policy on transfer pricing could lead to a sizable accumulation of profits in the DISC. Many countries that had indirect tax systems strongly objected to the DISC legislation, claiming it broke the GATT rules and gave U.S. exporters a competitive advantage. To meet some of those objections the DISC was replaced by FSC, or the Foreign Sales Corporation, in 1985. The benefits of the FSC are better insofar as they give a permanent exemption from federal taxes compared to the deferral benefit under DISC. Now a real foreign presence is required, however, and the FSC must perform real functions in the export business, for example, solicitation of business, negotiation,

Prices, Taxes, and Exchange Risks

or contracting. The big difference between the DISC and the FSC is that the latter must have a minimum percentage of its transaction costs identifiable as foreign direct costs and be incurred by the FSC outside the United States. The group of activities in the foreign direct-cost test are

- A. Advertising and sales promotion
- B. Processing orders to the supplier and arranging for shipment to the customer
- C. Transportation costs
- D. Invoicing and receipt of payment
- E. Assumption of credit risk

An FSC meets the foreign-direct cost test if 50 percent, or more, of direct costs of all these activities, or 85 percent of each of two of them, are incurred in the foreign location. So, a significant increase in activity is required of the FSC compared to the DISC, and it requires a foreign location, but for the exporter the tax benefit may make it well worthwhile.

Licensing Fees

If you collect royalties or fees from the licensing of your technology overseas, the foreign government may withhold taxes on the fee. However, this is usually allowed as a credit against U.S. income taxes due on the fee.

Foreign Branches

If you set up a branch overseas, for tax purposes, it is really regarded as an extension of the mother company, and its income is taxed as if it were earned at home. The same applies to a loss. The parent is allowed to deduct the loss of the branch, a fact that might be significant for your entry decision if you are expecting losses in the early years of a foreign operation. You might be able to convert the branch into a different structure for tax purposes at a later date.

Joint Ventures

The U.S. partner has to include a share of its foreign-source income on its U.S. tax return. Again, a credit is allowed for tax paid in the foreign location. Alternatively, if there is a loss the U.S. partner is allowed to reduce U.S. taxable income by the amount of the foreign losses.

Foreign Corporations

When a U.S. firm or individual establishes a foreign corporation the income earned by that corporation is not subject to U.S. income tax until dividends are actually paid to the U.S. firm or individual. However, the matter is complicated by the efforts of the U.S. government to block loopholes and abuses of tax havens. Here two distinctions are important: 1. The difference between a controlled foreign corporation, or CFC, and a non-CFC and 2. the difference between passive and active income. Differences apply on when income is taxed depending on whether it is regarded as active or passive or whether the foreign corporation is controlled or not.

How the Government Can Help in Financing and Protecting the Investment

Three government institutions can help you here:

1. OPIC
2. Export-Import Bank
3. USAID

OPIC gives both direct loans and loan guarantees to U.S. firms interested in investing in more than 100 developing countries. The direct loans are reserved exclusively for small businesses or cooperatives. The loan guarantees reassure financial institutions in providing loans in countries that are perceived as risky. The investment has to meet certain basic criteria, as must the sponsor, and the project must contribute to the economic and social development of the host country and not have a negative effect on the U.S. economy or employment. To apply for a loan or a loan guarantee you need to submit, at least in broad outline, the information covered in Chapter 5 as part of the outline for a feasibility study. As indicated in Chapter 4 on political risk, OPIC also offers a number of insurance programs to encourage investment in the developing countries. From the point of view of financial management, the most important insurance is that associated with exchange controls. The coverage insures that earnings, capital, or principal, interest, and other payments are available for transfer back to the United States. In the developing economies, where there are large markets and attractive opportunities combined with high inflation and scarce foreign exchange, this insurance is what may make an otherwise unacceptable level of risk acceptable. And, the insurance extends further than the foreign exchange control policies that might be introduced by the government. If, for example, your foreign exchange is not released within 60 days of receipt of the local currency, OPIC pays in dollars. You can also get insurance against expropriation and losses from war, revolution, and civil strife. OPIC also issues letters of credit and on-demand bonds required as bid performance or advance payments. For smaller companies nervous of arbitrary drawing, this gives them the protection they need.

Export-Import Bank provides financing assistance for U.S. exports. It covers exports that are so large that they are normally financed over a period of five years. This long-term financing can be given in the form of a direct credit to an overseas client or as a financial guarantee to a private lender. The terms and conditions may vary depending on the financing being provided to other suppliers by their governments. In large-scale purchases what swings the deal is often not the price but the financing, and when you make a bid you can get a preliminary commitment from the Export-Import Bank that outlines the amount and terms of the financial assistance being offered. In late 1985 the government was planning to go even further by setting up a special fund to try and boost exports in order to lower protectionist sentiment in Congress.

The Agency for International Development (USAID) may offer assistance through several channels. All kinds of projects are eligible, but a high priority is given to agribusiness projects. USAID's Bureau of Private Enterprise will consider direct financing of U.S. firms or citizens or host country nationals for certain development-type projects in certain countries. It also, on occasion, has allocated funds to banks that then provide project financing for joint ventures between U.S. and local investors. Right now, for instance, such funding is being provided by AID to the Caribbean Development Bank for a variety of projects in the Caribbean Basin.

CONCLUSION

As we have seen throughout the chapters of this book, doing business in a foreign environment is distinctively different and requires distinctive skills. There may be weakness or failure at other levels and you can still do well, but in handling the money you cannot afford too many mistakes. And the problems you have to handle are unique to international business. That is why knowing the forces that move the foreign-exchange markets is so important and why it is so important for you to know how to react and protect yourself. It's of little use having an efficient production facility, excellent salespeople, a good product, and an expanding market unless the profits end up in the right amount in your currency in your bank. You have a certain degree of control over pricing, how you structure your investment, and how you handle taxes. But the foreign exchange markets are outside your control because they are free and subject to rumor and speculation. And it's there that you can make or break your profit goals. Of course, you could be very conservative and hedge everything. But that is, to a degree, a suspension of judgment and could lead to a lost opportunity and to a loss in competitiveness if rates went the other way. The challenge is to achieve a balance between risk, cost, and expected returns, something that can be done only when you have a full awareness of the environment you are working in and the tools at your disposal to manage it.

1. "By Trading Currencies Kodak's Eric R. Nelson Saves the Firm Millions," *The Wall Street Journal,* March 5, 1985, p. 1.

EPILOGUE

As this book goes to production in mid-1986, two events of major significance to international marketing are occurring. First, the major industrialized countries are applying a sustained effort to drive the dollar down in value against other currencies. This is making U.S. exports cheaper and making imports into the United States more expensive. Previous efforts to manipulate floating exchange rates did not endure over time. But this time the stakes are higher because many U.S. and foreign leaders realize that without a lower dollar protectionist legislation is inevitable in the United States, and that could lead to retaliation abroad. So, overall for the firms wanting to go international the news is good on two counts: Their products will be more competitive overseas, and there is less likelihood of interference with free trade.

The second major event is the dramatic drop in oil prices in the first six months of 1986. While this negatively affects importing demand in the oil-producing countries, it is great news for the rest of the world and particularly great news for the countries whose scarce foreign earnings were eaten up by oil imports. Their savings are now becoming available for other imports and for domestic production. This could lead to faster growth and greater demand for goods and services in most importing countries.

Such fundamental changes in exchange rates and oil prices, in such a short period, show how necessary it is in international marketing to stay on top of the trends and to have the tools to analyze them. That is what this book was intended to help you do.

SELECTED BIBLIOGRAPHY

Apart from the U.S. government and other publications mentioned in the text, there are several other books that you may wish to consult to get a complementary or different approach than the one offered here. Below are a few resource books that I consider particularly helpful.

Delphon, William (ed.). *Washington's Best Kept Secrets: A Guide to International Business.* New York: John Wiley and Sons, 1983.
Moyer, R. Charles, James R. McGuigan, and William J. Kretlow. *Contemporary Financial Management*, 2nd ed. St. Paul, Minnesota: West Publishing Company, 1984.
Robinson, Richard D. *Internationalization of Business: An Introduction.* New York: The Dryden Press, 1984.
Root, Franklin R. *Foreign Market Entry Strategies.* New York: Amacon, 1982.
Terpstra, Vern. *International Marketing.* New York: The Dryden Press, 1983.

Index

Agency for International Development (USAID), 28, 37
  Bureau of Private Enterprise, 96, 102
  feasibility study, financing of, 102
  financial assistance, 257
  service contracts, 161
Agents
  formal agreements, 129–36
  guidelines in choice of, 127–28
  locating agents, 126
  role of, 125
Agreements
  with agents/distributors, 129–36
  licensing agreement, 157–60
American firms
  Asia as market, 3–4
  current markets, 1–2
Asia
  future population, 5
  importance as market, 3–4
Attitudes, cultural aspects, 231–34
Average income, 10

Balance of payments, 52-59, 119
  double entry, 53–54
  explanation of, 52
  government intervention, trade deficits, 54, 56
  IMF format for, 53
  interpretation of balances, 54, 56
  packaging of project, 74
  signs to monitor, 57–59
Bangladesh, 6
Brazil, 72, 81
  GNP, 8
Bureau of Census
  information supplied by, 30
Bureau of Private Enterprise of USAID, 96
Business Environment Risk Index, 83

Capital account, IMF format, 54, 55
Capital budgeting, 191–94
  steps in financial analysis, 192, 194

Carrier, piggyback exporter, 112
Cash in advance, 137
Change, cultural aspects, 233
China
  import figures, 3
  negotiations with, 106–7
Color, cultural aspects, 233–34
"Commerce Business Daily," 37, 161
Commercial invoice, 142
Commodity Series, "Market Share Report," 30
Communication, 225–29
  barriers to, 226–27
  guidelines to overcoming barriers, 228–29
  process of, 225–26
Compensation
  performance incentives, 218
  to overseas managers, 213
  to workers, 217–18
  voluntary fringe benefits, 218
Competition, 17–20
  advantages of competitors, 18–19
  identification of, 18
  overcoming competitors, 20
  product life cycle and, 15
  product type and, 120–21
Concession agreements, 86
Confiscation, danger of, 70–71
Consular invoice, 142
Consumption, equation for, 23
Contract manufacturing, 163–64
Countertrade, 162–63
Credit, balance of payments, 53
Cultural factors, 222–41
  Arab style of business, 238–40
  attitudes of culture, 231–34
  communication, 225–29
  cultural distances from U.S. markets, 223–25
  Filipinos style of business, 240–41
  guidelines for entering market, 236–38
  religion, 234–35
  social organization, 233–36

267

technology of country, 230-231
Currency
  devaluing of, 56
  See also Exchange rate; World currency.
Current account, IMF format, 54, 55
Customs invoice, 142

Debit, balance of payments, 52, 53, 54
Demand
  income distribution and, 10
  market potential, determining, 3–20
  prediction of, 22–28
    consumption equation, 23
    government purchases, 28
    income elasticity of demand, 25–27
    regression analysis, 25
    use of home market for, 23–25
Department of Agriculture, 33
  Economic Research Service, 33
  Foreign Agricultural Service, 33
Department of Commerce, 22, 30, 33, 37, 40
  Agent/Distributor Service, 126
  country specialists, 91
  District Office, 91
  feasibility study, financing of, 102–3
  Foreign Traders Index (FTI), 40, 95
  International Market Search Program, 40
  trade missions, 91–92, 102
  Trade Opportunities Program (TOP), 40
Devaluing of currency, 56
Direct exporting, 113
Direct foreign investment, *See* Wholly owned subsidiaries.
Distribution of income, 8, 10
  demand for product and, 10
  measurement of, 10
Distributors
  formal agreements, 129–36
  guidelines in choosing, 127–28
  role of, 125
District Office, Department of Commerce, 91
Dollar, tied to gold standard, 60–62

Domestic International Sales Corporation (DISC), 254–255
Double entry, balance of payments, 53–54

Economic Research Service, 33
Egypt, 6, 37
Employment, creation of, 74–75
Entry decisions, 48
  determining factors, 117–22
    expected returns, 121–22
    foreign environment, 118–19
    investment of company resources, 121
    market characteristics, 117–18
    product type, 119–21
  exporting, 110–13
  franchising, 155–56
  joint ventures, 114–15
  licensing and contracting, 113–14
  wholly owned subsidiaries, 115–16
  See also specific types of entry.
European Currency Unit (ECU), 62
European Economic Community, 4
  as information source, 42
  rise of, 18–9
European Trading Companies, 113
Exchange controls, 56
Exchange permits, 143–44
Exchange rate, 63–64
  changes, investment decisions and, 199
  forecasting of, 67–68
  foreign exchange, 63–64, 67–68
  multiple, 65
  reflections of, 12
Export declarations, 142
Export documentation, 113, 141–46
Export-Import Bank, financial assistance, 257
Export Management Company (EMC), 111–12
  advantages in use, 111
  conflicts of system, 111
Export Trading Act of 1918, 112
Exporting, 110–13
  direct exporting, 113

Index

Export Management Company (EMC), 111–12
    indirect exporting, 111–13
    piggyback exporting, 112
    tariff barrier documentation, 113
    Webb-Pomerene Associations, 112
Exports
    balance of payments, 52–59
    import/export imbalance, 22
    limitations by federal government, 48
    tax incentives, 255

Family structure problems, on-site market research, 100–101
Feasibility study, 98
    financing of, 102–103
    outline for, 99
    steps for, 98
Federal government
    exports
        interest in, 22
        limiting of, 48
    trade deficits, intervention in, 54, 56
Federal government information
    advantages of, 41–42
    Agency for International Development, 37
    Census Bureau, 30, 33
    Department of Agriculture, 33
    Department of Commerce, 30, 33, 37, 40
    Government Printing Office, 29
    State Department, 28, 30, 37
    See also individual agencies.
Financial aspects, 50, 51–68
    balance of payments, 52–59
    capital budgeting, 191–94
    foreign exchange, 63–68
    internal rate of return, 197–98
    net present value, 195, 197
    payback period, 195
    pricing, 242–53
    profitability index, 198
    taxes, 253–57
    world currency, 59–62
    See also Payment; specific topics.

Financial assistance, 256–57
    Agency for International Development (USAID), 257
    Export-Import Bank, 257
    OPIC, 256–57
Financial risk, foreign currencies, 51–52
Folklore, cultural aspects, 234
Food and Agriculture Organization, as information source, 46
Foreign Agricultural Service, 33
Foreign branches, tax incentives, 255
Foreign commercial officials, 95
Foreign corporations, tax incentives, 256
Foreign Corrupt Practices Act, 144–45
Foreign environment, and entry decision, 118–19
Foreign exchange
    currency-rate change, 63
    exchange rates, 63–64, 67–68
    interest rates and, 66
    international commercial banks and, 66
    market speculation, 66–67
    risk associated with, 51–52
    risk, management of, 249–53
Foreign governments
    frequent changes in, 71–72
    price controls, 245–46
    purchases, predicting demand from, 28
Foreign representative, locating, 94–95
Foreign Sales Corporation (FSC), 254–55
Foreign Traders Index (FTI), 40, 95
Forward market, exchange rate and, 63, 65, 67
France, 71
Franchising, 155–56
Free market rate, 56
Futures market, foreign currency, 67

General Agreement on Tariffs and Trade, 46
German mark, historical view, 60
Ghana, 72, 203
Gold standard
    breakdown of, 61–62
    dollar tied to, 60–62

Governments, *See* Federal government; Foreign governments.
Government Printing Office, 29
Gross National Product (GNP)
  ranking of top ten countries, 8–9
  size of economy and, 8
  statistical distortions, 12

Hedging, 252, 253
Hong Kong, 4
Host country
  barriers presented by, 47–48
  as information source, 46, 47
  special agreements, 86
  visiting country, 88–108

Import documentation, 143–44
  exchange permits, 143–44
  import licenses, 143
  quotas, 144
Import licenses, 143
Imports
  balance of payments, 52–59
  current restrictions, 165
  import/export imbalance, 22
Incentives, *See* Taxes, incentives.
Income elasticity of demand, 25–27
  limitations in, 27
  steps in, 27
Incomes
  average, 10
  distribution of, 8, 10
  Gross National Product (GNP), use of, 8
  less developed countries, 7–8
  market potential and levels of, 4
  per capita income, 4, 8, 10
  purchasing power, 12-13
  size of economy and, 8
Indirect exporting, 111–13
Indonesia, 4, 28
Information sources
  area-specific banks, 44
  federal government, 28–41
  host country, 46, 47
  United Nations, 44, 46
  World Bank, 42, 44

Intangible property rights, 114
Interest rates
  foreign exchange, 66
  investment decisions and, 199
Intermediate production, 76–77
Internal rate of return, 197–98
International Market Search Program, 40
International Monetary Fund (IMF), balance of payments format, 53
International commercial banks, foreign exchange, 66
International Labor Organization, as information source, 46
International Monetary Fund, 46
  beginning of, 61
Investment, and entry decision, 121
Investments
  and entry decision, 121
  ranking of, 195–98
    internal rate of return, 197–98
    net present value, 195, 197
    payback period, 195
    profitability index, 198
Italy, 71

Jamaica, 71
Japanese
  joint ventures, 166–67, 177
  management training, 211
  negotiation with, 107
Joint ventures, 114–15, 166–81
  advantages of, 115, 170–71
  control of, 175–80
    dummy shareholders, 178
    key functions, 177
    local managers, 179–80
    local partners, 178–79
  decision-making guidelines, 172–76
  disadvantages of, 171
  tax incentives, 255–56
  types of, 167–69

Korea, 4
Kuwait, GNP, 8

Labor laws, 215–16

Index

Language problems, on-site market research, 100
Latin America, future population, 5
Less developed countries
  age structure of population, 5
  future demands, 5
  GNP, 12
Letters of credit, 138–40
  guidelines for, 138–39
  sample letter, 139–40
Liberia, 75
Licensing, 147–65
  advantages for licensee, 150–51
  ancillary services/earnings and, 152–53
  contracting without license, 161–65
  controversial nature of, 147–48
  determining factors for, 149–50, 151
  franchising, 155–56
  licensing agreement, 157–60
  payment, 153, 160
  pitfalls to avoid, 152–53
  tax incentives, 255
Licensing and contracting, 113–14
  intangible property rights, 114
Loans, 256–57
Local resources, use of, 74
Logistical problems, on-site market research, 101–102

Malaysia, 4
Management
  compensation to workers, 217–18
  knowledge of work force required, 214–15
  labor laws and, 215–16
  motivating workers, 216–17
  performance evaluation, 218–19
  unions (foreign), relations with, 220
Management contracts, 161
Managers, 202–21
  advantages/disadvantages in use of, 206–7
  cost of, 213
  home country managers, 204–5
  locating foreign manager, 203–4
  role of, 202

  selection criteria, 207–9
  training procedure, 209, 211–12
Market characteristics, and entry decision, 117–18
Market potential, 3–20
  competition and, 7–13
  income levels and, 4, 17–20
  market segments and, 4–5
  population density and, 6–7
  population growth rate and, 4
  products and, 13–17
  rural versus urban areas, 6
  services, sale of, 15–16
  statistics, use of, 12–13
Market research
  foreign markets, information collection, 29
  market potential, 3-20
  on-site, 98, 100–2
  narrowing choices, 21–48
  See also specific topics.
Market segments, 4–5
  age structure, importance of, 5
  categories of populations, 4
  of less developed countries, 5
  use of, 4–5
  Commodity Series, 30
  Country Series, 30
Market speculation, foreign exchange, 66–67
Marketing, social organization of country and, 236
Mexico, 6, 48, 51–52, 215
  balance of payments example, 53, 54
Middle East
  business customs, 238–40
  market opportunities, 4–5
Money-market hedge, 253
Music, cultural aspects, 234

Narrowing choices, 21–48
  demand, prediction of, 22–28
  information sources, 28–47
  supplying the market, 47–50
Negotiations, 103–8
  case examples, 105–8
    China, 106–7

Japan, 107
  Saudia Arabia, 105–6
 goals of, 103
 guidelines for, 104–5
Net present value, 195, 197
NICs (New Industrializing Countries), 9–10

Officers in the Agency for International Development, 96
On-site market research, 98, 100–2
 family structure problems, 100–101
 language problems, 100
 logistical problems, 101–2
Open account, 137–38
Options, 252
Organization for Economic Corporation and Development, as information source, 42
Overseas Private Investment Corporation, 84
 trade missions, 84
Overseas Private Investment Corporation (OPIC), 37
 financial assistance, 256–57
 political insurance, 84
 trade missions, 84
Ownership, divesting, 86

Packaging of project, 73–77
 balance of payments in, 74
 capital, transfer of, 74
 employment, creation of, 74–75
 exporter as intermediary, 76–77
 investor/host country, goals of, 74
 local resources, use of, 74
 taxation issues, 76
Patents, sale of, 16, 114
Payback period, 195
Payment, 137–41
 bill of exchange, 140-41
 cash in advance, 137
 letters of credit, 138–40
 open account, 137–38
 royalties from licensing, 153, 160

Per capita income
 ranking of top ten countries, 8–9
 rate of growth and, 10
 statistical distortions, 12
Performance evaluation, 218–19
Performance incentives, 218
Personnel, expertise of, 49–50
Philippines, 6, 28, 74, 167
 business customs, 240–41
 GNP, 10
Piggyback exporting, 112
Political insurance, 84
 guidelines for use, 84
 Overseas Private Investment Corporation, 84
Political risk, 69–87
 assessment of, 78–83
  Business Environment Risk Index, 83
  comparison of countries, 81, 83
  general risks, 79
  sources of risk, 79
  specific risks, 79
  subjectivity in, 83
 as growth industry, 69
 investment decisions and, 199
 minimizing risk, 84–86
  agreements with host government, 86
  divesting ownership, 86
  local involvement, 84
  political insurance, 84
  shift of assets, 86
 myths about, 68–73
 packaging of project and, 73–77
 principles for international manager, 70
Populations
 density, importance of, 6–7
 growth rates, significance of, 4
 market segments, 4–5
Price controls, 56
Pricing, 242–53
 controlling prices, methods of, 246–47
 cost decisions, 243–44
 escalator effect, 244–45

Index

foreign-exchange risk, management of, 249–53
government, role of, 245–46
transfer pricing, 247–48
Pro forma invoice, 142
Production
  employment, creation of, 74–75
  intermediate production, 76–77
  local resources, use of, 74
Production skills, sale of, 16, 114
Products, 13–17
  and entry decision, 119–21
  for export, systematic approach to, 14–15
  modifications for foreign markets, 14, 120
  product life cycle, 14–15
  related products, 16–17
  services, 15–16
  world brands, 120
Profitability index, 198
Profits, and entry decision, 121–22
Purchase order, 142
Purchasing power, statistical distortions, 12–13

Religion, 234–235
Reserves account, IMF format, 54, 55
Resource nationalism, 70
Rider, piggyback exporter, 112
Royalties, licensing, 153, 160
Rural areas, scanning for market potential, 6

Saudi Arabia, negotiations with, 105–6
Saving face, meanings of, 224–25
Severance pay, 215
Singapore, 4
Social organization, 235–36 and marketing effort, 236
Special Drawing Rights (SPRs), 62
State Department, 30
State enterprises, joint ventures, 168
Statistical information
  consumption equation, 23
  distortions in, 12–13

Supplying the market, 47–50
  financial factors, 50
  home-country barriers, 48
  host-country barriers, 47–48
  long run vs. short run, 48–49
  personnel expertise and, 49–50
  production, 50
Surplus, balance of payments, 52

Taiwan, 4
Tariff barrier, 54
  advantages of competitors, 18–19
  documentation required, 113
  non-tariff barrier, 47–48, 54
  reason for, 47
Taxes, 253–57
  credits, 76
  incentives, 254–57
    exports, 255
    foreign branches, 255
    foreign corporations, 256
    joint ventures, 255–56
    licensing fees, 255
  investment decisions and, 199
Technical Assistance contracts, 161
Technology, cultural aspects, 230–31
Thailand, 28
  designation, as strategic country, 37
Third World countries, 2
  urban population of, 6
Third World multinational, joint ventures, 168
Time, cultural aspects, 232–33
Trade, post World War II, 124–25
Trade deficits, government intervention, 54, 56
Trade fairs, 91–92
  value of, 92
Trade missions
  Department of Commerce, 91–92, 102
  Overseas Private Investment Corporation, 84
Trade Opportunities Program (TOP), 40
Trade statistics, use of, 23
Training, of overseas managers, 209, 211–12
Turnkey contracts, 16, 163

Index

Unions, 219–220
United Nations Development Program, as information source, 46
United Nations information, 44, 46
  from specialized agencies, 46
    General Agreement on Tariffs and Trade, 46
    International Monetary Fund, 46
    United Nations Statistical Yearbooks, 46
Urban areas, scanning for market potential, 6
USAID, *See* Agency for International Development (USAID).

Visiting the country, 88–108
  contact persons
    Bureau of Private Enterprise of USAID, 96
    feasibility study, 98, 99, 102
    foreign commercial officials, 95
    foreign government officials, 96–97
    foreign representatives, 94–95
    Officers in the Agency for International Development, 96
    other firms, 96
  financing of, 102–3
  negotiations, 103–8
  on-site market research, 98, 100–2
  sources of advice, 91
  trade fairs/exhibitions, 91–92
Voluntary fringe benefits, 218

Wholly owned subsidiaries, 115–16, 182–201
  decision making guidelines, 199–200
  financial analysis, 190–98
    capital budgeting, 191–94
    internal rate of return, 197–98
    net present value, 195, 197
    payback period, 195
    profitability index, 198
  firm specific advantages, 185–86
  incentives for, 187–90
  location advantages, 183–84
  risks, 185–87
Workers
  compensation, 217–18
  labor laws, 215–16
  manager's knowledge of, 214–15
  motivating workers, 216–17
  severance pay, 215
World Bank, 28
World Bank information, 42, 44
  value of, 44
World currency, 59–62
  foreign exchange, management of, 63–68
  historical view
    British pound, 59–60
    dollar and gold standard, 60–62
    European Currency Unit (ECU), 62
    German mark, 60
    Special Drawing Right (SDRs), 62
World Health Organization, as information source, 46
World market
  agents/distributors, 125–26
  entry decisions, 110–22
  financial aspects, 51–68
  information sources for, 28–47
  market potential, 3–20
  most popular countries, 3–4
  narrowing choices, 21–48
  payment, 137–41
  political risk, 69–87
  population of, 3
  visiting the country, 88–108
  See also specific topics.

Yeman Arab Republic, 71